Cultures in Babylon

THE HAYMARKET SERIES

Editors: Mike Davis and Michael Sprinker

The Haymarket Series offers original studies in politics, history and culture with a focus on North America. Representing views across the American left on a wide range of subjects, the series will be of interest to socialists both in the USA and throughout the world. A century after the first May Day, the American left remains in the shadow of those martyrs whom the Haymarket Series honors and commemorates. These studies testify to the living legacy of political activism and commitment for which they gave their lives.

RECENT AND FORTHCOMING TITLES

The Invention of the White Race, Volume 2: The Origin of Racial Oppression in Anglo-America by Theodore Allen

Pickup Artists: Street Basketball in America by Lars Anderson and Chad Millman

Glitter, Stucco and Dumpster Diving: Reflections on Building Production in the Vernacular City by John Chase

Prisoners of the American Dream: Politics and Economy in the History of the US Working Class (new edition) by Mike Davis

Mechanic Accents: Dime Novels and Working-Class Culture in America (new edition) and *The Cultural Front: The Laboring of American Culture in the Twentieth Century* by Michael Denning

The Sixties Chicano Movement: Youth, Identity, Power (new edition) by Carlos Muñoz

Red Dirt: Growing Up Okie by Roxanne Dunbar Ortiz

Structures of the Jazz Age: Mass Culture, Progressive Education and Racial Discourse in American Modernist Fiction by Chip Rhodes

The Wages of Whiteness: Race and the Making of the American Working Class (new edition) by David R. Roediger

A Plague on Your Houses: How New York was Burned Down and National Public Health Crumbled by Deborah Wallace and Rodrick Wallace

From Pearl Harbor to Saigon: Japanese American Soldiers and the Vietnam War by Toshio Whelchel

Development Arrested: The Blues and Plantation Power in the Mississippi Delta by Clyde Woods

Cultures in Babylon

Black Britain
and
African America

HAZEL V. CARBY

V

VERSO

London • New York

for Stuart Hall

First published by Verso 1999
© Hazel Carby 1999
All rights reserved

Verso
UK: 6 Meard Street, London W1V 3HR
US: 180 Varick Street, New York, NY 10014–4606

Verso is the imprint of New Left Books

ISBN 1–85984–884–2
ISBN 1–85984–281–X (pbk)

British Library Cataloguing in Publication Data
A catalogue record for this book is available from the British Library

Library of Congress Cataloging-in-Publication Data
A catalog record for this book is available from the Library of Congress

Typeset by Set Systems Ltd, Saffron Walden
Printed by Biddles Ltd, Guildford and King's Lynn

Contents

Dispatches from the Multicultural Wars

Introduction

The essays collected in *Cultures in Babylon* span the eighteen years of my transatlantic journeying from the United Kingdom to the United States. I arrived in America as a black Briton of Welsh and Jamaican parentage searching for an audience for *The Empire Strikes Back: Race and Racism in Seventies Britain*, written while I was a member of the Race and Politics group at the Centre for Contemporary Cultural Studies in Birmingham, England.[1] The response was not gratifying. The irrational rationale of publishing companies was patiently explained to this obviously ignorant European: the majority of Americans were totally unaware of the existence of black communities in the UK; those few who might be interested in such a phenomenon would be African American; but African Americans did not constitute a sufficient reading public to warrant the publication of *Empire* in the USA.

The response from the black American intellectual establishment to the concerns of this eager and aggressively feminist "black Brit" was mixed. It is strange to write these words while being Chair of African American Studies at Yale University because the occupant of that position then was Charles Davis, the man most responsible for my coming to America. Professor Davis was a "founding father" of the field of African American Studies, his intellectual vision was broad and international and he greeted me and my work with enthusiasm, warmth and support. As a visiting graduate student I worked closely with and was supported by John Blassin-game and Robert B. Stepto, who were both very generous with their time and inspired me with their intellectual energy and commitment.

But apart from these exceptions, twenty years ago the black male intellectual community was sceptical that there were sufficient black women writers to constitute a field of research, and as black female scholars we worked in relative isolation from each other. Of course, once the men were persuaded by our collective efforts, black women writers became a market-able commodity, and the rest, shall we say, is history.

When I ventured outside of the libraries and left the early drafts of what was to become *Reconstructing Womanhood* on my desk, many black American intellectuals, both men and women, were very suspicious of black "outsiders" writing and speaking about what they perceived as a very particular and peculiar African *American* experience.[2] I found that whereas I took for granted the importance of the concept of the black diaspora, many fledgling African American Studies programs, in the face of limited funding and resources, focused almost entirely on the history of black peoples in the continental United States. However, it was clear that there were virtually no opportunities to teach Black Studies in Margaret Thatcher's Britain. Having taught courses on the literature of black women and on Caribbean fiction as a lecturer in Yale's African American Studies Program, I joined the very progressive English Department at Wesleyan University in 1982.

What follows does not start with the work from this period; rather the book works backward toward the roots of my theoretical and political interests. Within each section I have followed a chronological ordering of the chapters. I decided that it would be most useful for the reader to start with the essays that addressed the issues that most concerned me as I finished *Reconstructing Womanhood*.

The chapters in "Women, Migration and the Formation of a Blues Culture" in various ways are an attempt to address the limitations inherent in concentrating upon the literary culture of black women. In them, I was seeking to broaden the ways in which I had been defining intellectual practices and to challenge the perception and definitions of women's culture and cultural presences in *Reconstructing Womanhood*. Each essay, in its own way, addresses the political dilemmas of representing black women as sexual subjects. They were written not only as historical pieces but as responses to the cultural politics of the 1980s, when issues of black women's sexuality became part of a regressive discourse of cultural pathology which advocated the surveillance of racialized bodies, rather than reform of racialized economic markets, as a means to address urban crises.

I was also interested in addressing questions of performance within the context of the culture industry, and the essays move from the blues recordings of the 1920s to the publication in 1986 of Tina Turner's explosive autobiography. All of them negotiate the terrain of feminist debate about how far female sexuality is exploited by, or triumphs in spite of, the consumerism of performance entertainment. They by no means provide a yes or no answer to this dilemma but argue that black women in the culture industry have to constantly live these contradictions. Collectively, the essays represent an unfinished project, for as I delved further and further into questions of black female sexuality I became convinced that I needed to have my say about black masculinity, and that resulted in the publication of *Race Men*.[3]

The essays in "Black Feminist Interventions" are occasional. They articulate my concerns about the terms and conditions under which black women exist in the academy, from their representation on a syllabus to the conditions of their employment, whether as dining hall workers or as graduate students. (The exception is "National Nightmares," which was originally written as a response to the essays contained in a book entitled *Race, Identity and Representation in Education* and was my first attempt to think about the relations between concepts of race, nation and masculinity in an obviously pedagogical film, Lawrence Kasdan's *Grand Canyon*.[4]) What ties each of the essays to the others is an abiding interest in pedagogic practices and theories of education, and it is this interest which links the essays in this section to those in "Dispatches from the Multicultural Wars." My experiences as a high school teacher of English and political activist in the dockland area of East London from 1972 to 1979 shape all my work, but my conclusions about the relations between theory and practice in the classroom are most easily grasped in these two sections.

"Fictions of the Folk" brings together work on black intellectual imaginings of the folk and folk culture. I question the political as well as intellectual motives which form the basis for the creation of black literary and cultural traditions out of reinventions of an unadulterated or pure rural past. I believe that the ways in which all of us, as black intellectuals, imagine and reproduce the roots of contemporary black culture have very real consequences for the ways in which we imagine the future. Consequently, these processes of thought in the production of our cultural histories and cultural analyses need to be self-consciously evident and open for critique. I can only hope that the essays in *Cultures in Babylon* may contribute to such self-consciousness about the political and cultural effect of what we write and teach.

Notes

1. Centre for Contemporary Cultural Studies, *The Empire Strikes Back: Race and Racism in Seventies Britain*, London: Hutchinson, 1982. This book was reprinted by Routledge in 1992.
2. Hazel V. Carby, *Reconstructing Womanhood: The Emergence of the Afro-American Woman Novelist*, New York: Oxford University Press, 1987.
3. Hazel V. Carby, *Race Men*, Cambridge, MA: Harvard University Press, 1998.
4. This essay was originally titled "Encoding White Resentment: *Grand Canyon* – A Narrative for Our Times," in Cameron McCarthy and Warren Crichlow, eds, *Race, Identity and Representation in Education*, New York: Routledge, 1993, pp. 236–47.

Women, Migration and the
Formation of a Blues Culture

1

The Sexual Politics of Women's Blues

This essay considers the sexual politics of women's blues and focuses on black women as cultural producers and performers in the 1920s. Their story is part of a larger history of the production of African American culture within the North American culture industry. My research so far has concentrated almost exclusively on black women intellectuals who were part of developing an African American literate culture, and thus it reflects the privileged place we accord to writers in African American Studies.[1] Feminist theory has analyzed the cultural production of black women writers in isolation from other forms of women's culture and cultural presence and has neglected to relate particular texts and issues to a larger discourse of culture and cultural politics. I want to show how the representation of black female sexuality in black women's fiction and in women's blues is clearly different. I will argue that different cultural forms negotiate and resolve very different sets of social contradictions. However, before considering the particularities of black women's sexual representation, we should consider its marginality within a white-dominated feminist discourse.

In 1982, at the Barnard conference on the politics of sexuality, Hortense Spillers condemned the serious absence of consideration of black female sexuality from various public discourses, including white feminist theory. She described black women as "the beached whales of the sexual universe, unvoiced, misseen, not doing, awaiting *their* verb." The sexual experiences of black women, she argued, were rarely depicted by themselves in what she referred to as "empowered texts": discursive feminist texts. Spillers complained of the relative absence of African American women from the academy and thus from the visionary company of Anglo-American women feminists and their privileged mode of feminist expression.

The collection of the papers from the Barnard conference, the *Pleasure and Danger* anthology, has become one of these empowered feminist theoretical texts, and Spillers' essay continues to stand within it as an important black feminist survey of the ways in which the sexuality of black

American women has been unacknowledged in the public/critical discourse of feminist thought.[2] Following Spillers' lead, black feminists continued to critique the neglect of issues of black female sexuality within feminist theory, and, indeed, I as well as others directed many of our criticisms toward the *Pleasure and Danger* anthology itself.[3]

As black women we have provided articulate and politically incisive criticism which is there for the feminist community at large to heed or to ignore – upon that decision lies the future possibility of forging a feminist movement that is not parochial. As the black feminist and educator Anna Julia Cooper stated in 1892, a woman's movement should not be based on the narrow concerns of white middle-class women under the name of "women"; neither, she argued, should a woman's movement be formed around the exclusive concerns of either the white woman or the black woman or the red woman but should be able to address the concerns of all the poor and oppressed.[4]

But instead of concentrating upon the domination of a white feminist theoretical discourse which marginalizes non-white women I am going to focus on the production of a discourse of sexuality by black women. By analyzing the sexual and cultural politics of black women who constructed themselves as sexual subjects through song, in particular the blues, I want to assert an empowered presence. First, I am going to situate the historical moment of the emergence of women-dominated blues and establish a theoretical framework of interpretation, and then I will consider some aspects of the representation of feminism, sexuality and power in women's blues.

Movin' On

Before World War I the overwelming majority of black people lived in the South, although the majority of black intellectuals who purported to represent the interest of "the race" lived in the North. At the turn of the century black intellectuals felt they understood and could give voice to the concerns of the black community as a whole. They were able to position themselves as spokespeople for the "race" because they were at a vast physical and metaphorical distance from the majority of those they represented. The mass migration of blacks to urban areas, especially to the cities of the North, forced these traditional intellectuals to question and revise their imaginary vision of "the people" and directly confront the actual displaced rural workers who were, in large numbers, becoming a black working class in front of their eyes. In turn, the mass of black workers became aware of the range of possibilities for their representation. No longer were the "Talented Tenth," the practitioners of policies of racial uplift, the undisputed "leaders of the race." Intellectuals and their constituencies fragmented: black union organizers, Marcus Garvey and the

Universal Negro Improvement Association, radical black activists, the Sanctified Churches, the National Association of Colored Women, the Harlem
creative artists, all offered alternative forms of representation and each
strove to establish that the experience of their constituency was representative of the experience of the race.

Within the movement of the Harlem cultural renaissance black women
writers established a variety of alternative possibilities for the fictional
representation of black female experience. Zora Neale Hurston chose to
represent black people as the rural folk; the folk were represented as being
both the source of African American cultural and linguistic forms and the
means for its continued existence. Hurston's exploration of sexual and
power relations was embedded in this "folk" experience and avoided the
cultural transitions and confrontations of the urban displacement. As
Hurston is frequently situated as the foremother of contemporary black
women writers, the tendency of feminist literary criticism has been to
valorize black women as "folk" heroines at the expense of those texts which
explored black female sexuality within the context of urban social relations.
Put simply, a line of descent is drawn from *Their Eyes Were Watching God* to
The Color Purple. But to establish the black "folk" as representative of the
black community at large was and still is a convenient method for ignoring
the specific contradictions of an urban existence in which most of us live.
The culture industry, through its valorization in print and in film of *The
Color Purple*, for example, can *appear* to comfortably address issues of black
female sexuality within a past history and rural context while completely
avoiding the crucial issues of black sexual and cultural politics that stem
from an urban crisis.

"There's No Earthly Use in Bein' Too-ga-tha if it Don't Put Some Joy in Yo Life"[5]

However, two other women writers of the Harlem Renaissance, Jessie Fauset
and Nella Larsen, did figure an urban class confrontation in their fiction,
though in distinctly different ways. Jessie Fauset became an ideologue for a
new black bourgeoisie; her novels represented the manners and morals
that distinguished the emergent middle class from the working class. She
wanted public recognition for the existence of a black elite that was urbane,
sophisticated and civilized, but her representation of this elite implicitly
defined its manners against the behavior of the new black proletariat.
While it must be acknowledged that Fauset did explore the limitations of a
middle-class existence for women, ultimately each of her novels depicts
independent women who surrender their independence to become suitable wives for the new black professional men.

Nella Larsen, on the other hand, offers us a more sophisticated dissection
of the rural/urban confrontation. Larsen was extremely critical of the

Harlem intellectuals who glorified the values of a black folk culture while being ashamed of and ridiculing the behavior of the new black migrant to the city. Her novel *Quicksand* (1928) contains the first explicitly sexual black heroine in black women's fiction. Larsen explores questions of sexuality and power within both a rural and an urban landscape; in both contexts she condemns the ways in which female sexuality is confined and compromised as the object of male desire. In the city Larsen's heroine, Helga, has to recognize the ways in which her sexuality has an exchange value within capitalist social relations while in the country Helga is trapped by the consequences of woman's reproductive capacity. In the final pages of *Quicksand* Helga echoes the plight of the slave woman who could not escape to freedom and the cities of the North because she could not abandon her children and, at the same time, represents how a woman's life is drained through constant childbirth.

But Larsen also reproduces in her novel the dilemma of a black woman who tries to counter the dominant white cultural definitions of her sexuality: ideologies that define black female sexuality as primitive and exotic. However, the response of Larsen's heroine to such objectification is also the response of many black women writers: the denial of desire and the repression of sexuality. Indeed, *Quicksand* is symbolic of the tension in late nineteenth- and early twentieth-century black women's fiction in which black female sexuality was frequently displaced onto the terrain of the political responsibility of the black woman. The duty of the black heroine toward the black community was made coterminous with her desire as a woman, a desire which was expressed as a dedication to uplift the race. This displacement from female desire to female duty enabled the negotiation of racist constructions of black female sexuality but denied sensuality, and in this denial lies the class character of its cultural politics.

It has been a mistake of much black feminist theory to concentrate almost exclusively on the visions of black women as represented by black women writers without indicating the limitations of their middle-class response to black women's sexuality. These writers faced a very real contradiction for they felt that they would publicly compromise themselves if they acknowledged their sexuality and sensuality within a racist sexual discourse, thus providing evidence that indeed they were primitive and exotic creatures. But because black feminist theory has concentrated upon the literate forms of black women's intellectual activity, the dilemma of the place of sexuality within a literary discourse has appeared as if it were the dilemma of most black women. On the other hand, what a consideration of women's blues allows us to see is an alternative form of representation, an oral and musical women's culture that explicitly addresses the contradictions of feminism, sexuality and power. What has been called the "Classic Blues," the women's blues of the twenties and early thirties, is a discourse that articulates a cultural and political struggle over sexual relations: a struggle that is directed against the objectification of female sexuality within a patriarchal order but which also tries to reclaim women's bodies as the sexual and sensuous objects of women's song.

Testifyin'

Within black culture the figure of the female blues singer has been reconstructed in poetry, drama, fiction and art and used to meditate upon conventional and unconventional sexuality. A variety of narratives both fictional and biographical have mythologized the woman blues singer and these mythologies become texts about sexuality. Women blues singers frequently appear as liminal figures that play out and explore the various possibilities of a sexual existence; they are representations of women who attempt to manipulate and control their construction as sexual subjects. In African American fiction and poetry the blues singer has a strong physical and sensuous presence. Sherley Anne Williams wrote about Bessie Smith:

> the thick triangular
> nose wedged
> in the deep brown
> face nostrils
> flared on a last hummmmmmmm.
>
> Bessie singing
> just behind the beat
> that sweet sweet
> voice throwing
> its light on me
>
> I looked in her face
> and seed the woman
> I'd become. A big
> boned face already
> lined and the first line
> in her fo'head was
> black and the next line
> was sex cept I didn't
> know to call it that
> then and the brackets
> round her mouth stood fo
> the chi'ren she teared
> from out her womb. . . .[6]

Williams has argued that the early blues singers and their songs "helped to solidify community values and heighten community morale in the late nineteenth and early twentieth centuries." The blues singer, she says, uses song to create reflection and creates an atmosphere for analysis to take place. The blues were certainly a communal expression of black experience which had developed out of the call and response patterns of work songs from the nineteenth century and have been described as a "complex interweaving of the general and the specific" and of individual and group experience. John Coltrane has described how the audience heard "we" even if the singer said "I." Of course the singers were entertainers, but the blues were not an entertainment of escape or fantasy and sometimes directly represented historical events.[7]

Sterling Brown has testified to the physical presence and power of Ma Rainey, who would draw crowds from remote rural areas to see her "smilin' gold-toofed smiles" and to feel like participants in her performance which articulated the conditions of their social existence. Brown, in his poem "Ma Rainey," remembers the emotion of her performance of "Backwater Blues," which described the devastation of the Mississippi flood of 1927. Rainey's original performance becomes in Brown's text a vocalization of the popular memory of the flood, and Brown's text constructs itself as a part of the popular memory of the "Mother of the Blues."[8]

Ma Rainey never recorded "Backwater Blues," although Bessie Smith did, but local songsters would hear the blues performed in the tent shows or on record and transmit them throughout the community. Ma Rainey and Bessie Smith were among the first women blues singers to be recorded, and with Clara Smith, Ethel Waters, Alberta Hunter, Ida Cox, Rosa Henderson, Victoria Spivey and Lucille Hegamin they dominated the blues recording industry throughout the twenties. It has often been asserted that this recording of the blues compromised and adulterated a pure folk form of the blues, but the combination of the vaudeville, carnival and minstrel shows and the phonograph meant that the "folk-blues" and the culture industry product were inextricably mixed in the twenties. By 1928 the blues sung by blacks were only secondarily of folk origin, and the primary source for the group transmission of the blues was by phonograph, which was then joined by the radio.

Bessie Smith, Ma Rainey, Ethel Waters and the other women blues singers traveled in carnivals and vaudevilles which included acts with animals, acrobats and other circus performers. Often the main carnival played principally for white audiences but would have black sideshows with black entertainers for black audiences. In this way black entertainers reached black audiences in even the remotest rural areas. The records of the women blues singers were likewise directed at a black audience through the establishment of "race records," a section of the recording industry which recorded both religious and secular black singers and black musicians and distributed these recordings through stores in black areas; they were rarely available in white neighborhoods.

When a Woman Gets the Blues . . .

This, then, is the framework within which I interpret the women blues singers of the twenties. To fully understand the ways in which their perform-ance and their songs were part of a discourse of sexual relations within the black community it is necessary to consider how the social conditions of black women were dramatically affected by migration, for migration had distinctively different meanings for black men and women. The music and song of the women blues singers embodied the social relations and contra-dictions of black displacement: of rural migration and the urban flux. In this sense, as singers, these women were organic intellectuals; not only were they a part of the community that was the subject of their song but they were also a product of the rural to urban movement.

Migration for women often meant being left behind: "Bye bye baby" and "Sorry I can't take you" were the common refrains of male blues. In women's blues the response is complex: regret and pain expressed as "My sweet man done gone and left me dead," or "My daddy left me standing in the door," or "The sound of the train fills my heart with misery." There was also an explicit recognition that if the journey were to be made by women it held particular dangers for them. It was not as easy for women as it was for men to hop freight trains, and if money was saved for tickets it was men who were usually sent. And yet the women who were singing the songs had made it North and recorded from the "promised land" of Chicago and New York. So, what the women blues singers were able to articulate were the possibilities of movement for the women who "have ramblin' on their minds" and who intended to "ease on down the line" for they had made it – the power of movement was theirs. The train, which had symbolized freedom and mobility for men in male blues songs, became a contested symbol. The sound of the train whistle, a mournful signal of imminent desertion and future loneliness, was reclaimed as a sign that women too were on the move. In 1924 both Trixie Smith and Clara Smith recorded "Freight Train Blues." These are the words Clara Smith sang:

> I hate to hear that engine blow, boo, hoo.
> I hate to hear that engine blow, boo, hoo.
> Everytime I hear it blowin', I feel like ridin' too.
>
> That's the freight train blues, I got box cars on my mind.
> I got the freight train blues, I got box cars on my mind.
> Gonna leave this town, 'cause my man is so unkind.
>
> I'm goin' away just to wear you off my mind.
> I'm goin' away just to wear you off my mind.
> And I may be gone for a doggone long long time.
>
> I'll ask the brakeman to let me ride the blind.
> I'll ask the brakeman to please let me ride the blind.
> The brakeman say, "Clara, you know this train ain't mine."

When a woman gets the blues she goes to her room and hides.
When a woman gets the blues she goes to her room and hides.
When a man gets the blues he catch the freight train and rides.[9]

The music moves from echoing the moaning, mournful sound of the train whistle to the syncopated activity of the sound of the wheels in movement as Clara Smith determines to ride. The final opposition between women hiding and men riding is counterpointed by this musical activity and the determination in Clara Smith's voice. "Freight Train Blues" and then "Chicago Bound Blues," which was recorded by Bessie Smith and Ida Cox, were very popular so Paramount and Victor encouraged more "railroad blues." In 1925 Trixie Smith recorded "Railroad Blues," which directly responded to the line "had the blues for Chicago and I just can't be satisfied" from "Chicago Bound Blues." Trixie Smith replied with "If you ride that train it'll satisfy your mind." "Railroad Blues" encapsulated the ambivalent position of the blues singer caught between the contradictory impulses of needing to migrate North and the need to be able to return, for the "Railroad Blues" were headed not for the North but for Alabama. Being able to move both North and South, the women blues singer occupied a privileged space: she could speak the desires of rural women to migrate and voice the nostalgic desires of urban women for home which was both a recognition and a warning that the city was not, in fact, the "promised land."

Men's and women's blues shared the language and experience of the railroad and migration but what that meant was different for each sex. The language of the blues carries this conflict of interests and is the cultural terrain in which these differences were fought over and redefined. Women's blues were the popular cultural embodiment of the way in which the differing interests of black men and women were a struggle of power relations. The sign of the train is one example of the way in which the blues were a struggle within the language itself to define the differing material conditions of black women and black men.

Baad Sista

The differing interests of women and men in the domestic sphere were clearly articulated by Bessie Smith in the "In the House Blues," a popular song for the mid-twenties which she wrote herself but didn't record until 1931. Although the man gets up and leaves, the woman remains, trapped in the house like a caged animal pacing up and down. But at the same time Bessie's voice vibrates with tremendous power which implies the eruption that is to come. The woman in the house is only barely restrained from creating havoc; her capacity for violence has been exercised before and resulted in her arrest. The music, which provides an oppositional counterpoint to Bessie's voice, is a parody of the supposed weakness of women. A vibrating cornet contrasts with the words that ultimately cannot be contained and roll out the front door.

> Sitting in the house with everything on my mind.
> Sitting in the house with everything on my mind.
> Looking at the clock and can't even tell the time.
>
> Walking to my window and looking outa my door.
> Walking to my window and looking outa my door.
> Wishin' that my man would come home once more.
>
> Can't eat, can't sleep, so weak I can't walk my floor.
> Can't eat, can't sleep, so weak I can't walk my floor.
> Feel like calling "murder" let the police squad get me once more.
>
> They woke me up before day with trouble on my mind.
> They woke me up before day with trouble on my mind.
> Wringing my hands and screaming, walking the floor hollerin' an' crying.
>
> Hey, don't let them blues in here.
> Hey, don't let them blues in here.
> They shakes me in my bed and sits down in my chair.
>
> Oh, the blues has got me on the go.
> They've got me on the go.
> They roll around my house, in and out of my front door.[10]

The way in which Bessie growls "so weak" contradicts the supposed weakness and helplessness of the woman in the song and grants authority to her thoughts of "murder." The rage of women against male infidelity and desertion is evident in many of the blues. Ma Rainey threatened violence when she sang that she was "gonna catch" her man "with his britches down," in the act of infidelity, in "Black Eye Blues." Exacting revenge against mistreatment also appears as taking another lover, as in "Oh Papa Blues," or taunting a lover who has been thrown out with "I won't worry when you're gone, another brown has got your water on" in "Titanic Man Blues." But Ma Rainey is perhaps best known for the rejection of a lover in "Don't Fish in My Sea," which is also a resolution to give up men altogether. She sang:

> If you don't like my ocean, don't fish in my sea,
> If you don't like my ocean, don't fish in my sea,
> Stay out of my valley, and let my mountain be.
>
> Ain't had no lovin' since God knows when,
> Ain't had no lovin' since God knows when,
> That's the reason I'm through with these no good triflin' men.

The total rejection of men as in this blues and in other songs such as "Trust No Man" stands in direct contrast to the blues that concentrate upon the bewildered, often half-crazed and even paralyzed response of women to male violence.

Sandra Lieb has described the masochism of "Sweet Rough Man," in which a man abuses a helpless and passive woman, and she argues that a distinction must be made between reactions to male violence against women in male- and female-authored blues. "Sweet Rough Man," though recorded by Ma Rainey, was composed by a man and is the most explicit description of sexual brutality in her repertoire. The articulation of the possibility that women could leave a condition of sexual and financial dependency, reject male violence, and end sexual exploitation was embodied in Ma Rainey's recording of "Hustlin' Blues," composed jointly by a man and a woman, which narrates the story of a prostitute who ends her brutal treatment by turning in her pimp to a judge. Ma Rainey sang:

> I ain't made no money, and he dared me to go home.
> Judge, I told him he better leave me alone.
>
> He followed me up and he grabbed me for a fight.
> He followed me up and he grabbed me for a fight.
> He said, "Girl, do you know you ain't made no money tonight."
>
> Oh Judge, tell me I'm through.
> Oh Judge, tell him I'm through.
> I'm tired of this life, that's why I brought him to you.

However, Ma Rainey's strongest assertion of female sexual autonomy is a song she composed herself, "Prove It On Me Blues," which isn't technically a blues song but which she sang accompanied by the Tub Jug Washboard Band. "Prove It On Me Blues" was an assertion and an affirmation of lesbianism. Though condemned by society for her sexual preference, the singer wants the whole world to know that she chooses women rather than men. The language of "Prove It On Me Blues" engages directly in defining issues of sexual preference as a contradictory struggle of social relations. Both Ma Rainey and Bessie Smith had lesbian relationships and "Prove It On Me Blues" vacillates between the subversive hidden activity of women loving women with a public declaration of lesbianism. The words express a contempt for a society that rejected lesbians. "They say I do it, ain't nobody caught me, They sure got to prove it on me." But at the same time the song is a reclamation of lesbianism as long as the woman publicly names her sexual preference for herself in the repetition of lines about the friends who "must've been women, cause I don't like no men."[11]

But most of the songs that asserted a woman's independence did so in relation to men not women. One of the most joyous is a recording by Ethel Waters in 1925 called "No Man's Mamma Now." It is the celebration of a divorce that ended a marriage defined as a five-year "war." Unlike Bessie Smith, Ethel Waters didn't usually growl, although she could; rather her voice, which is called "sweet-toned," gained authority from its stylistic enunciation and the way in which she almost recited the words. As Waters said, she tried to be "refined" even when she was being her most outrageous.[12]

You may wonder what's the reason for this crazy smile,
Say I haven't been so happy in a long while
Got a big load off my mind, here's the paper sealed and signed,
And the judge was nice and kind all through the trial.
This ends a five year war, I'm sweet Miss Waters once more.

I can come when I please, I can go when I please.
I can flit, fly and flutter like the birds in the trees.
Because, I'm no man's mamma now. Hey, hey.

I can say what I like, I can do what I like.
I'm a girl who is on a matrimonial strike;
Which means, I'm no man's mamma now.

I'm screaming bail
I know how a fella feels getting out of jail
I got twin beds, I take pleasure in announcing one for sale.

Am I making it plain, I will never again,
Drag around another ball and chain.
I'm through, because I'm no man's mamma now.

I can smile, I can wink, I can go take a drink,
And I don't have to worry what my hubby will think.
Because, I'm no man's mamma now.

I can spend if I choose, I can play and sing the blues.
There's nobody messin' with my one and my twos.
Because, I'm no man's mamma now.

You know there was a time,
I used to think that men were grand.
But no more for mine,
I'm gonna label my apartment "No Man's Land."

I got rid of my cat cause the cat's name was Pat.
Won't even have a mail box in my flat.
Because, I'm no man's mamma now.[13]

Waters' sheer exuberance is infectious. The vitality and energy of the performance celebrates the unfettered sexuality of the singer. The self-conscious and self-referential lines "I can play and sing the blues" situate the singer at the center of a subversive and liberatory activity. Many of the men who were married to blues singers disapproved of their careers: some felt threatened; others, like Edith Johnson's husband, eventually applied enough pressure to force them to stop singing. Most, like Bessie Smith, Ethel Waters, Ma Rainey and Ida Cox, did not stop singing the blues, but their public presence, their stardom, their overwhelming popularity and their insistence on doing what they wanted caused frequent conflict with the men in their personal lives.

Funky and Sinful Stuff

The figure of the woman blues singer has become a cultural embodiment of social and sexual conflict from Gayl Jones' novel *Corregidora* to Alice Walker's *The Color Purple*. The women blues singers occupied a privileged space; they had broken out of the boundaries of the home and taken their sensuality and sexuality out of the private and into the public sphere. For these singers were gorgeous and their physical presence elevated them to being referred to as Goddesses, as the high priestesses of the blues, or, like Bessie Smith, as the Empress of the blues. Their physical presence was a crucial aspect of their power; the visual display of spangled dresses, of furs, of gold teeth, of diamonds, of all the sumptuous and desirable aspects of their body, reclaimed female sexuality from being an objectification of male desire to a representation of female desire.

Bessie Smith wrote about the social criticism that women faced if they broke social convention. "Young Woman's Blues" threads together many of the issues of power and sexuality that have been addressed so far. "Young Woman's Blues" sought possibilities, possibilities that arose from women being on the move and confidently asserting their own sexual desirability.

> Woke up this morning when chickens were crowing for day.
> Felt on the right side of my pillow, my man had gone away.
> On his pillow he left a note, reading I'm sorry you got my goat.
> No time to marry, no time to settle down.
>
> I'm a young woman and ain't done running around.
> I'm a young woman and ain't done running around.
>
> Some people call me a hobo, some call me a bum,
> Nobody know my name, nobody knows what I've done.
> I'm as good as any woman in your town,
> I ain't no high yella, I'm a deep killer brown.
>
> I ain't gonna marry, ain't gonna settle down.
> I'm gonna drink good moonshine and run these browns down.
> See that long lonesome road, cause you know it's got a end.
> And I'm a good woman and I can get plenty men.[14]

The women blues singers have become our cultural icons of sexual power, but what is often forgotten is that they could be great comic entertainers. In "One Hour Mama" Ida Cox used comedy to intensify an irreverent attack on male sexual prowess. The women blues singers had no respect for sexual taboos, for breaking through the boundaries of respectability and convention. The comic does not mellow the assertive voice, but, on the contrary, undermines mythologies of phallic power, and establishes a series of woman-centered heterosexual demands. Many women heard the "we" when Ida Cox said "I."

I've always heard that haste makes waste,
So I believe in takin' my time.
The highest mountain can't be raced
It's something you must slowly climb.

I want a slow and easy man;
He needn't ever take the lead,
Cause I work on that long time plan
And I ain't a lookin' for no speed.

I'm a one hour mama, so no one minute papa
Ain't the kind of man for me.
Set your alarm clock papa, one hour that's proper,
Then love me like I like to be.

I don't want no lame excuses,
Bout my lovin' being so good,
That you couldn't wait no longer
Now I hope I'm understood.

I'm a one hour mama so no one minute papa
Ain't the kind of man for me.

I can't stand no greenhorn lover
Like a rookie going to war,
With a load of big artillery,
But don't know what it's for

He's got to bring me reference
With a great long pedigree
And must prove he's got endurance
Or he don't mean snap to me.

I can't stand no crowing rooster
What just likes a hit or two
Action is the only booster
Of just what my man can do.

I don't want no imitation,
My requirements ain't no joke,
Cause I got pure indignation
For a guy what's lost his stroke.

I'm a one hour mama, so no one minute papa
Ain't the kind of man for me.
Set your alarm clock papa, one hour that's proper.
Then love me like I like to be.

I may want love for one hour,
Then decide to make it two.
Takes an hour fore I get started,
Maybe three fore I'm through.

I'm a one hour mama, so no one minute papa
Ain't the kind of man for me.[15]

But this moment of optimism, of the blues as the exercise of power and control over sexuality, was short-lived. The space occupied by these blues singers was opened up by race records, but race records did not survive the Depression. Some of these blues women, like Ethel Waters and Hattie McDaniels, broke through the racial boundaries of Hollywood films and were inserted into a different aspect of the culture industry where they occupied not a privileged but a subordinate space and articulated not the possibilities of black female sexual power but the "Yes, Ma'am's" of the black maid. The power of the blues singer was resurrected in a different moment of black power, re-emerging in Gayl Jones' *Corregidora*, and the woman blues singer remains an important part of our twentieth-century black cultural reconstruction.

1987

Notes

1. Hazel V. Carby, *Reconstructing Womanhood: The Emergence of the African American Woman Novelist*, New York: Oxford University Press, 1987.
2. Hortense Spillers, "Interstices: A Small Drama of Words," in Carol Vance, ed., *Pleasure and Danger: Exploring Female Sexuality*, Boston and London: Routledge & Kegan Paul, 1984, pp. 73–100.
3. Hazel V. Carby, "'On the Threshold of Woman's Era': Lynching, Empire and Sexuality in Black Feminist Theory," in Henry Louis Gates, Jr, ed., *Race, Writing and Difference*, Chicago: University of Chicago Press, 1986, pp. 301–15.
4. Anna Julia Cooper, *A Voice from the South*, Zenia, OH: Aldine Publishing House, 1892, p. 125.
5. Sherley Anne Williams, "The House of Desire," in Erline Stetson, ed., *Black Sister: Poetry by Black American Women 1746–1980*, Bloomington: Indiana University Press, 1981, p. 255.
6. Sherley Anne Williams, "Fifteen," in *Some One Sweet Angel Chile*, New York: William Morrow and Company Inc., 1982, p. 40.
7. Sherley Anne Williams, "The Blues Roots of Contemporary African American Poetry," in Michael S. Harper and Robert B. Stepto, eds, *Chant of Saints*, Chicago: University of Illinois Press, 1979, pp. 123–35.
8. Sterling Brown, "Ma Rainey," in *The Collected Poems of Sterling A. Brown*, New York: Harper & Row, 1980, p. 62.
9. Clara Smith, "Freight Train Blues," *Women's Railroad Blues*, Rosetta Records, 1980, RR1301.
10. Bessie Smith, "In House Blues," *Bessie Smith: The World's Greatest Blues Singer*, Columbia Records, CG33.
11. Ma Rainey, *Ma Rainey*, Milestone Records, 1974, M47021; Sandra Lieb, *Mother of the Blues: A Study of Ma Rainey*, Amherst: University of Massachusetts Press, 1981.
12. Ethel Waters and Charles Samuels, *His Eye is on the Sparrow*, New York: Doubleday, 1951.

13. Ethel Waters, "No Man's Mama," *Big Mamas*, Rosetta Records, 1982, RR1306.
14. Bessie Smith, "Young Woman's Blues," *Nobody's Blues But Mine*, Columbia Records, 1972, CG31093.
15. Ida Cox, "One Hour Mama," *Mean Mothers*, Rosetta Records, 1980, RR1300.

2

Policing the Black Woman's Body in an Urban Context

The problem of the unemployed negro woman in New York city is probably more serious than that of any other class of worker. She is unquestionably shut out from many lines of occupation, and through her increasing inefficiency and desire to avoid hard work, the best households and hotels and restaurants are gradually supplanting her with whites. This means in many instances that she must rely upon odd jobs and employment in the questionable house. . . .

Negro women who are led into immoral habits, vice and laziness, have in too many instances received their initiative from questionable employment agencies. . . . Some preventive measure must be taken for the colored girl going to work for the first time, and for the green helpless negro woman brought up here from the South – on promises of "easy work, lots of money and good times."

Frances A. Kellor, "Southern Colored Girls in the North"[1]

The migration of black people to cities outside of the Secessionist states of the South in the first half of the twentieth century transformed America socially, politically, and culturally. Of course, the migration of black people is not a twentieth-century phenomenon. In the antebellum period the underground railroad was the primary conduit out of the slave-holding states; in the late 1870s there was significant black migration to Kansas and in the 1880s to Oklahoma. Before 1910 there were major changes in the distribution of the black population between rural and urban areas within the South. The proportion of black people in southern cities more than doubled between 1870 and 1910 and, consequently, the proportion of the black population that continued to live in rural areas decreased significantly from 81 to 70 percent.[2] Historians and demographers seem to agree that what is now called the Great Migration needs to be viewed in the context of these earlier migratory patterns and in light of the fact that black people were becoming increasingly urbanized before they left for northern cities.

When considering the complex cultural transformations that not only accompany but are an integral part of these demographic shifts, it is important to challenge simplistic mythologies of how a rural black folk without the necessary industrial skills, untutored in the ways of the city, "green" and ignorant, in Frances Kellor's opinion, were exploitable fodder for the streets of New York, Chicago, Detroit, Cleveland, Philadelphia and Pittsburgh.[3] Certainly, male and female black migrants suffered economic and political exploitation, but it is important to separate the structural forces of exploitation from the ways in which black migrants came to be regarded as easily victimized subjects who quickly succumbed to the forces of vice and degradation.

I am going to argue that the complex processes of urbanization had gender-specific and class-specific consequences for the production of African American culture, in general, and for the cultural representation of black women, in particular. The movement of black women between rural and urban areas and between southern and northern cities generated a series of moral panics. One serious consequence was that the behavior of black female migrants was characterized as sexually degenerate and, therefore, socially dangerous. By using the phrase "moral panic" I am attempting to describe and to connect a series of responses, from institutions and from individuals, that identified the behavior of these migrating women as a social and political problem, a problem that had to be rectified in order to restore a moral social order.[4] These responses were an active part of a 1920s bourgeois ideology that not only identified this moral crisis but also produced a language that provided a framework of interpretation and referentiality that appeared to be able to explain for all time the behavior of black women in an urban environment. Kellor's indictment of the sexual behavior of black migrant women registers the emergence of what would rapidly become a widely shared discourse of what was wrong with black urban life.

Frances Kellor was the general director of the Inter-Municipal Committee on Household Research in New York City, and her "Southern Colored Girls in the North" appeared in *Charities*, "A Review of Local and General Philanthropy." Her article provides important evidence that as early as 1905 the major discursive elements were already in place that would define black female urban behavior throughout the teens and twenties as pathological.[5] The subjects of Kellor's article are migrating black women who are looking for work, and she implicitly assumes that these women are alone, either single or, at least, without men. Therefore, according to Kellor, they need "protection." On the surface, it looks as if Kellor is inciting moral alarm in defence of the rather abstract quality of female virtue, but it is quickly evident that she does not believe that black women have any moral fiber or will of their own that can be mobilized in the defense of their own interests. On the contrary, she believes that they become prostitutes because they are unable to protect themselves. Kellor's report makes a strong case for the creation of an alternative set of institutions to police the actual bodies of migrating black women. While Kellor is apparently condemning the existence of employment agencies that create a situation of economic dependency and exploitation in order to channel black women into houses of prostitution, she is actually identifying the "increasing inefficiency and desire [of black women] to avoid hard work" as the primary cause of the "problem."

Kellor has three major recommendations to make in addition to the establishment of more respectable and law-abiding agencies. First, she suggests the use of "practical and sympathetic women," like those on Ellis Island "who guide and direct the immigrant women," to "befriend" and act as "missionaries" toward black women when they arrive from the South. Second, she advocates the institution of a controlled system of lodging houses where black women can be sent at night and kept from going off on their own into the streets. Finally, she argues for the creation of training schools to make black women "more efficient."[6] This discourse, however, establishes a direct relationship between the social supervision of black women migrants and the control of their moral and sexual behavior, between the morally unacceptable economics of sex for sale and a morally acceptable policing of black female sexuality. In other words, Kellor characterizes the situation not as the lack of job possibilities for black women with the consequent conclusion that the employment market should be rigorously controlled, but, on the contrary, as a problem located in black women themselves, who, given the limited employment available to them and their "desire to avoid hard work," will sell their bodies.[7] Therefore, the logic of her argument dictates that bodies, not economic markets, need stringent surveillance.

The need to police and discipline the behavior of black women in cities, however, was not only a premise of white agencies and institutions but also a perception of black institutions and organizations, and the black middle class. The moral panic about the urban presence of apparently uncontrolled black women was symptomatic of and referenced aspects of the more general crises of social displacement and dislocation that were caused by migration. White and black intellectuals used and elaborated this discourse so that when they referred to the association between black women and vice, or immoral behavior, their references carried connotations of other crises of the black urban environment. Thus the migrating black woman could be variously situated as a threat to the progress of the race; as a threat to the establishment of a respectable urban black middle class; as a threat to congenial black and white middle-class relations; and as a threat to the formation of black masculinity in an urban environment.

Jane Edna Hunter, who was born in 1882 on the Woodburn plantation in South Carolina and trained as a nurse in Charleston and then at the Hampton Institute, arrived in Cleveland in May 1905 with little money. In an attempt to find accommodations she mistakenly arrived at a brothel, and her search for a place to live, she says, gave her an insight into the conditions that a black girl, "friendless and alone," had to face.[8] Hunter reflects that at home on the plantation she was well aware that some girls had been seduced, but she was totally unaware of what she calls a "wholesale organized traffic in black flesh" (*NP*, p. 68). When she goes to a dance she is shocked to see that the saloon on the first floor of Woodluff Hall is "the resort of bad women," and that the Hamilton Avenue area is the home of "vice." Hunter's discovery of what she identifies and criticizes as organized vice is interspersed with a description of her own difficult search for legitimate employment. Although highly trained, she cannot find a doctor who wants to employ a black nurse, and she depends on a cousin to find cleaning jobs for her.[9] Eventually, Hunter alternates work as a domestic with temporary nursing assignments until she finds a permanent position in the office of a group of doctors.

In her autobiography, *A Nickel and a Prayer*, Hunter states that her experiences led her to conclude that "a girl alone in a large city must needs know the dangers and pitfalls awaiting her" (*NP*, p. 77). While Hunter never situates herself as a helpless victim, she carefully creates a narrative that identifies and appears to account for the helplessness of other black migrating women, and as she does so she incorporates Kellor's analysis, strategies and conclusions. Hunter turned the death of her mother, from whom she had become estranged, into a catalyst to devote her life to political and social activity on behalf of the black women she designated as helpless. As a young woman Hunter was forbidden to see the man she loved, and she blamed her mother for forcing her into marriage with a man forty years older than herself. However, she walked out of the marriage fifteen months later and went to Charleston to find work, declaring that "a great weight rolled from my mind as I left him, determined to find and keep the freedom which I so ardently desired" (*NP*, p. 50). Hunter's mother died in 1911, after Hunter had lived in Cleveland for four years, and the realization that reconciliation was now impossible occasioned deep despair. In the midst of contemplating suicide Hunter found herself asking the question: "how could I best give to the world what I had failed to give her?" (*NP*, p. 81). Hunter's self-interrogation resulted in her making her mother, rather than herself, a symbol for the helplessness of all migrant women. Hunter characterized her mother as both "immature and impulsive" and imagined that her mother would have been totally helpless if she had been a migrant. What Hunter cannot explicitly acknowledge is that a figure of such helplessness stands in direct contrast to the way she writes with confidence and self-determination about her own need to gain and retain her freedom through urban migration. But the designation of her mother as helpless enables Hunter to occupy the absent maternal space. The daughter becomes mother as Hunter listens to the strains of a spiritual and is moved by the words, "ah feels like a motherless child." At this moment she decided on her "supreme work," dedicating her life to helping "the young Negro girl pushed from the nest by economic pressure, alone and friendless in a northern city; reduced to squalor, starvation; helpless against temptation and degradation" (*NP*, p. 83).

The fruit of Hunter's labors and the institutionalization of her maternal role into that of a matriarch is the formation of the Working Girls' Home Association, which later became the Phillis Wheatley Association, with Hunter as president. The Phillis Wheatley Association was the equivalent of the "controlled system of lodging houses" that Kellor recommended in her report, but under black not white control. In cooperation with the National Association of Colored Women other similar institutions were established in cities across the country with Hunter as chair of the Phillis Wheatley department of the NACW. The board that was established in 1913 to oversee the home included white as well as black patrons, and Hunter argued that the Phillis Wheatley Association was "one of the strongest ties between the Negro and white races in America" (*NP*, p. 165). It was not only at the level of management, however, that Hunter was proud of the association as a model of interracial cooperation. The home was a training ground to prepare young black women for domestic service, and one of Hunter's aims was to improve relations between white mistress and maid by producing a happy and efficient servant. As Hunter states:

> The most important factor in successful domestic service is a happy and human relation between the lady of the house and the maid – on the part of the maid, respect and affectionate regard for her employer; on the part of the employer, sympathy and imagination. Perhaps it is not going too far to say that the lady of the house should stand in the relation of a foster mother to the young woman who assists her in the household tasks. . . .
>
> The girl who is fairly well-trained and well-disposed will become interested in the life of the family that she serves, and will be devoted to its happiness. (*NP*, pp. 161–2)

Hunter asserted that the Phillis Wheatley Association was "an instrument for [the] social and moral redemption" of young black women (*NP*, p. 157). A prerequisite for this redemption, Hunter maintained, was surveillance over all aspects of the lives of the girls in the home:

> In fact it was necessary at all times to guard our girls from evil surroundings. I kept a vigilant ear at the switchboard in my office to catch conversations of a doubtful character, and to intercept assignations. No effort we made to restrict tenancy to girls of good character could exclude the ignorant, the foolish, and the weak, for these had to be protected as well. In the company of a policeman whom I could trust, I would sometimes follow couples to places of assignation, rescue the girl, and assist in the arrest of her would-be seducer. (*NP*, pp. 128–9)

There are extraordinary contradictions present in this narrative reconstructing the life of a woman who when young had declared her independence from both the patriarchal power of her husband and the maternal power of her mother by walking away from both of them to "find and keep the freedom [she] so ardently desired," only to find herself in her mature years thwarting the desires of other young women by lurking in hallways to eavesdrop on their telephone calls and marching off into the night accompanied by the police to have their lovers arrested. And, yet, Hunter clearly tries to establish a maternal framework to disguise and legitimate what are actually exploitative relations of power. Exploitation becomes nurturance when Hunter describes the white mistress acting as a "foster mother" to a young black domestic worker, and when she herself dominates the lives of her charges in the Phillis Wheatley Association. Hunter, remembering her own mother as weak and helpless, created the association as a matriarchy that allowed her to institutionalize and occupy a space of overwhelming matriarchal power over younger black women.

Although Hunter is uncritical of and, indeed, manipulates and abuses the possibilities of matriarchal power, she is explicit in her criticism of the ways in which an abusive patriarchal power becomes embedded in the corrupt legal and political machinery of city governance. Hunter is trenchant in her analysis of the mutually beneficial relations between "unscrupulous politicians," the "rapacity of realtors," the creation of the segregated ghetto, and organized vice in Cleveland. But urban blacks are situated as merely the victims of the forces of corruption: the politicians, Hunter felt, played "upon the ignorance of the Negro voter to entrench themselves in office, and then deliver[ed] the Negro over to every force of greed and vice which stalked around him" (NP, p. 121).

Hunter utilizes the force of matriarchal power to declare war on what she feels to be her most formidable enemy, "commercialized vice." She describes her battle in the most epic of biblical language, a battle in which she joins with a "dreadful monster . . . spawned by greed and ignorance . . . hideous to behold. 'Out of its belly came fire and smoke, and its mouth was as the mouth of a lion . . . and its wages were death'" (NP, p. 120). Corrupt city politics enables and maintains the monstrous network that feeds on the young female souls in Hunter's charge, but at its heart is a single patriarchal figure whom she refers to only as "Starlight."[10] If Hunter sees herself as the matriarchal savior of young black women, she describes "Starlight" as the "'Great Mogul' of organized vice." He is the epitome of the seducer of young black women whom he manipulates, betrays and then drags as "prisoners" down into the depths of "shame and degradation" (NP, p. 122). But, although the war is figuratively between these forces of patriarchal power and maternal influence, Hunter's matriarchal power is aimed directly at other women. Black female sexual behavior, because according to Hunter it is degenerate, threatens the progress of the race: threatens to "tumble gutterward," in her words, the "headway which the Negro had made toward the state of good citizenship" (NP, p. 126).

Dance halls and nightclubs are particular targets of Hunter's reformist zeal, and she identifies these cultural spaces, located in the "heart of [the] newly created Negro slum district[s]," as the site of the production of vice as spectacle: "Here, to the tune of St. Louis voodoo blues, half-naked Negro girls dance shameless dances with men in Spanish costumes. . . . The whole atmosphere is one of unrestrained animality, the jungle faintly veneered with civilized trappings" (NP, pp. 132–3). Places of amusement and of recreation for black people are condemned as morally dangerous and described as being filled with "lewd men and wretched women" (NP, p. 132). Nightclubs where black women perform for a white audience threaten the very foundations of Hunter's definitions of acceptable interracial relations:

> Interracial co-operation built the Phillis Wheatley Association and is carrying on its work; a co-operation of Negroes and whites for worthy purposes; which can gauge the spiritual contribution the Negro has made to American life, since his arrival in America. But in the meeting of blacks and whites in night clubs . . . there is to be found only cause for regret and head-hanging by both races. On the one side an exhibition of unbridled animality, on the other a blase quest for novel sensations, a vicarious gratification of the dark and violent desires of man's nature, a voluntary return to the jungle. (NP, p. 133)

There are deep fears being expressed in this passage in which the exploitation of black women is only one concern among many. These fears haunt the entire narrative and are also embedded in Kellor's account of young, black migrating women: fears of a rampant and uncontrolled female sexuality; fears of miscegenation; and fears of the assertion of an independent black female desire that has been unleashed through migration. If a black woman can claim her freedom and migrate to an urban environment, what is to keep her from negotiating her own path through its streets? What are the consequences of the female self-determination evident in such a journey for the establishment of a socially acceptable moral order that defines the boundaries of respectable sexual relations? What, indeed, is to be the framework of discipline and strategies of policing that can contain and limit black female sexuality? These are the grounds of contestation in which black women became the primary targets for the moral panic about urban immorality.

St Clair Drake and Horace Cayton in their history of Chicago, *Black Metropolis*, describe how the existence of residential restrictive convenants made middle-class neighborhoods in Bronzeville "the beach upon which broke the human flotsam which was tossed into the city streets by successive waves of migration from the South."[11] They also describe the deep ambivalence in the attitudes of the black middle class toward the black working class, who, as Drake and Cayton insist, perform "the essential digging, sweeping, and serving which make Metropolitan life tolerable" (*BM*, p. 523). This ambivalence, they argue, caused the black upper class to live a contradictory existence. On the one hand they defined their social position by emphasizing their *difference* from the lower class:

> But, as Race Leaders, the upper class must [also] identify itself psychologically with "The Race," and The Race includes a lot of people who would never be accepted socially. Upper-class Negroes, too, depend upon the Negro masses for their support if they are business or professional men. The whole orientation of the Negro upper class thus becomes one of trying to speed up the processes by which the lower class can be transformed from a poverty-stricken group, isolated from the general stream of American life, into a counterpart of middle-class America. (*BM*, p. 563)

Hunter, clearly, lives this contradiction: her self-definition and her right to control her own behavioral boundaries are beyond question. But, by positioning herself as part of the emergent black bourgeoisie, Hunter secures her personal autonomy in the process of claiming the right to circumscribe the rights of young black working-class women and to transform their behavior on the grounds of nurturing the progress of the race as a whole.

What Drake and Cayton fail to recognize, however, is the extent to which the behavioral transformation of this lower class was thought to be about transforming the behavior of black working-class women. Hunter's accounts of the women who represented the success stories of the Phillis Wheatley Association, for example, are narratives of the transformation of the behavior of migrant working-class black women to conform to middle-class norms of acceptable sexual behavior while actually being confirmed in their subordinate, working-class status as female domestics. These success stories represented the triumphant fulfilment of the mission of the Phillis Wheatley Association, a mission that declared itself to be "to discover, protect, cherish, and perpetuate the beauty and power of Negro Womanhood," but which was primarily concerned with shaping and disciplining a quiescent urban, black, female, working-class population.

The texts that draw on aspects of this discourse of black female sexuality as a way to respond to northern urban migration are multiple and varied. In two important novels about Harlem during the twenties, Carl Van Vechten's *Nigger Heaven* (1926) and Claude McKay's *Home to Harlem* (1928), both authors use their female characters as the terrain on which to map a relation between the sexual and class politics of urban black life.[12] While neither author appears to be overtly interested in prescribing a program of social engineering, both novels are fictions of black urban classes in formation. Central to the success of the emergent black middle class in these two novels is the evolution of urban codes of black masculinity. In each text representations of urban black women are used as both the means by which male protagonists will achieve or will fail to achieve social mobility and as signs of various possible threats to the emergence of the wholesome black masculinity necessary for the establishment of an accept-able black male citizenship in the American social order.

The first part of *Nigger Heaven* focuses on Mary Love, a figure of virginal purity. The failure of Byron Kasson, the male protagonist, to recognize the worth of Mary to the social security of his own future leads directly to his social disintegration. Van Vechten, a white patron of black culture and black artists, describes Mary as "cold":

> She had an instinctive horror of promiscuity, of being handled, even touched, by a man who did not mean a good deal to her. This might, she sometimes argued with herself, have something to do with her white inheritance, but Olive [her friend], who was far whiter, was lacking in this inherent sense of prudery. At any rate, whatever the cause, Mary realized that she was different in this respect from most of the other girls she knew. The Negro blood was there, warm and passionately earnest: all her preferences and prejudices were on the side of the race into which she had been born. She was as capable, she was convinced, of amorous emotion, as any of her friends, but the fact remained that she was more selective. Oh, the others were respectable enough; they did not involve them-selves too deeply. On the other hand, they did not flee from a kiss in the dark. A casual kiss in the dark was a repellent idea to Mary. What she wanted was a kiss in the light. (*NH*, p. 54)

Van Vechten appears to dismiss, or put in doubt, the classic nineteenth-century literary explanation of blood "admixture" for these opposing aspects of Mary's fictional personality in favor of using a more contempor-ary, and urban, explanation that uses Mary's "horror of promiscuity" as a sign of her secure class position.

Mary's middle-class existence is initially defined through her job: she works as a museum curator gathering together collections of African art. But Van Vechten also carefully defines her difference from migrant and working-class black women in a variety of more complex ways. When Mary attends a rent party, for example, she is figuratively defiled by the gin and juice that is spilled over her and stains her clothes. When she regretfully wonders why she danced at this party until two in the morning, Van Vechten has her mentally discipline herself by reflecting on a long, directly quoted passage from Gertrude Stein's "Melanctha." The passage is an extended reflection on the dangers of "colored people" getting excited and "running around and . . . drinking and doing everything bad they can think of" instead of "working hard and caring about their working and living regular with their families and saving up all their money, so they will have some to bring their children up better" (*NH*, p. 57). Mary carefully differentiates herself culturally and ideologically from the black working class. On the one hand, she defines spirituals, which deeply affect her, as a cultural form produced from "real faith," which has the power to "touch most of us . . . and make us want to cry or shout." But on the other hand, she sees the culture of "servant girls and the poor" as being very different.

The latter, she is convinced, don't really "feel faith – except as an escape from the drudgery of their lives. They don't really stop playing Numbers or dancing on Sunday or anything else that their religion forbids them to do. They enjoy themselves in church on Sunday as they do in the cabarets on week-days" (*NH*, pp. 60, 59). Mary's disdain of sexual promiscuity is firmly embedded, by Van Vechten, in a middle-class ideology of endlessly deferred gratification.

The counterpoint to Mary is a character called Lasca Sartoris, who uses her sexuality to negotiate her way through her life. Unlike Mary, who has never even been to the South, Lasca, the daughter of a country preacher, "began by teaching school in the backwoods down in Louisiana" and then migrated north when an uncle left her an inheritance. In the city Lasca is said to "cut loose" dancing, playing the piano and singing in Harlem clubs all night (*NH*, pp. 83–4). Lasca's sexuality ensnares a rich and much older husband whose death leaves her a rich heiress. Van Vechten uses Lasca as a figure of overt and degenerate sexuality whose behavior is absolutely outside of all moral boundaries. She attracts, then physically and emotion-ally destroys and discards a series of male lovers, including Byron Kasson, having embroiled them in an intense bacchanalia of alcoholic, drug and sexual abuse. For Byron, the would-be intellectual and writer, his choice of the influence of Lasca, rather than Mary, brings a certain end to all his hopes and ambition.

Claude McKay in *Home to Harlem* has a rather more subtle but, for women, an equally damning approach to the relation between black sexual politics, masculinity and the securing of social position. McKay's protago-nist, Jake, is ultimately saved by Felice, the woman he loves, in an interest-ing narrative sleight of hand that transforms Felice from the position of prostitute to a figure of wholesome sexuality. Jake arrives in Harlem and meets Felice in a bar. He spends the night with her, pays her and leaves the following morning thinking he will never see her again. Wondering if he can afford breakfast, Jake discovers that Felice has returned all his money to his pocket, thus proving that her sex is not for sale. This gesture convinces Jake that he must return to Felice, but he is quickly lost in the unfamiliar city streets, and it takes the whole course of the novel for him to find her again. On the journey back toward this "true" woman, however, Jake has to negotiate the vice and temptations of the city, which are embodied in a series of other women that he meets.

McKay has a much deeper, richer and more complex understanding of the cultural forms of the black urban landscape on which he draws than Van Vechten. But, despite this formal complexity, McKay situates his female figures in a very simplistic manner in various degrees of approxi-mation to an uncontrolled and, therefore, problematic sexual behavior. For Jake's journey is not just a journey to find the right woman; it is, primarily, a journey of black masculinity in formation, a sort of *Pilgrim's Progress* in which a number of threatening embodiments of the female and the feminine have to be negotiated. The most significant of these female figures is Rose, a nightclub singer at a cabaret called the Congo. As its name implies, the Congo is "a real throbbing little Africa in New York. It was an amusement place entirely for the unwashed of the Black Belt. . . . Girls coming from the South to try their future in New York," McKay stresses, "always reached the Congo first" (*HH*, pp. 29–30). These "chippies [that] come up from down home," a male friend of Jake's advises him, represent "the best pickings" in Harlem (*HH*, p. 35). Felice, of course, is never seen there. At the heart of what McKay describes as the "thick, dark-colorful, and fascinating" Congo, he situates the blues and Rose, the blues singer (*HH*, p. 36). As far as Jake is concerned, Rose is "a wonderful tissue of throbbing flesh," though he neither loves nor feels "any deep desire for her" (*HH*, pp. 42, 114). The assumption of the novel is that male love and desire could not be generated for, or be sustained by, a woman like Rose, who is characterized as bisexual because she lacks the acceptable feminine qualities of "tenderness . . . timidity . . . [and] aloofness." Indeed, Rose's sexual ambiguity is positioned as a threat to the very existence of black masculinity, reducing Jake to the role of a "big, good slave" (*HH*, pp. 42, 41). McKay proposes that only a pathological and distorted form of masculine power could exist in such a relationship when Rose makes masochistic demands that Jake brutalize her, confirming his belief "that a woman could always go further than a man in coarseness, depravity, and sheer cupidity" (*HH*, p. 69). Jake's refusal to beat Rose is a triumph of wholesome masculinity over the degenerate female element and allows Jake to proceed on his journey to become a man.

The dance hall and the cabaret, in the texts that I have been discussing, are the most frequently referenced landscapes in which black female promiscuity and sexual degeneracy were described. In William H. Jones's sociological study of black urban recreation and amusement (1927), the dance hall was a complex and a contested social space. Jones could not condemn the dance hall as an "essentially antisocial institution" because it was possible that a dance hall could be a place in which "romantic love of the most idealistic type" could blossom. But dance halls encouraged a quick intimacy that could also lead the young "on the downard path to crime."[13] What Jones condemned without compromise was the dancing that took place in the dance halls. He saw modern dances as nothing more than "sexual pantomimes. They are similar to many of the ancient and primitive methods of publicly arousing human passions in preparation for lascivious orgies." He asserted that the results of his "careful investigation disclosed the fact that . . . a large amount of illicit sex behavior is unquestionably the natural sequence of certain modern forms of dancing" (*RA*, p. 122).

Jones reserved his greatest vehemence for the cabaret, where

> excess in dancing, jungle laughter, and semi-alcoholic beverages are character-
> istic features of their life. Here, jazz music is carried to extremes. In general,

there is more abandon achieved by the dancers than in the formal dance hall, and more of a tendency toward nakedness on the part of the female entertainers. (*RA*, p. 131)

What Jones particularly feared was what he called "social demoralization." He designated these recreational social spaces as places where "the most powerful human impulses and emotions are functioning," impulses and emotions that threatened the deterioration of the fragile social fabric of the black urban community (*RA*, p. 122).

The existence of dance halls and cabarets was particularly dangerous to the moral health of the black middle class, Jones maintained, because of "the rapidity and ease with which the anti-social forms of dancing spread upwards into and engross the so-called higher classes." He viewed the social fabric of the black urban community as fragile because of the lack of "adequate bulwarks against the encroachment of such behavior forms upon the life of the more advanced groups of Negroes" (*RA*, p. 122). "Class stratification" within the black community, Jones continued, only "seems to be strong." If black middle-class public opinion could generate disapproval of "the vulgar, sexually-suggestive modern dances ... they would be compelled to confine themselves to the lower anti-social cultural groups in which they originated" (*RA*, p. 123). His appeal to the mobilization of social disapproval appears to be as much about generating a black middle-class ideology of solidarity and coexistence as about challenging threats to the social mores of that group. If middle-class hegemony could be established in the black community, it could more effectively discipline the black working class through the implementation of what Jones refers to as "mechanisms of control whereby forces which tend to disintegrate and demoralize the higher forms of culture may be excluded or annihilated" (*RA*, p. 123).

Between Kellor's report for *Charities* and Jones's book the moral panic about the lack of control over the sexual behavior of black women had become absorbed into the fundamental assumptions of the sociological analysis of urban black culture, which thus designated many of its forms of entertainment and leisure "pathological" and in need of greater institutional control.[14] Kathy Peiss, in her recent analysis of white working-women's leisure and recreation in New York, describes how white reformers in the early decades of the twentieth century believed that "the primary purpose of reform for working women was to inculcate standards of respectable behavior." Perceptions of "a rising tide of promiscuity and immorality" and panics over "white slavery and commercialized prostitution," she argues, motivated Progressive reformers whose prime target was increasingly "the growing menace of commercial amusements."[15] But the black urban community was constructed as pathological in very specific ways. Black urban life was viewed as being intimately associated with commercialized vice because black migrants to cities were forced to live in or adjacent to areas previously established as red-light districts in which prostitution and gambling had been contained. The existence of restrictive covenants enforced black residential segregation and limited the expansion of what became identified as black urban ghettos.[16] It was within the confines of East St Louis, the south side of Chicago, the tenderloin in Kansas City, and Harlem in New York that an entertainment industry that served both a white and a black clientele was located and from which an urban blues culture emerged.

On the eve of the Depression black women who had migrated to urban areas were still overwhelmingly limited to employment in domestic service and as laundresses. In Chicago, for example, between the First World War and the onset of the Depression, over 40 percent of white women workers but only 5 percent of black women workers who entered the labor force obtained "clean" work (see *BM*, pp. 220–9). The category "clean" work referred to jobs like office secretary and department store clerk; "clean" work was the type of employment from which black women were rigorously excluded. From the biographies and autobiographies of the black women who eventually became entertainers it is clear that joining a touring vaudeville troupe or tent show was an important avenue of geographic mobility for young black women who were too poor to pay for train fares and for whom hopping a freight car was dangerous. In addition, being a member of a vaudeville show or performing in a nightclub was not attractive primarily because it offered a mythic life of glamor but because it was a rare opportunity to do "clean" work and to reject the life of a domestic servant.

When she was eight years old Josephine Baker started her first job and discovered that working as a maid for a white mistress was not "the happy and human relation" that Jane Edna Hunter maintained it should be. Baker was assured by her mistress, Mrs Keiser, that she loved children, and she promised Baker the shoes and a coat that her own family were too poor to provide. However, Baker had to start to work at five in the morning so she could be at school by nine, and when she arrived home in the afternoon she had to work again until ten o'clock at night, when she was sent to bed in the cellar to sleep with the dog. One day when Baker made a mistake Mrs Keiser punished her by plunging the little girl's arms into boiling water. This story and Baker's account of how she watched white people murder and torture her relatives and neighbors during the East St Louis riot of 1917 are situated in her autobiography as the preface to her decision to leave St Louis when she was thirteen years old and get on a train with a vaudeville troupe called the Dixie Steppers.[17]

Alberta Hunter left Memphis when she was thirteen because she had heard that young girls in Chicago were being paid ten dollars a week to sing.[18] In 1912 she started working in a club called Dago Frank's, singing to an audience of pimps and prostitutes, and then moved to Hugh Hoskins, a club for "confidence men and their girls who were pickpockets." In many ways Alberta Hunter's story of her early years in Chicago epitomizes the life from which Jane Edna Hunter wanted to save young black women in the name of maternal protection. But Alberta Hunter emphasizes how she found maternal care and nurturance from the prostitutes in her audience and describes how "the prostitutes were so wonderful, they'd always make the 'Johns' give me money you know. . . . They'd go out and buy me little dresses and things to put on me so I'd look nice."[19]

Ethel Waters agreed to join the act of two vaudevillians she met in a Philadelphia saloon because she was offered ten dollars a week playing the Lincoln Theatre when she was "getting three fifty a week as a scullion and chambermaid [at the Harrod Apartments] and a dollar and a quarter more for taking home some of the guests' laundry."[20] Waters grew up in the red-light districts of Philadelphia, and in her autobiography she asserts that she "always had great respect for whores" (*H*, p. 17). Like Alberta Hunter she utilizes the language of maternal nurturance when she describes how her friendship with a young prostitute blossomed:

> Being hardly more than a child herself, Blanche often played with me, read me stories, and sang little songs with me. Her beauty fascinated me. I loved her. There was a great camaraderie between us, and that young prostitute gave me some of the attention and warm affection I was starving for. Whenever I tipped off the sporting world that the cops were just around the corner I felt I was doing it for Blanche and her friends. (*H*, p. 18)

Waters reveals a consciousness of being part of a world in which women were under surveillance and has little hesitation in declaring her allegiance. The images and figures of the sources of both exploitation and nurturance in the lives of these young black women are in direct contrast to and, indeed, in direct conflict with the attempts of the black middle class to police and discipline female sexuality.

Black women blues singers, musicians and performers dominated the black recording industry and vaudeville circuit throughout the twenties, and they are the central figures in the emergence and establishment of an urban blues culture. However, in order to acknowledge their roles as the primary cultural mediators of the conditions of transition and the producers of a culture of migration we have to challenge the contemporary histories of the formation of a black urban culture as a history of the black middle class. The dominance of the conceptual paradigm of the Harlem Renaissance with its emphasis on the practices of literature and fine art relies on a belief that the black middle class did, in fact, accomplish and secure its own cultural and political dominance within black America. However, as Houston A. Baker, Jr, argues, what is called the Renaissance actually marks the historical moment of the failure of the black bourgeoisie to achieve cultural hegemony and to become a dominant social force.[21]

The contradictory nature of the culture that was produced in black urban America between the teens and the Depression has not been retained or absorbed within black urban cultural histories. The twenties must be viewed as a period of ideological, political and cultural contestation between an emergent black bourgeoisie and an emerging urban black working class. The cultural revolution or successful renaissance that did occur stemmed from this terrain of conflict in which the black women who were so central to the formation of an urban blues culture created a web of connections among working-class migrants. The possibilities of both black female liberation and oppression were voiced through a music that spoke to the desires which were released in the dramatic shift in social relations that occurred in a historical moment of crisis and dislocation.[22]

Women's blues were not only a central mechanism of cultural mediation but also the primary means of the expression of the disrupted social relations associated with urban migration. The blues women did not passively reflect the vast social changes of their time; they provided new ways of thinking about these changes, alternative conceptions of the physical and social world for their audience of migrating and urban women and men, and social models for women who aspired to escape from and improve their conditions of existence. I have already described how hopping freight cars, because of the inherent dangers associated with that form of travel, was not a viable option for women and that traveling tent shows and vaudeville on the Theater Owners' Booking Association circuit (TOBA) offered an alternative way to achieve mobility for young women – Mamie Smith, for example, started dancing when she was ten, and Ida Cox left home to join the Black and Tan Minstrel Show when she was fourteen. This increase in their physical mobility parallels their musical challenges to sexual conventions and gendered social roles. However, the field of blues history is dominated by the assumption that "authentic" blues forms are entirely rural in origin and are produced by the figure of the wandering, lone male. Thus the formation of mythologies of blues masculinity, which depend on this popular image, has obscured the ways in which the gendering of women was challenged in the blues. The blues women of the twenties, who recorded primarily in urban centers but who employed and modified the full range of rural and urban blues styles, have come to be regarded as professionalized aberrations who commercialized and adulterated "pure" blues forms. But as Chris Albertson insists, the blues "women were all aggressive women [who] knew what they wanted and went after it."[23] The blues women brought to the black, urban, working class an awareness of its social existence and acted creatively to vocalize the contradictions and tensions of the terrain of sexual politics in the relation of black working-class culture to the culture of the emergent black middle class. In doing so they inspired other women to claim the "freedom [they] so ardently desired."

1992

Notes

1. Frances A. Kellor, "Southern Colored Girls in the North: The Problem of Their Protection," *Charities*, Mar. 18 1905, pp. 584–5.
2. See Daniel M. Johnson and Rex R. Campbell, *Black Migration in America: A Social Demographic History*, Durham, NC: Duke University Press, 1981.
3. Carole Marks argues two important points in *Farewell – We're Good and Gone*. The first is that the majority of migrants at this stage of migration were from urban areas and left not just to "raise their wages but because they were the displaced mudsills of southern industrial development." Second, the level of a laborer's skill was less important "than institutional barriers in determining migrant assimilation and mobility." While there is a dispute about whether the majority of migrants were from rural or urban areas in the South it is clear that a significant number of migrants were urbanized and had previous experience of wage labor, skilled and unskilled, and that a number were professionals following their clients (Carole Marks, *Farewell – We're Good and Gone: The Great Black Migration*, Bloomington: Indiana University Press, 1989, p. 3). See also Johnson and Campbell, *Black Migration in America*, p. 79.
4. See Stuart Hall et al., *Policing the Crisis: Mugging, the State, and Law and Order*, London: Macmillan, 1978, pp. 16–20. Hall and his co-authors draw on the work of Stanley Cohen, who argues that

   > societies appear to be subject, every now and then, to periods of moral panic. A condition, episode, person or group of persons emerges to become defined as a threat to societal values and interests; its nature is presented in a stylized and stereotypical fashion by the mass media; the moral barricades are manned by editors, bishops, politicians and other right-thinking people; socially accredited experts pronounce their diagnoses and solutions; ways of coping are evolved or (more often) resorted to; the condition then disappears, submerges or deteriorates and becomes more visible. Sometimes the object of the panic is quite novel and at other times it is something which has been in existence long enough, but suddenly appears in the limelight. (Stanley Cohen, *Folk Devils and Moral Panics: The Creation of the Mods and Rockers*, London: MacGibbon and Kee, 1972, p. 9).

5. Kellor, "Southern Colored Girls," pp. 584–5.
6. Ibid., p. 585.
7. Another unspoken assumption here, of course, is that selling sex is not hard but easy work.
8. Jane Edna Hunter, *A Nickel and a Prayer*, Cleveland, 1940, p. 67; hereafter abbreviated *NP*. I am very grateful to Darlene Clark Hine for telling me about Hunter, her autobiography and her papers.
9. Hunter maintains that she was one of only two black professional nurses in Cleveland. See *NP*, p. 87.
10. This figure was Albert D. "Starlight" Boyd, whom Katrina Hazzard-Gordon refers to as a "political strongman." He owned and operated Woodluff Hall, the dance hall that Hunter felt was so disreputable, and the Starlight Café. Boyd had numerous estate holdings and links to prostitution and gambling and helped to deliver the black votes of the Eleventh Ward to the Republican boss

Maurice Maschke (Katrina Hazzard-Gordon, *Jookin': The Rise of Social Dance Formations in African-American Culture*, Philadelphia: Temple University Press, 1990, p. 127; see also pp. 128, 130–2 and 136–7).

11. St Clair Drake and Horace R. Cayton, *Black Metropolis: A Study of Negro Life in a Northern City*, New York: Harcourt, Brace and Company, 1945, p. 577; hereafter abbreviated *BM*.

12. See Carl Van Vechten, *Nigger Heaven*, New York: Knopf, 1926, hereafter abbreviated *NH*; and Claude McKay, *Home to Harlem*, New York: Harper & Brothers, 1928, hereafter abbreviated *HH*.

13. William H. Jones, *Recreation and Amusement among Negroes in Washington, D.C.: A Sociological Analysis of the Negro in an Urban Environment*, Washington, DC: n.p., 1927, p. 121; hereafter abbreviated *RA*.

14. Jones acknowledged his greatest debt to Robert E. Park and others of the Department of Sociology at the University of Chicago.

15. Kathy Peiss, *Cheap Amusements: Working Women and Leisure in Turn-of-the-Century New York*, Philadelphia: Temple University Press, 1986, pp. 178–9. The focus of my analysis is rather different than Peiss's. She describes her book as "a study of young working women's culture in turn-of-the-century New York City – the customs, values, public styles, and ritualized interactions – expressed in leisure time" (p. 3). Not only am I concentrating on black women rather than white women, but also I am most interested here in the black women for whom the site of leisure was a place of work rather than recreation.

16. See William Barlow, *Looking Up at Down: The Emergence of Blues Culture*, Philadelphia: Temple University Press, 1989, pp. 240–3 (on Kansas City), 250–1 (on St Louis) and 287–92 (on Chicago). See also *BM*, pp. 174–213.

17. See Josephine Baker and Jo Bouillon, *Josephine*, trans. Mariana Fitzpatrick, New York: Harper and Row, 1977, pp. 3–4. See also Phyllis Rose, *Jazz Cleopatra: Josephine Baker in Her Time*, New York: Doubleday, 1989, p. 12.

18. See Frank C. Taylor and Gerald Cook, *Alberta Hunter: A Celebration in Blues*, New York: McGraw-Hill, 1987, pp. 20–3.

19. Alberta Hunter, quoted in Stuart Goldman (producer), *Alberta Hunter: My Castle's Rockin'*, 1988.

20. Ethel Waters and Charles Samuels, *His Eye is on the Sparrow*, New York: Doubleday, 1951, p. 72; hereafter abbreviated *H*.

21. See Houston A. Baker, Jr *Modernism and the Harlem Renaissance*, Chicago: University of Chicago Press, 1987.

22. Virginia Yans-McLaughlin argues that the new scholarship in immigration and migration studies has moved away from questions about

> individual and group agency toward the social relations of exchange. So, instead of individuals assimilating or achieving, we have group strategies and networks. What we might call a network-exchange theory seems to be emerging as a potential alternative to assimilation and human-capital theory. In network-exchange theory, an ethnic group's human capital is not simply transported from one place to another by individuals who fold their riches into the American system. Although it is true that the groups are sometimes portrayed as holders of assets, these are transformed to new purposes; indeed, immigrant groups seem capable of creating new advantages for themselves. The network structure that originally functioned as the grid connecting Old

World kin might, for example, transform itself in ethnic subeconomies to provide jobs, housing, or even business opportunities. (Virginia Yans-McLaughlin, introduction, *Immigration Reconsidered: History, Sociology and Politics*, Virginia Yans-McLaughlin, ed., New York: Oxford University Press, 1990, p. 12)

Using such a methodology Suzanne Model argues that because of their very limited access to the job market black migrants were unable, or failed, to establish such a system of mutual assistance. Although it is clear that networks of exchange did indeed exist within black urban migrant enclaves, my argument here is that network-exchange theory is unnecessarily limited if it is applied only to access to the labor market and to alternative economies that existed within migrant communities. I would argue that urban blues culture could profitably be regarded as a network of exchange or web of connection rather than as a conglomeration of individual achievement. See Suzanne W. Model, "Work and Family: Blacks and Immigrants from South and East Europe," in ibid., pp. 130–59. It would seem to me that the role of the *Chicago Defender* would be important in writing a history that documented the system of mutual exchange in black communities that provided information about and access to the job market. See, for example, Emmett J. Scott, "Letters of Negro Migrants of 1916–1918," *Journal of Negro History*, no. 4, July 1919, pp. 290–340, and "Additional Letters of Negro Migrants of 1916–1918," *Journal of Negro History*, no. 4, Oct. 1919, pp. 412–65.

23. Chris Albertson, quoted in Carole van Falkenburg and Christine Dall (producers), *Wild Women Don't Have the Blues*, 1989.

3

Black Women's Blues, Motown and Rock and Roll

On October 10 1977, Alberta Hunter opened at the Cookery, a nightclub run by Barney Josephson in New York City. "This is the first song I have sung professionally in twenty years," she told her audience before she let go with her own composition, "My Castle's Rockin'." Hunter had been forced to retire from a nursing career that she really loved because she was thought to be seventy years old. "I fooled them though," she declared to the peopled gathered that night, "I lied. I'm eighty-two." The nurses who had been her colleagues and had come to the opening night cheered raucously. She followed "My Castle's Rockin'" with "Down Hearted Blues," which Bessie Smith recorded in 1923, "a song I wrote before most of your children were born. . . . Men were dragging women's hearts around then, and they're still doing it," Hunter asserted.[1]

The reviews of Hunter's show were raves; she was described as "the hottest thing in town." The white press recognized her as a "national treasure," and as an "overnight sensation," though the "night" had been sixty-six years long. Even Hunter's biographer, Frank Taylor, did not come to hear of her before 1978 and did not meet her until 1983 when she was on tour in São Paulo, Brazil.

Alberta Hunter was born April 1 1895 and grew up in Memphis, a city which belatedly recognized the talent of its black daughter in 1978 when the Mayor gave her a bunch of flowers and a key to the city. Hunter remembered vividly how as a child she had not been allowed to walk on the sidewalks of Memphis, and after the ceremony she told reporters how happy she was to see that there were no "COLORED ONLY" signs at restrooms and water fountains. Hunter was not one to romanticize such a moment of recognition. "I was always equal," she said; "I always felt I was good enough to do anything else that anybody else could do, but I was not given a chance to do."[2]

In 1911, when Hunter was sixteen, she left Memphis for Chicago and started singing at Dago Frank's, a bordello. Her pianist could only play Stephen Foster songs but Hunter describes the pimps as "gentlemen" and the clients as so proper in appearance "You would think they were all ministers . . . not that ministers are so grand and good." For the next few years Hunter sang at various clubs, including the Panama Café, where she worked with George Hall, "who could play a mess of a piano," Florence Mills, Cora Green and Bricktop (Ada Smith). By 1917 she could be said to have "made it" as she began what became a five-year engagement at the Dreamland Ballroom, singing with King Oliver's Band, which at the time included Lil Hardin and Sidney Bechet.

Hunter made her first record, "How Long, Sweet Daddy, How Long?," in May 1921 for Black Swan, the first black-owned label. By 1922 Louis Armstrong had moved to Chicago and in 1924 Hunter recorded "Nobody Knows the Way I Feel Dis Mornin'," and "Early Every Morn" with Armstrong, Bechet and Lil (Hardin) Armstrong. Frank C. Taylor, in his biography of Hunter's career, *Alberta Hunter: A Celebration in Blues*, charts in careful detail when each of Hunter's songs was recorded and who played with her.[3] But those who are unfamiliar with Hunter's work, or only know of it since the late seventies, need a critical perspective to guide them through the gradual but dramatic changes in Hunter's style throughout her career, a perspective that Taylor, like most biographers, fails to provide, preferring to amass detail than exercise critical judgment.

The most pleasurable and informative way to read *A Celebration in Blues* is to listen to a careful selection of recordings at the same time. Hunter's early recording years were collected on *Young Alberta Hunter: The Twenties* (Stash, 1984, ST123), an invaluable collection that established Hunter's distinct contribution to women's blues.[4] Hunter did not have the power of Bessie Smith or the rumbling depth of Ma Rainey; her clear diction with an occasional tremulous waver in "How Long?" has the range of Ethel Waters combined with the mannered dignity of Adelaide Hall. But Hunter could growl when she wanted to, as in the slower, more sustained pace of "Nobody Knows," and when she moans "I could kill you with an express train," she plumbs the depths of the blues. This collection also manages to capture some of the sensuality which was a key element of Hunter's performances: songs like "Your Jelly Roll is Good," "Take that Thing Away" and "I'm Hard to Satisfy" are strong and sexually suggestive. In her early years as an entertainer Hunter was a sexy table singer, "always strolling from table to table and singing to one small group of people at a time. . . . I made it more intimate by stopping here and there, because that way the people felt I was singing just for them and the tips were bigger."[5] "Alberta wore heavily beaded dresses that glittered and sparkled as she shimmied around the room and sang. . . . Every now and then she'd make her breasts jump, and then the cats really loosened up on their bankrolls."[6]

Taylor argues that Hunter constructed a public version of her life (she herself insisted that she "never shared [her] private life with anybody in the world") and he admits that at times "she knowingly mixed up details of her past simply because she had always done it that way." In *A Celebration in*

Blues Taylor is self-consciously satisfied that he has reconstructed the private as well as the public persona, but it is obvious, particularly in relation to issues of sexuality, that Hunter is very cautious with her biographer. She consistently underplays any and all references to the sensual aspects of her performances and refuses to discuss her lesbian relationships. Consequently, Taylor can tell us little about the years Hunter spent with Lottie Tyler or Carrie Mae Ward and concentrates instead upon her friendships with men.

In 1927 Hunter went to Paris and then to London, where she starred in *Showboat* with Paul Robeson. Much of the thirties was spent commuting between Europe, where she felt she was loved, and the States, where her ambitions were frustrated. Hunter's style changed in Europe, as can be heard on *The Legendary Alberta Hunter* (DRG, n.d., SL5195), a collection of recordings made in London in 1934. Singing with Jack Johnson and his orchestra, the microphone allows Hunter to achieve the intimacy she had sought to project by directing her voice toward particular tables in Chicago clubs, though, of course, the movements which had been a crucial part of her performance were curbed. Her voice, recorded at the Dorchester Hotel, is sophisticated, softer, more mellow and "polished," as it is described in the liner notes. Hunter has gained more control over her voice but she is also more restrained. Nevertheless, it is a beautiful set of recordings.

Popularity in Paris and London and a greater sophistication did not help Hunter to find glamorous jobs Stateside, where she was "just another 'little colored gal,' a little older and far too refined for most club owners in the United States."[7] Taylor argues that the greater barrier to Hunter's success was her refusal to "play the game, to go to bed with the guys controlling the shows." On the contrary, in Hunter's view, "she wanted to be respected as the talented individual she was without all the bullshit associated with show business."[8] Hunter did do some radio broadcasts, however, and landed a part in *Mamba's Daughters* (1939). When Hunter was on tour in Europe she wrote a regular column which was sent back home for publication in the *Afro-American*.

Hunter spent the war years traveling for the United Service Organizations (USO). In 1944 she left for a tour of China, Burma and India, and by 1952 she was on her seventh USO tour in Korea. But in the mid-fifties she found herself occasionally having to collect unemployment benefit and playing the bit part of a "happy Negro servant" in an unsuccessful play, so Hunter decided to quit the entertainment business while she was ahead; she became a volunteer worker at Harlem Hospital and then persuaded the director of the YWCA school to enroll her in a course for licenced practical nurses. They put her age back twelve years and Hunter started her second career.

Taylor was able to work with Hunter for five months before she died, taping her reminiscences and reconstructing her life from the "boxes and grocery bags filled with photos, theater programs, correspondence, and scraps of paper she had saved over her long life." With the assistance of Gerald Cook, Hunter's last pianist, Taylor created a biography that reflects the great respect he has for her talent, her achievements and the progress of her life. Unfortunately this respect borders upon an awe that puts Alberta Hunter, the woman, at an almost unreachable distance from the reader. We seem to have all the "facts" about her life while as a person she escapes our understanding, retaining the intangibility that is an essential ingredient of stardom in American culture. I constantly found myself wishing that Taylor would spend less time on the creation of an indomitable but daunting figure and more time concentrating on hearing and understanding the cultural meaning of the history of Alberta Hunter's life; but it didn't happen. The result is less a process of reflection than an assemblage of undigested data.

The major problem is Taylor's approach to the boxes and bags of memorabilia to which Hunter granted him access. He regards them as the repository of the "really important facts of her life" and reconstructs this life by linking together these "facts" into a frequently dry chronicle of events. He argues that Hunter hadn't saved this material to ensure herself a place in history but "simply because she wanted people to believe she had done what she had." Taylor does not accept Hunter's reasoning but imposes his own psychological interpretation upon the process of amassing the details of her life. Taylor insists that Hunter needed the proof of her existence because she

> grew up without much nurturing of her sense of self-worth. There was no daddy to tell her to dream and to believe her dreams would come true. Her mother favored Alberta's older sister; whites made her come to their back doors; her stepfather beat up her mother and despised her; a school principal molested her; uppity, lighter-skinned blacks kept her at a distance . . . some people in the record business cheated her of royalties and American vaudeville theaters denied her top billing.[9]

Taylor's interpretation is shaped by and dependent upon an ideology of black pathology. His inability to separate the effects of institutionalized racism, sexual harassment and familial relations is irritating and it means that he misses opportunities to relate Hunter's experiences to those of other black performers (most of whom were cheated out of royalties, for example). Taylor automatically equates poverty and blackness with low self-esteem, but when Hunter's own voice bursts through his carefully controlled narrative it contradicts him and aggressively denies such limitations. As a white male writing the story of a black woman, Taylor should have been more conscious of the racist, patriarchal ideologies that structure his perceptions of what it means to be poor and black and female in America.

Hunter herself is clear about the relation between the material conditions of her existence and her music. "Many people think a woman sings the blues only when she is in love with a man who treats her like a dog," she explained to reporters in Brazil.

> I've never had the blues about no man, never in my life honey. If a man beats me, I'll take a broomstick and beat him to death. . . . We sing the blues because our hearts have been hurt. Blues is when you're hungry and you don't have money to buy food. Or you can't pay your rent at the end of the month. Blues is when you disappoint somebody else: if you owe some money to your best friend, and you know he needs it, but you don't have it to give to him. . . . Blues is like milk to a baby.[10]

It is moments like this, in *A Celebration in Blues*, which free black music from the cultural assumptions of white America and which make it worth reading.

In stark contrast to Taylor, who cares very much about his subject and tries very hard to get it right, Jim Haskins seems to care very little about Dinah Washington. Unlike *A Celebration in Blues*, *Queen of the Blues: A Biography of Dinah Washington* reveals scant respect and no love.[11] Haskins reproduces unquestioningly the mythology of Washington created by the culture industry and remains adamantly ignorant of the subtleties of the oppressive sexual politics that shaped her existence. His narrative is structured through an account of Washington's marriages and relations with men. She is represented as a tragic figure because these relationships are designated by Haskins simply as "failures." Gossip and anecdotes about drinking, diet pills and sleeping pills are reproduced for the unreflective consumption of the reader. "She was always hitting somebody over the head with his instrument, or being hit over the head, or throwing a glass at some woman, or being sued by some woman."[12] What Haskins does know is the entertainment industry – he has previously written biographies of Scott Joplin, Diana Ross, and Bricktop and the Cotton Club – but his few insightful commentaries on the Jim Crow institutional structure of record companies and radio stations are not sufficient to salvage what appears as a hastily written, careless and often sexist biography.

In 1924 when Alberta Hunter was recording for Paramount in New York and popularizing a new dance, the Black Bottom, Dinah Washington was born, Ruth Jones, in Tuscaloosa, Alabama. The nineteen years which separates their ages signifies a generational difference with specific consequences for their music. Like Hunter, Washington first recorded blues within the confines of "race records" produced for the "race market." Her earliest recordings were made available on the offensively named *Dinah Washington: A Slick Chick (on the Mellow Side)* (EmArcy, 1983, 814 184 1) and *Wise Woman Blues: Dinah Washington Rare and Early* (Rosetta Records, 1984, RR1313). But unlike Hunter, Washington began her career as a gospel singer by joining the first all-woman gospel group, the Sallie Martin Colored Ladies Quartet, when she was sixteen. Washington was influenced by both Mahalia Jackson and the Reverend C. L. Franklin (father of Aretha Franklin). After two years she left the world of gospel music for the "Devil's music" and sang blues in Chicago's south side jazz clubs until she joined Lionel Hampton's band late in 1942.

Leonard Feather, songwriter, agent and late jazz critic of the *Los Angeles Times*, described Washington as having

> a very biting tone quality to her voice, a unique timbre. . . . She had a style that reflected her church and gospel background and the whole tradition of the blues. She didn't sound like Bessie Smith, but it was in the same tradition, just a generation later.[13]

Hunter made a distinct attempt in the thirties to acquire a sophisticated tone and quality; Washington's earliest recordings are sophisticated and smooth but also deeply emotive.

Though Washington was quickly hailed as a modern Bessie Smith, she traced her own musical heritage somewhat differently. In her first records she sings without hesitation; the confidence that she projects and the tone of authority in her voice, even though she was only nineteen, must have come from her gospel singing. But her power and clarity, the ways in which the musical conventions of the early blues are blended with gospel, is only one aspect of Washington's particular contribution to the blues; the fusing of emotion and sensitivity comes from Billie Holiday. Holiday was the idol of the young Washington; she went to see Holiday perform as often as she could during those early years working the blues clubs and incorporated her style and phrasing into her performance.

Washington left Hampton's band and rapidly became a star in the "race" market. Record companies designated and promoted blues for sale and distribution in black areas only, and by 1946 *Billboard* was charting these sales on their "Honor Roll of Hits," the first form of popular charts. These records were played primarily on jukeboxes for communal rather than private consumption. As part of her contract for the Mercury company, Washington recorded "covers" of popular songs previously recorded by white singers. (In the segregated recording industry popular songs could not be distributed to a black buying public unless sung by a black singer.) A variety of phrases were developed in the forties by the record companies to replace "race" with a market category that would signify that a black singer was singing for a black audience. The term chosen by RCA-Victor, "rhythm and blues," was eventually used throughout the industry after *Billboard* adopted it as the title for their black music chart in 1949. Rhythm and blues was a euphemism for "black" rather than the name of a distinct musical genre, and while it covered a wide variety of musical forms the term did describe a particularly urban music. By 1950 Washington's records dominated the R & B charts and she was Mercury's best-selling artist to a black audience, earning the name "Queen of the Blues."

But stardom in the fifties was strictly segregated, and a position in the charts, having hit records, increasingly determined the quality and quantity of bookings. The black music market was not as lucrative as the white music market and Washington's records were not promoted to become "crossovers" or given much air time on white radio stations. Washington was a severe critic of the structure of the industry and grew steadily more angry as rock and roll, which had its source in black rhythm and blues forms, came to dominate the white charts. Television was an increasingly important avenue for marketing musical talent, but even singers like Nat King Cole, whose records were "crossovers," were not offered much air time because advertisers did not want their products associated with black performers. Washington found herself limited to local shows. As television came to dominate the presentation of hit records, she discovered that she was not good at lip-sychronization.

In 1959, Washington finally had a "crossover" record: "What a Difference a Day Makes" reached number 9 in the mainstream charts at the same time as she received a Grammy for the best R & B record. Unfortunately, her bookings did not bring in enough money to stave off financial problems. Hard work and a severe regime of diet pills and mercury shots to lose weight resulted in mental stress, physical deterioration and sickness. Washington's death at Christmas in 1963 was sudden and accidental, the result of a lethal mixture of chemicals ingested at a moment when she felt that at last everything in her life, private and public, was going right. Rosetta Reitz has argued that Washington was a victim of ideologies of beauty expressed in anxieties about her weight:

> ... fat is fatal for popularity. That was over twenty years ago, in 1963, before anorexia became the idealized form of beauty; but thin was in.... [S]he internalized the national hysteria for thinness. ... [H]er death was a waste.[14]

Perhaps the cultural expression of American mythologies is most poignantly epitomized by the Supremes. Mary Wilson closes *Dreamgirl: My Life as a Supreme* with a description of the final farewell concert of Diana (Diane) Ross and the Supremes as if it were the empty consummation of the ideology of the American dream.[15] Wilson, Ross and Florence Ballard

> had created the Supremes; we'd made ourselves into our image of what we could be, in our homemade dresses and fake pearls. Now here Diane and I were, dripping in real diamonds and adorned in black velvet and pearls. ... And this was the end.[16]

In Wilson's final emphatic assertion that the Supremes made themselves in their own image we can see her reaction against the legend that three little girls, "giggly and immature," were taken from a Detroit ghetto by Berry Gordy and groomed into sophistication. The most interesting aspects of *Dreamgirl* concern this story, the relation between Wilson, Ross and Ballard, an ambitious singing group, and the intensely patriarchal Motown organization.

Charlie Gillett has argued in *The Sound of the City* that in the fifties the connection between the emotion of gospel singing and the expectations of adolescent listeners to popular music was being realized by various singers, record company executives and composers.[17] Both gospel styles and the styles of new singing groups were worked out through complex vocal harmonies; Wilson talks about the hours that the "Primettes," their first group name, spent practicing harmonies after school. But while gospel music, and of course the blues, had been developed mostly by migrants from the South, the new group singers were not only of another generation but entirely urban in orientation, working out their harmonies on city streets.

Between the mid-fifties and the late sixties girl groups are arguably the most interesting phenomenon produced by rock and roll. The Chantals, the Shirelles, the Marvelettes, the Crystals and countless others sang with emotion and sentiment of teenage sexuality and desire which was nearly always focused on a heterosexual, idealized love directed toward a male figure of mythic proportions, *The Boy, The Leader of the Pack*. What *Dreamgirl* documents is how these utopian songs were produced under very oppressive conditions.

Berry Gordy's Motown, "Hitsville USA," in 1960 is described as "running very much like a family. Loyalty, honesty and obedience were demanded and often gladly given," and careers were discussed and planned over family meals. But Wilson, Ross and Ballard were undemanding teenagers who didn't question receiving pocket money instead of wages and never knew how much profit their hit records accrued. After their first number 1 hit they were told they had made no money. Motown did not disclose its sales or profits to anyone, not even the Recording Industry Association of America (the organization that certified the award of gold records). It was structured for total control, being booking agent, manager, accountant, financial adviser and everything else for each of its performers.

Motown, Wilson argues, was grooming its performers to produce stars, not just records. The Artist Development Department under Harvey Fuqua was at the heart of creating the Motown myth. It was patterned after the Hollywood studio "charm" schools of the thirties and forties, and to the young performers of the sixties, Wilson recalls, it seemed archaic. Wilson describes as "insulting" the idea that Berry took "a bunch of ghetto kids with no class, no style and no manners" and transformed them:

> The truth is that Berry never signed anyone to Motown who needed to be "remade." The uncouth, boisterous, and slovenly couldn't get a foot in the door

anyway. . . . [E]veryone . . . wanted to move up in the world. None of us came from homes that didn't teach manners. We were all trying to get ahead, and it's always bothered me that some people have assumed that by accepting what some consider "white" values, we sold out.[18]

Wilson, Ross and Ballard were tightly bound, however, by their initiation into "ladyhood." As they themselves had spent years creating their "sophisticated style," they were Motown's star pupils.

In a tale in which competitiveness, jealousy and distrust are elevated to become the leading protagonists, success means the defeat of the Supremes' early egalitarian relationship as they became Motown's greatest commodity and Ross its "first lady." Despite its fascination as a biography that reveals the cultural contradictions of the entertainment industry, *Dreamgirl* is a very unpleasant reading experience indeed. Ultimately, it is a consummate act of revenge against Diana Ross. The narrative is framed and punctuated by events that are meant to signify Wilson's total disillusionment with Ross, who is characterized as completely ego-centered. Ross is made the wicked witch of the tale; Wilson has faith in and loves everybody; Ballard is the victim. The tragic demise of Ballard, from star to welfare recipient, the story of her unsuccessful suit against Motown and the eventual loss of her house received national publicity. But Wilson's attitude toward Ballard is ambiguous. She is critical of gossip that blamed the behavior of Gordy and Ross for Ballard's untimely death; but, at the same time, she herself seems to blame Gordy and Ross and uses the occasion of Ballard's funeral to create a vindictive portrait of Ross, interpreting her every action as that of a heartless publicity seeker. In the opening pages Wilson describes the taping of the Motown 25th Anniversary Special and blames Ross for catering to the desire of the audience to witness a cat fight between the ex-Supremes – *Dreamgirl* is one of the rounds in just such a fight.

In stark contrast *I, Tina* is a pleasure to read.[19] The autobiography actually uses a multiple-voice structure. The narrative voice of Kurt Loeder, an editor at *Rolling Stone* magazine, is perhaps the least successful. At times Loeder is extremely heavy-handed in his provision of potted histories of international events for background and at his worst when waxing lyrical in the creation of atmosphere. If you can get through the first chapter, with its sentimental description of Nut Bush, Tennessee, complete with "deep rural repose: the occasional buzz of a hornet, the halfhearted peck of an odd stray hen . . . the soft flip-and-splash of a hooked perch . . . and the unhurried clop of a family field horse" without losing your lunch you are home and dry![20]

Tina Turner, born Anna Mae Bullock in November 1939, brings the autobiography alive as soon as her voice enters. She is captivating. All the Turner sequences have the vitality, enthusiasm and directness of a superb oral history, and the structure of her narrative with its pauses, hesitations and rhetorical questions positions the reader as listener and participant: "Were we poor? I don't remember being poor. . . . I remember the white people as being friendly then. Now, a lot of that was because the blacks 'knew their place,' right?"[21] The immediacy and frequently the urgency of her voice makes Turner a tangible narrative figure who appears very much in control of her own tale.

Turner grew up with the radio not a record player, listening to country and western and the black radio station WDIA out of Memphis, playing B. B. King, and then in the fifties a few women like Faye Adams and La Vern Baker, "women with a certain style." In 1956 Turner moved to St Louis with her mother, and in one of the clubs over the Mississippi in East St Louis she heard and then joined Ike Turner and the Kings of Rhythm.

The story of the Turners' relationship can be characterized from the first battering Tina Turner received at his hands:

> [He] grabbed one of those [shoe stretchers] and started beating me with it. After that he made me go to bed, and then he had sex with me. . . . And that was the beginning, the beginning of Ike instilling fear in me. He kept control of me with *fear*. Why didn't I leave him? It's easy now to say I should've. But . . . I already had one child, and I was pregnant with another by him. Singing with Ike was how I made my living.[22]

The batterings continued and got worse; he would beat her with anything – telephones, shoes, wire hangers – and choke her and punch her. One night in Los Angeles in 1968 Tina Turner was ready to die: she had to sing with a broken jaw and blood gushing in her mouth, and she tried to kill herself. However, Tina Turner did not leave Ike Turner until 1976. When she did she quickly found out she had no money available to her; Ike had never provided her with the means to access the money their records made and by leaving him she became financially liable for the losses promoters suffered through canceled performances. She stayed with a series of women friends housekeeping and cleaning for them until she put together her own road show.

Freedom from Ike Turner meant not only a liberation from mental and physical torture but a freedom to develop her own artistic direction. The only record that Tina Turner had made without Ike Turner was "River Deep, Mountain High" produced by Phil Spector in 1966. A spectacular production, it was "too black for the pop stations and too pop for the black stations" and failed to make significant sales in the US, though it was a great success in Europe. Turner returned there to establish her second career as a soloist and record the *Private Dancer* album in London.

Tina Turner's voice had always broken through the expected confines of the female voice in rock and roll. While "girl" songs were harmonious fetishizations of the boy who was the meaning of life, while singers like Brenda Lee and Connie Francis were idolized for their restrained, feminine

and shallow vocal range, and while the Supremes were grooming themselves and their voices with lady-like fastidiousness, Turner screamed and
shouted with overt sexuality about the men she "could keep satisfied." In
its own contemporary terms, *Private Dancer* was a significant challenge to
the spaces occupied by Madonna and Cyndi Lauper.

Feminist debate is unlikely to resolve the question of how far female
sexuality is exploited by, or triumphs in spite of, the consumerism of
performance entertainment – the cultural contradiction remains. But the
sight and sound of Tina Turner is unquestionably awesome, and watching
her you *know* that now she is in control. Perhaps her awareness of the
exploitative nature of the social relations of the culture industry are most
aptly expressed by her refusal of Steven Spielberg's offer to play the starring
role of Celie in *The Color Purple*: "I've *lived* that story," she said.

1987

Notes

1. Frank C. Taylor with Gerald Cook, *Alberta Hunter: A Celebration in Blues*, New
   York: McGraw-Hill, 1987, pp. 238–9.
2. Ibid., p. 12.
3. Taylor records these details both in the body of the text and in a discography.
4. Recording information is given for vinyl but can be used to track CD
   compilations.
5. Quoted in the liner notes to *The Legendary Alberta Hunter*, DRG, n.d., SL5195.
6. Taylor, *A Celebration in Blues*, p. 40.
7. Ibid., p. 109.
8. Ibid., p. 115.
9. Ibid., pp. xvii–xviii.
10. Ibid., pp. 263–4.
11. Jim Haskins, *Queen of the Blues: A Biography of Dinah Washington*, New York:
    William Morrow and Company, 1987.
12. Ibid., pp. 123–4.
13. Ibid., p. 33.
14. Rosetta Reitz, liner notes to *Wise Woman Blues*, Rosetta Records, 1984, RR1313.
15. Mary Wilson with Patricia Romanowski and Ahrgus Juilliard, *Dreamgirl: My Life
    as a Supreme*, New York: St Martin's Press, 1986.
16. Ibid., p. 234.
17. Charlie Gillett, *The Sound of the City*, New York: Pantheon, 1983.
18. Wilson, *Dreamgirl*, p. 150.
19. Tina Turner with Kurt Loeder, *I, Tina*, New York: William Morrow and
    Company, 1986.
20. Ibid., p. 9.
21. Ibid., p. 15.
22. Ibid., p. 76.

4

They Put a Spell on You

Wild Women Don't Have the Blues is a slick, professional, general introduction to the subject of black women blues singers who dominated the production of "race" records in the twenties and thirties.[1] It is a visually rich record of the earliest years of the entertainment industry in North America because it includes early vaudeville stills and film from traveling tent shows. This visual material can be complemented by the publicity photographs and record company newspaper advertisements (taken mainly from the *Chicago Defender*) in Daphne Duval Harrison's book *Black Pearls: Blues Queens of the 1920s*,[2] itself a general survey of a number of singers and some of their lyrics. Books on individual performers – Chris Albertson's *Bessie* and *Bessie Smith: Empress of the Blues*, Edward Brooks's *The Bessie Smith Companion* and Sandra Lieb's *Mother of the Blues: A Study of Ma Rainey*[3] – offer more biographical detail, discussion of lyrics and discographies. However, the most indispensable resource for introducing students to the blues women and their music are the records produced by Rosetta Reitz. Reitz, based in New York, has for a number of years compiled collections of women singers and instrumentalists and has reproduced them on her own label, Rosetta Records. The collection features albums organized by individuals and by theme; each record is accompanied by liner notes which are well researched and more informative than any books currently available.

William Barlow, author of *Looking Up at Down*,[4] has written the most fascinating regional history of the emergence of a blues culture in the United States. Barlow argues, quite rightly, that blues music "resisted cultural domination in both form and content" and that blues singers "acted as proselytizers of a gospel of secularization in which the belief in freedom became associated with personal mobility – freedom of movement in this world here and now, rather than salvation in the next."[5] However, Barlow is outrageous in his analysis of the reasons for the success and popularity of blues women. He argues that most of the early recording stars were women because: "Black women tended to be more socially acceptable than black men to the white men running the music industry. They were less threatening physically, usually less experienced in business matters, and presumably easier to control. There may also have been some white male sexual fantasies at work in the equation."[6] Unfortunately, *Wild Women Don't Have the Blues* is a film that does little to counter the misconceptions and mythologies that abound about women in most histories of the blues. It acts to establish their presence but lacks any substantial historical analysis of their relation to a blues culture in general.

The blues women of the twenties and thirties are usually collectively referred to as the "Classic Blues Singers," but this label is inadequate. On the one hand, it does not effectively describe the wide variety of blues and popular songs that they performed, and, on the other hand, the label acts to separate the musical production of men from that of women. Women, like Memphis Minnie, who sang blues that are not classified as "Classic Blues" and who utilized musical structures that have been associated by blues critics with male performers are consequently neglected in histories of the blues. The field of blues history is dominated by an assumption that "authentic" blues forms are entirely rural in origin and are produced by the figure of the wandering, lone male. The blues women of the twenties, who recorded primarily in urban centers, are regarded as commercialized aberrations who compromised and adulterated "pure" blues. *Wild Women Don't Have the Blues* does not reproduce this analysis explicitly but neither does it address and challenge the discursive boundaries that position blues women as exceptions to the history of "authentic" blues. The film stresses their popularity and credits the blues women for "opening up a whole new future for the blues" by integrating them into traditions of theatrical entertainment. But, in traditional blues histories, it is precisely this commercial success, and the fact that these women were professionals, that justifies their marginalization or the neglect of their impact on the development of a blues culture as a whole. What is needed is an analysis of the creative role of the blues women in the massive transformation of black culture that occurred as black people moved from rural to urban areas in the North and the South.

If *Wild Women Don't Have the Blues* is used in conjunction with Rosetta Records, however, it is possible to counter some of the more pervasive mythologies. The lyrics of the songs on the collection of *Women's Railroad Blues* (Rosetta Records, 1980, RR1301), for example, explicitly address issues of the personal freedom of black women. Hopping freight cars was particularly difficult and dangerous for women, and traveling tent shows and vaudeville offered an alternative way to achieve mobility for young black women like Mamie Smith, who started dancing when she was ten, and Ida Cox, who left home to join the Black and Tan Minstrel Show when she was fourteen. This increase in the physical mobility of these women is paralleled by the challenge to sexual conventions and gendered social roles that is found in their music. Unfortunately, in the script of *Wild Women Don't Have the Blues* is the statement that Bessie Smith's portrayal of a woman done wrong (in the film *St Louis Blues*) "dramatically captured the heart of the Classic Blues." The mythology that blues women sang obsessively about the passive female victims of male indifference or violence has been sustained by patriarchal histories and the lack of availability of alternative recordings. The existence of Rosetta Records means that these myths can be aggressively countered. Far from being the songs of passive victims, women's blues are a highly contested and contradictory cultural form. This music and lyrics confronted conventional expectations of male/ female sexual relationships and challenged the narrow boundaries and limits of compulsory heterosexuality.

The interviews in *Wild Women Don't Have the Blues* are far more interesting than the frequently unimaginative and misleading narrative of the voice-over. Chris Albertson insists that, indeed, the blues "women were all aggressive women [who] knew what they wanted and went after it." The film also includes direct testimony of the influence that the blues women had over the young women and girls who listened to them. Blue Lu Barker describes how she learned to sing the blues from the records that her mother bought; they would carry the phonograph all over the house while they were working and sing. Koko Taylor argues that women blues singers, like Ma Rainey and Bessie Smith, hypnotized their audience: "It's like they put a spell on you. They would capture their audience in the palm of their hands." Doll Thomas adds that the women blues singers captivated audiences because "everybody in the public figured that they were singing exactly to them." Raised on a cotton farm, the daughter of sharecroppers, Koko Taylor listened to records of the blues women and determined to sing the blues herself. "They were the inspiration, women like Ma Rainey were the foundation of the blues, they brought the blues up from slavery to today." Taylor is convinced that the early women blues singers got the ideas for their songs from the same place that she now gets hers: "When I write a song, I'm thinking about people in general, everyday living, just look around you, you know." The subject of any particular blues song is like a pair of shoes, Taylor adds, "They may not fit my feet, know what I'm saying? That shoe may not fit your feet, but that shoe do fit somebody's feet. . . . If some woman out there is really feeling this way, then these are the words she would like to say." Ida Goodson talks about how she grew up in a religious household with parents who believed that "the Devil got his work and God got his work," and concluded that the blues was the Devil's work. Consequently, they were not allowed to play the blues in the house. As a child, Goodson would play the blues on the piano while her parents were out until she was warned by her ever-vigilant look-out that they were returning and blue notes would rapidly be transformed into the chords of a respectable hymn.

Cissy Houston began singing when she was only five years old. In the film *Cissy Houston: Sweet Inspiration*[7] she recalls how her elder sister Marie taught her siblings to sing in spite of the fact that they were not aware of any other children's groups that they could emulate. Using their family name

– Drinkard – Marie, Ann, Cissy and brother Nicholas, who played the piano, formed a gospel group called the Drinkard Singers. A climax in their career together came when they were invited, along with Mahalia Jackson and Clara Ward, to perform at the Newport Jazz Festival in 1967. It was the first time that gospel had been presented at Newport, and as Ann Drinkard Moss remembers, the primarily white audience unnerved them. Their appearance at the Festival led to an increase in their popularity and their bookings, but this success also led to Cissy Houston's eventual departure from the group.

For the Drinkard Sisters, as for many African Americans, their singing began in the church. It is widely understood that the influence of spirituals and gospel music can be felt across a spectrum of black American musical forms, but it is also clear that popular forms of secular music have influenced gospel music. Thomas A. Dorsey, the "father" of gospel music, used to write for and accompany Ma Rainey, who is commonly referred to as the "mother" of the blues. When Dorsey stopped writing blues songs, it was not because he wanted to abandon popular musical forms; rather he wanted to take into the church the traditions of black popular music that were present in vaudeville and blues performances. In the early years of gospel both Dorsey and Willie Mae Ford Smith, his protégée, were accused of bringing the Devil's music into God's house.

To be a performer of both sacred and secular music has, historically, often involved making difficult choices, choices that can result in living with a permanent sense of dual and conflicting loyalties. Whitney Houston was aware that the demands of "serving two Gods," as she described it, "plagued" her mother because "the church people never want to let you go." However, the Drinkard Singers could not earn enough from gospel singing to support themselves; they had to have day jobs in order to survive. As Ann Drinkard Moss explains, you performed gospel songs because you loved it, but "secular music was attractive because it presented you with more money. Those that saw a chance of making their living went over to secular music . . . but it never set with me, I was never comfortable with it." For Cissy Houston the extra money was a necessity, and she formed a group called the Sweet Inspirations who sang together for almost ten years performing background arrangements for the vast array of singers associated with the "soul" sound of Atlantic Records produced in Muscle Shoals, Alabama. She wanted and needed more money so that she could educate her children. "I've taken a lot of flak from church people for singing pop," she explains; "it comes with the territory, but my base is the church."

Dave Davidson has anchored his filmic perception of Cissy Houston in his vision of her as a woman who has both her roots and her heart in the church. His film opens and closes in the New Hope Baptist Church in Newark, New Jersey, where Houston is minister of music and director of the choir, a choir repeatedly referred to as *her* choir. The narrative of the film is the progress of an 8:00 A.M. Sunday service, a service that is broadcast on the radio to the community. The service begins with the choir entering the hall, and the camera focuses on Cissy Houston emerging into their midst. This is an important visual image that signals the major preoccupation of the film: Houston's relation to the choir of the New Hope Baptist Church – a relation that is variously established as leader, teacher, nurturer and mentor. Her artistic "inspiration" is established as being both derived from and sustained by her involvement with the Baptist Church and the choir, but the main subject of the film is Houston's "inspiration" of others.

Whitney Houston and her brother, Gary Garland, both attest to the ways in which their mother inspired them to achieve success. As Whitney Houston says, "I had a mother, I had a teacher, all in one, which was great. . . . The reason I am a singer is because of her." But what is most interesting about the way in which Dave Davidson has decided to reproduce particular cultural meanings of "mothering" in his film is that he abandons the conventional signifiers of "home," like filming women in kitchens, to represent aspects of nurturance and motherhood. Instead, the visual representation of mutual inspiration between mother and children takes place in one of the most public of spaces – on the stage. Whitney Houston, Cissy Houston and Gary Garland, in concert, perform the song "You Are My Dreams," and Dave Davidson uses this performance as if it were the embodiment and culmination of Cissy Houston's motherhood.

Cissy Houston: Sweet Inspiration concentrates almost exclusively upon the public presences of Cissy Houston. Visually, she is consistently situated in public, as opposed to private, or intimate, spaces. The strength of this approach is obvious: Cissy Houston as "mother," for example, is not viewed in isolation from Cissy Houston's multiple "public" roles as artist, performer and teacher. But Davidson is clearly uninterested in the important issues that arise for women who must occupy multiple subject positions. The film is infuriatingly silent about the difficulties that Houston must have faced as she constantly negotiated the conflicting demands of her children and her work. The decision to limit the representation of Houston to public spaces and to public faces, I would argue, is a mistake. It is not that women exist either in a public or in a private or domesticated space but that they exist in both, and it is the relation and interdependence between them that need to be explored. Davidson neglects this relationship and the conflicting demands that women face, and this neglect is the film's greatest weakness.

The weakness of *Cissy Houston: Sweet Inspiration* can be most aptly demonstrated if the absences of that film are compared to issues that arise in *Say Amen, Somebody,*[8] a film about the gospel careers of Willie Mae Ford Smith and Thomas A. Dorsey. Davidson elicits information about Houston directly from her or from friends, colleagues or family, in the formal visual interview where people respond to questions that the audience does not hear being asked and which are posed by an interviewer whom the audience never sees. The effect is to create a subject, Cissy Houston, whose life is to be reflected upon and judged individually and, as it were, at a distance. George T. Nierenberg, on the other hand, frequently attempts to make the camera part of communal exchanges and conversations which take place between his subjects rather than between an individual, isolated subject and the camera. Using the camera in this way creates as well as mimics the more intimate effect of eavesdropping. These differences in the formal cinematic techniques of Dave Davidson and George T. Nierenberg, I would suggest, enable very different political approaches to their subjects.

Nierenberg confronts the conflicts that women gospel singers face as they have divided themselves between the sacred and the secular demands of home and work. Because he filmed in intimate as well as public spaces, these tensions are directly apparent and, in some segments of filmed conversations, actually surface as filming is taking place. Willie Mae Ford Smith asks her grandson to drive her around the neighborhood where she started as a gospel singer. In the course of the journey she tells him that she started singing because the church "didn't want women preachers." Her grandson replies that he agrees that women should not be allowed to preach and then asserts, "a woman's place is behind the man." Willie Mae Ford Smith is visibly shocked and surprised by these statements, but her response is immediate and spontaneous: "If a woman is nice enough to cook your food, make your beds, clean your house, care for your children, and *you*, how come she can't take the word and carry it. . . . God did not take me out of a man's back."

The conflict and tension that arise within the family and that are played out in this particular scene are then elaborated upon in a following scene in which Willie Mae Ford Smith, called "Mother Smith," talks to a young female gospel singer who is seeking advice on how to balance the needs of her family with her own desire to travel away from home to sing. The two women are filmed sitting at a kitchen table, and they transform the kitchen from a place that women are not supposed to leave into a space for the subversion of patriarchal and familial demands. Rather than visually abandoning domestic space, Nierenberg utilizes it, and what emerges in this particular conversation is an intimacy that allows for the expression of deep emotional response to the problems that both women have faced in the past and continue to face in the present.

Willie Mae Ford Smith tells a story of leaving her family to attend a revival, and while she is telling it, the camera focuses on the conflicting emotions revealed in her face as she relives both the heartbreak of the occasion and the strength of her determination to go anyway:

> It's hard being a gospel singer having a career. I have been down to Union Station, getting on the train, and look at my little kids, they've been brought down there. "Oh, Mother don't leave us!"

[She cries.]

And I said, "Well, I'll see you later."

I went to Springfield, Missouri. . . . I called home. I talked to my husband, he said, "You ought to be ashamed of yourself, these little children are here and you are running around the town. What good are you doing?"

I told him on the phone, "Look, I'm gonna leave you in the hands of the Lord 'cause I can't do anything about what I'm doing right now. God has given me this work."

The response of Willie Mae Ford Smith's husband is to threaten to be after her when she returns on the next Saturday.

I got off the train Saturday morning, my husband was looking up in one coach for me and the Lord made him know, "Let her alone." He fell down the elevator shaft, looking for me, not paying attention to this elevator that takes the baggage down in the basement. He was injured so bad he couldn't get up after he sat down, and that man stayed that way about eight years. Well, he said he was through, he wasn't going to bother me anymore.

What is so powerful about these moments in the film is that they allow us to recognize and establish the connections between the history of women who are tormented by the demands of living multiple subjectivities but who refuse to neglect their own needs and desires and the way that these conflicts still have to be negotiated. However, in *Cissy Houston: Sweet Inspiration*, when Houston states that "I have heard things that have devastated me so bad there was no place to go but to God. . . . I can go to my story cabinet back there and bring it all out," as an audience we have no way of situating such devastation because no room has been provided for these stories to be told within the film. Without hearing Houston's stories, it is also impossible to fully comprehend the depth of emotion that is expressed through her voice. Davidson fails to provide the space for what Houston asserts is so important when she declares, "You have to make people feel what you feel in order to generate the kind of enthusiasm that it takes to generate the spirit."

It is possible to establish the connections between the spoken and unspoken tensions in the lives of Willie Mae Ford Smith and Cissy Houston in the twentieth century and the narratives of the lives of black women preachers and evangelists in the nineteenth century. A collection of the spiritual autobiographies of black women entitled *Sisters of the Spirit*, edited by William Andrews,[9] contains the narratives of Jarena Lee, Zilpha Elaw and Julia Foote. All three women were determined to preach, to carry the Word, as Willie Mae Ford Smith describes it, in the face of opposition from church and state and family. Jarena Lee's narrative contains the story of how she was condemned when she left her son in the care of others, and Zilpha Elaw used the authority of God to enable her to refuse to recognize the authority that society had invested in her husband. What is important in these spiritual autobiographies is not just the liberation of these women from domestic space but the ways in which they also usurped the privileged space of the male voice; each woman liberates her own voice in the process of establishing her own right to speak and interpret the Word. It has become conventional in the study of African American culture to recognize, on the one hand, that black women have been the backbone of the church while, on the other, to concentrate scholarly energy entirely toward the intellectual contributions of the male preacher. If texts like *Cissy Houston: Sweet Inspiration, Say Amen, Somebody* and *Sisters of the Spirit* are used in conjunction with each other, it is possible to pose a direct challenge to the paternalistic gestures which only apparently recognize the contributions of black women to the formation of African American culture and which, in fact, have effectively silenced the history of their spiritual activity.

Alberta Hunter states that she was born "in Memphis, Tennessee, April 1st, 1895. . . . I went to Auction Street School, what school I went to, and they told me I could sing, you know." Unlike Cissy Houston and Willie Mae Ford Smith, Hunter was alienated by her experience of church: "My grandmother would take me to church. If the church opened up at five in the morning, my grandmother would have me there at five and I would stay there until the church closed, all day long, that's the reason I don't go to church!" At sixteen Hunter became part of the great migration of black people from cities and rural areas of the South to cities in the North when she traveled to Chicago. Her apprenticeship as a singer was undertaken in secular rather than sacred institutions, as noted previously: she started off singing to an audience of pimps and prostitutes in a club called Dago Frank's, and then moved to Hugh Hoskins, a club for "confidence men and their girls who were pickpockets." She was nurtured and encouraged by the women in her audience: "The prostitutes were so wonderful, they'd always make the 'Johns' give me money you know. . . . They'd go out and buy me little dresses and things to put on me so I'd look nice."

Alberta Hunter: My Castle's Rockin'[10] has two invaluable qualities. The more important is the extraordinary presence of Hunter herself. She is filmed at two different moments in her life: as a dynamic eighty-two-year-old woman who has just made the greatest show business comeback in history, and then again just before she died at eighty-nine, thinner, weaker, but as feisty as ever. The second important aspect of the film is that the script was written by Chris Albertson, who was able to situate a narrative of Alberta Hunter's career within a wider history of the rise of blues and jazz. The film documents with visual images Hunter's rise to international fame. There are stills of Chicago in the teens and twenties, of Harlem during the Harlem Renaissance, and of Paris and London during the twenties and thirties when Europeans were fascinated by "le jazz hot" and a variety of black performers. There are photographs of Hunter starring with Paul

Robeson in *Showboat* in 1928 and photographs from her United Service Organizations tours from World War II through the Korean War. The use of historical and archival material is visually interesting and extremely useful and includes some very rare footage from Britain's first feature film, *Radio Parade of 1935*, in which Hunter sang a song entitled "Black Shadows."

Alberta Hunter: My Castle's Rockin' opens with, and is punctuated by, Alberta Hunter performing at the Cookery, Barney Josephson's club in Manhattan. It includes eight songs sung live at the Cookery, many of them revised versions of songs from her earlier career as a blues singer, and a number of original recordings. Hunter's performances are utterly spellbinding. She establishes a sense of direct intimacy with the audience that the film has managed to retain. However, the film does not explore the difference between the dignity of Hunter's performance at the Cookery and the sexual exploitation and debasement that used to be an integral part of singing in clubs. In the early years of her career, Hunter, like many women blues singers, was a "table singer," which meant strolling from table to table singing to one small group at a time. Table singing often involved more than creating an atmosphere of intimacy with the audience; it was also the way that singers obtained tips. The men at the table would expect the singer to pick up their money with various parts of her body. (Billie Holiday is famous for refusing to pick up money from tables when the management demanded that she use her vulva.) But one of the stories that Hunter relates hints at the more sordid side of life in the clubs that the film refuses to confront. She describes how her tips were meant to be placed in a box on the piano so that they would be shared with the musicians at the end of the performance but that she would frequently try to hide the money by placing it inside the front of her low-cut dresses while pretending to place money in the box. One night the lights suddenly went out and she seized the opportunity to take money out of the box without being seen. When the lights just as suddenly went on again, Hunter was caught, predictably, bending over the piano with her hand in the box. But, lying next to her, there was also the body of a man who had been shot! In the segments filmed at the Cookery, Hunter re-creates the sensuality, sexuality and suggestive performance style that was uniquely her own and that ranges from the aggressively assertive "Rough and Ready Man" to the engagingly sensitive "The Love I Have for You."

The biography of Hunter re-created by the film is extremely selective, but she was always very cautious with her biographers. The major biography, Frank C. Taylor's *Alberta Hunter: A Celebration in Blues*,[11] is a reasonably good book about a fascinating woman that can fill some but not all of the gaps in the film. Taylor, unfortunately, assumes that he is successfully reconstructing the private as well as the public personality of Hunter, but it is clear that she is extremely reserved about many aspects of her life both in Taylor's book and with Chris Albertson in the film. Albertson and Taylor learn nothing, for example, about Hunter's long-term relationships with

Lottie Tyler and Carrie Mae Ward. Both biographers are far more comfortable making reference to her extremely brief marriage to Willard Saxby Townsend than to her committed relationships with women. But Hunter dismisses Townsend as being of little significance in her life: "Poor Willard, I didn't stay with Willard 'cause, Lawd, I wasn't cut out for no housewife. Stayed with him a week or two weeks."

The biographical strength of the film is that it provides the space for Hunter to tell her own stories. Whether these stories are elaborated or mix up the details of her life (as Taylor claims her stories did),[12] they are unforgettable. Visually, Hunter dominates the camera when she talks and sings. She had an extraordinarily expressive face and she would wink and grin impishly one minute and then grimace the next. What is unusual in the experience of watching the documentary film is to see how comfortable Hunter was in front of a camera, comfortable enough to take visible pleasure in and to be amused by her own re-creations of her youthful self.

Tiny and Ruby: Hell Divin' Women,[13] a film about Tiny Davis and Ruby Lucas (a.k.a. Renei Phelan), is a challenge to conventional perspectives on the relationship between women and jazz. Greta Schiller and Andrea Weiss are independent feminist filmmakers whose work is innovative in two important and interrelated ways: they revise and transform the formal cinematic practices that situate women as subjects and they confront issues of female subjectivity and sexuality that are usually silenced. The first challenge is that their subjects are not singers but instrumentalists. Sally Placksin has argued that what she calls "Western" traditions and African traditions parallel each other in the cultural expectation that, "keyboards and strings were appropriate for women whereas horns and drums were reserved for men."[14] Davis plays the trumpet and Lucas plays the drums, bass and piano.

Tiny Davis was born in Memphis, Tennessee, in 1909 and started playing the trumpet at thirteen. She describes how she saw boys at school with a trumpet and asked her mother to buy her one. Practicing took place on the top of her barn. Hearing this story, the interviewer asks if she knew "any other women who were wild and crazy like that." But the characterization of her desire to play the trumpet as being "wild and crazy" is language that Davis refuses to adopt, and she responds by naming herself very differently. She replies that "No," she was "the only *woman musician* down there." Ruby Lucas grew up in Kansas City and the first instrument that she learned to play was the piano. They eventually met in Kansas City, where Davis's husband held a job in the packing houses.

Davis and her group, called the Torrid Eight, earned between 75¢ and $1.25 a night playing in theaters and clubs in Kansas City. In 1935 she joined the Harlem Play Girls and toured the Midwest playing standards, blues and jazz for white audiences; then she joined the International Sweethearts of Rhythm, the first racially integrated band, which lasted throughout the forties. Rosetta Reitz describes in the liner notes to her collection of their music that, in 1938, the "International" aspect of the band was "apparent in the looks of Willie Mae Wong, Chinese saxophonist; Alma Cortez, Mexican clarinet player; Nina de LaCruz, Indian saxophonist; and Nova Lee McGee, Hawaiian trumpet player. They were all children of mixed parents; the rest were Afro-American." The first white musician, Reitz states, joined in 1943.[15] Tiny Davis was not one of the original members but became one of the group's star soloists. As Ruby Lucas characterizes the start of her relationship of forty-two years with Davis: "The way I met Tiny was the 'Sweethearts' come. . . . They used to come there every Easter and after they were through playing Tiny used to have some of the band over to her house 'cause she sold drinks and food." Davis interrupts to insist that she also sold "pussy," and then Lucas, slightly exasperated but also amused by the interruption, continues, "and so I came over . . . and never left."

Schiller and Weiss include their questions to Davis and Lucas in their film, but they do not challenge filmic convention enough to visually include their bodies as well as their voices. At times the voice that speaks from behind the camera emerges suddenly and unexpectedly and appears intrusive because, as an audience, we are unprepared for the apparently neutral camera to reveal a point of view and a direct manipulation of what is being filmed. What is so refreshing about *Tiny and Ruby: Hell Divin' Women* is that both the filmmakers and the subjects of the film are clearly engaged in a dialogue with each other. Greta Schiller and Andrea Weiss are interested in encouraging Tiny Davis and Ruby Lucas to talk about the stories that are carefully edited from conventional histories of the lives of women performers, and the latter are clearly amused by and interested in the feminist politics of the filmmakers.

> *Interviewer*: Tell me what the clubs were like in Kansas City?
>
> *Davis*: Oh, you enjoyed yourself and had a good time. They had clubs never closed . . . spots in houses with rooms to rent.
>
> *Lucas*: You could do whatever you wanted to, that was your business. You could bed in two women or two men, they didn't care who you had. Most of the women were married and they were doing it on the side. As long as they didn't get caught everything was cool. It wasn't quite as open as things are now, but people did what they wanted to do then. You understand what I'm saying? It's just that they were kind of cool with it.

Unfortunately, what we, as an audience, see of this dialogue is still one-sided. We have the reactions of Davis and Lucas to the questions of their interviewers, but when they return comments directly to Schiller and Weiss, their reactions remain invisible, which is a pity. When Lucas describes how they were both "run out of town" and Davis explains that, because of their relationship with each other, she had a confrontation with her husband and she had to leave "everything" in Kansas City, she looks at the women behind the camera and indicates how her experience was very different from theirs: "You can do anything. . . . You all pretty girls, you can do anything." Because of their invisibility, the filmmakers escape having to face this challenge in public. Their response, if there was one, was left on the cutting-room floor, but the moment signals a lost opportunity to have incorporated into their film the relationship between filmmaker and subject.

Schiller and Weiss chose to make a deeply personal film which displays both intense respect for and extraordinary sensitivity toward the complexity of the lives of Tiny Davis and Ruby Lucas. Their intimacy is presented as growing in a multitude of ways through the many aspects of their relationship – working together as talented female musicians, as business partners, and as friends and lovers. The poetic narration of Cheryl Clarke is an evocative thread that weaves its way through the film in a pattern of call and response to the life of Tiny Davis:

> If I had been a singer instead of a horn player. Maybe I'd still be cutting records. Be in magazines, in Vegas. On Broadway, playing nightly in the New York clubs. A professor. But it's been one night stands since the war was over. . . .
>
> I was mighty, the sensation of the century. But it was them girls, white, light, bright, brown, tan and yellow. Yes sir, that's who I ground my axe for. Times wasn't ready for us. Still ain't.

Though *Hell Divin' Women* is short, only thirty minutes, the camera lingers over moments of personal revelation and intimate detail. As an audience we become witnesses to the ways in which Tiny Davis and Ruby Lucas complete each other's thought and comments, offering not closures but elaborations, riffs that rework, expand upon and then offer back to each other fuller, richer and more tangible descriptions of their lives.

1991

Notes

1. *Wild Women Don't Have the Blues*, produced by Carole van Falkenburg and Christine Dall, 1989.
2. Daphne Duval Harrison, *Black Pearls: Blues Queens of the 1920s*, New Brunswick, NJ: Rutgers University Press, 1988.
3. Chris Albertson, *Bessie*, New York: Stein & Day, 1972, and *Bessie Smith: Empress of the Blues*, New York: Schirmer Books, 1975; Edward Brooks, *The Bessie Smith Companion*, London: Cavendish Publishing, 1982; Sandra Lieb, *Mother of the Blues: A Study of Ma Rainey*, Amherst: University of Massachusetts Press, 1981.
4. William Barlow, *Looking Up at Down: The Emergence of Blues Culture*, Philadelphia: Temple University Press, 1989.
5. Ibid., p. 5.

6. Ibid., p. 138. For a very different interpretation of the role of blues women in the formation of a blues culture, see Chapter 1 of the present volume.

7. *Cissy Houston: Sweet Inspiration*, produced by Dave Davidson, Hudson West Productions, 1987.

8. *Say Amen, Somebody*, produced by George T. Nierenberg, GTN Productions, 1983.

9. William Andrews, ed., *Sisters of the Spirit*, Urbana: University of Illinois Press, 1989.

10. *Alberta Hunter: My Castle's Rockin'*, produced by Stuart Goldman, Stuart Goldman Productions, Inc., 1988.

11. Frank C. Taylor with Gerald Cook, *Alberta Hunter: A Celebration in Blues*, New York: McGraw-Hill, 1987.

12. Ibid., p. xvii.

13. *Tiny and Ruby: Hell Divin' Women*, produced by Greta Schiller and Andrea Weiss, Jezebel Productions, 1988.

14. Sally Placksin, *American Women in Jazz: 1900 to the Present: Their Words, Lives and Music*, New York: Wideview Books, 1982, p. 41.

15. Rosetta Reitz, liner notes to *International Sweethearts of Rhythm*, Rosetta Records, 1984, RR1312.

Black Feminist Interventions

5

White Woman Listen!
Black Feminism and the Boundaries
of Sisterhood

> I'm leaving evidence. And you got to leave evidence too. And your
> children got to leave evidence.... They burned all the docu-
> ments.... We got to burn out what they put in our minds, like you
> burn out a wound. Except we got to keep what we need to bear
> witness. That scar that's left to bear witness. We got to keep it as
> visible as our blood.
>
> Gayl Jones, *Corregidora*[1]

The black women's critique of *his*tory has not only involved us in coming
to terms with "absences"; we have also been outraged by the ways in which
it has made us visible, when it has chosen to see us. *His*tory has constructed
our sexuality and our femininity as deviating from those qualities with
which white women, as the prize objects of the Western world, have been
endowed. We have also been defined in less than human terms.[2] Our
continuing struggle with *his*tory began with its "discovery" of us. However,
this chapter will be concerned with herstory rather than *his*tory. We wish to
address questions to the feminist theories which have been developed
during the last decade; a decade in which black women have been fighting,
in the streets, in the schools, through the courts, inside and outside the wage
relation. The significance of these struggles ought to inform the writing of
the herstory of women in Britain. It is fundamental to the development of
a feminist theory and practice that is meaningful for black women. We
cannot hope to reconstitute ourselves in all our absences, or to rectify the
ill-concealed presences that invade herstory from *his*tory, but we do wish to
bear witness to our own herstories. The connection between these and the
herstories of white women will be made and remade in struggle. Black
women have come from Africa, Asia and the Caribbean and we cannot do
justice to all their herstories in a single chapter. Neither can we represent
the voices of all black women in Britain; our herstories are too numerous

and too varied. What we will do is to offer ways in which the "triple" oppression of gender, race and class can be understood, in its specificity, and also as it determines the lives of black women.

Much contemporary debate has posed the question of the relation between race and gender, in terms which attempt to parallel race and gender divisions. It can be argued that as processes, racism and sexism are similar. Ideologically for example, they both construct common sense through reference to "natural" and "biological" differences. It has also been argued that the categories of race and gender are both socially constructed and that, therefore, they have little internal coherence as concepts. Furthermore, it is possible to parallel racialized and gendered divisions in the sense that the possibilities of amelioration through legislation appear to be equally ineffectual in both cases. Michèle Barrett, however, has pointed out that it is not possible to argue for parallels because as soon as historical analysis is made, it becomes obvious that the institutions which have to be analyzed are different, as are the forms of analysis needed.[3] We would agree that the construction of such parallels is fruitless and often proves to be little more than a mere academic exercise; but there are other reasons for our dismissal of these kinds of debate. The experience of black women does not enter the parameters of parallelism. The fact that black women are subject to the *simultaneous* oppression of patriarchy, class and "race" is the prime reason for not employing parallels that render their position and experience not only marginal but also invisible.

In arguing that most contemporary feminist theory does not begin to adequately account for the experience of black women we also have to acknowledge that it is not a simple question of their absence, consequently the task is not one of rendering their visibility. On the contrary we will have to argue that the process of accounting for their historical and contemporary position does, in itself, challenge the use of some of the central categories and assumptions of recent mainstream feminist thought. We can point to no single source for our oppression. When white feminists emphasize patriarchy alone, we want to redefine the term and make it a more complex concept. Racism ensures that black men do not have the same relations to patriarchal/capitalist hierarchies as white men. In the words of the Combahee River Collective:

> We believe that sexual politics under patriarchy is as pervasive in Black women's lives as are the politics of class and race. We also often find it difficult to separate race from class from sex oppression because in our lives they are most often experienced simultaneously. We know that there is such a thing as racial–sexual oppression which is neither solely racial nor solely sexual e.g. the history of rape of Black women by white men as a weapon of political repression.
>
> Although we are feminists and lesbians, we feel solidarity with progressive Black men and do not advocate the fractionalization that white women who are

separatists demand. Our situation as Black people necessitates that we have solidarity around the fact of race, which white women of course do not need to have with white men, unless it is their negative solidarity as racial oppressors. We struggle together with Black men against racism, while we also struggle with Black men about sexism.[4]

It is only in the writings by black feminists that we can find attempts to theorize the interconnection of class, gender and race as it occurs in our lives, and it has only been in the autonomous organizations of black women that we have been able to express and act upon the experiences consequent upon these determinants. Many black women have been alienated by the non-recognition of their lives, experiences and herstories in the women's liberation movement (WLM). Black feminists have been, and are still, demanding that the existence of racism must be acknowledged as a structuring feature of our relationships with white women. Both white feminist theory and practice have to recognize that white women stand in a power relation as oppressors of black women. This compromises any feminist theory and practice founded on the notion of simple equality.

Three concepts which are central to feminist theory become problematic in their application to black women's lives: "the family," "patriarchy" and "reproduction." When used they are placed in a context of the herstory of white (frequently middle-class) women and become contradictory when applied to the lives and experiences of black women. In a recent comprehensive survey of contemporary feminist theory, *Women's Oppression Today*, Michèle Barrett sees the contemporary family (effectively the family under capitalism) as the source of oppression of women:

> It is difficult to argue that the present structure of the family-household is anything other than oppressive for women. Feminists have consistently, and rightly, seen the family as a central site of women's oppression in contemporary society. The reasons for this lie both in the material structure of the household, by which women are by and large financially dependent on men, and in the ideology of the family, through which women are confined to a primary concern with domesticity and motherhood. This situation underwrites the disadvantages women experience at work, and lies at the root of the exploitation of female sexuality endemic in our society. The concept of "dependence" is perhaps the link between the material organisation of the household, and the ideology of femity: an assumption of women's dependence on men structures both of these areas.[5]

The immediate problem for black feminists is whether this framework can be applied at all to analyze our herstory of oppression and struggle. We would not wish to deny that the family can be a source of oppression for us but we also wish to examine how the black family has functioned as a prime source of resistance to oppression. We need to recognize that during slavery, periods of colonialism and under the present authoritarian state, the black family has been a site of political and cultural resistance to racism. Furthermore, we cannot easily separate the two forms of oppression because racist theory and practice is frequently gender-specific. Ideologies of black female sexuality do not stem primarily from the black family. The way the gender of black women is constructed differs from constructions of white femininity because it is also subject to racism. Black feminists have been explaining this since the last century when Sojourner Truth pointed to the ways in which "womanhood" was denied the black woman.

> That man over there says women need to be helped into carriages, and lifted over ditches, and to have the best place everywhere. Nobody ever helps me into carriages, and lifted over ditches, or over mud-puddles, or gives me any best place! And aint I a woman? Look at me! Look at my arm! I have ploughed, and planted, and gathered into barns, and no man could head me! And aint I a woman? I could work as much and eat as much as a man – when I could get it – and bear the lash as well! And aint I a woman? I have borne thirteen children, and seen most all sold off to slavery, and when I cried with my mother's grief, none but Jesus heard me! And aint I a woman?[6]

In our earlier examination of common sense we indicated the racist nature of ideologies of black female sexuality. Black women are constantly challenging these ideologies in their day-to-day struggles. Asian girls in schools, for example, are fighting back to destroy the racist mythology of their femininity. As Pratibha Parmar has pointed out, careers officers do not offer them the same interviews and job opportunities as white girls. This is because they believe that Asian girls will be forced into marriage immediately after leaving school. The common-sense logic of this racism dictates that a career for Asian girls is thought to be a waste of time. But the struggle in schools is not just against the racism of the careers service:

> "Yes, and then there are some racist students who are always picking on us. Recently, we had a fight in our school between us and some white girls. We really showed them we were not going to stand for their rubbish."
>
> Sangeeta and Wahida's statements reflect a growing confidence and awareness amongst young Asian girls about themselves and their situations in a climate of increased racist attacks on black people generally.
>
> Many Asian girls strongly resent being stereotyped as weak, passive, quiet girls, who would not dare lift a finger in their own defence. They want to challenge the idea people have of them as girls "who do not want to stand out or cause trouble but to tip-toe about hoping nobody will notice them".[7]

The use of the concept of "dependency" is also a problem for black feminists. It has been argued that this concept provides the link between the "material organization of the household, and the ideology of feminity." How then can we account for situations in which black women may be heads of households, or where, because of an economic system which structures high black male unemployment, they are not financially dependent upon a black man? This condition exists in both colonial and metropolitan situations. Ideologies of black female domesticity and motherhood have been constructed through their employment (or chattel position) as domestics and surrogate mothers to white families rather than in relation to their own families. West Indian women still migrate to the United States and Canada as domestics and in Britain are seen to be suitable as office cleaners, National Health Service domestics, and so on. In colonial situations Asian women have frequently been forced into prostitution to sexually service the white male invaders, whether in the form of armies of occupation or employees and guests of multinational corporations. How then, in view of all this, can it be argued that black male dominance exists in the same forms as white male dominance? Systems of slavery, colonialism and imperialism have systematically denied positions in the white male hierarchy to black men and have used specific forms of terror to oppress them.

Black family structures have been seen as pathological by the state and are in the process of being constructed as pathological within white feminist theory. Here, ironically, the Western nuclear family structure, and related ideologies of "romantic love" formed under capitalism, are seen as more "progressive" than black family structures. An unquestioned common-sense racism constructs Asian girls and women as having absolutely no freedom, whereas English girls are thought to be in a more "liberated" society and culture. However, one Asian schoolgirl points out:

> Where is the freedom in going to a disco, frightened in case no boy fancies you, or no one asks you to dance, or your friends are walked home with boys and you have to walk home in the dark alone?[8]

The media's "horror stories" about Asian girls and arranged marriages bear very little relation to their experience. The "feminist" version of this ideology presents Asian women as being in need of liberation, not in terms of their own herstory and needs, but *into* the "progressive" social mores and customs of the metropolitan West. The actual struggles that Asian women are involved in are ignored in favor of applying theories from the point of view of a more "advanced," more "progressive" outside observer. In fact, it is very easy for this ideology to be taken up and used by the state in furtherance of racist and sexist practices. The way in which the issue of arranged marriages has been used by the British Conservative government to legitimate increased restrictions on immigration from the Indian subcontinent is one example of this process.

Too often concepts of historical progress are invoked by the left and feminists alike, to create a sliding scale of "civilized liberties." When barbarous sexual practices are to be described, the "Third World" is placed on display and compared to the "First World," which is seen as more "enlightened" or "progressive." The metropolitan centers of the West define the questions to be asked of other social systems and, at the same time, provide the measure against which all "foreign" practices are gauged. In a peculiar combination of Marxism and feminism, capitalism becomes the vehicle for reforms which allow for progress toward the emancipation of women. The "Third World," on the other hand, is viewed as retaining pre-capitalist forms expressed at the cultural level by traditions which are more oppressive to women. For example, in an article comparing socialist societies, Maxine Molyneux falls straight into this trap of defining "Third Worldism" as "backwardness."

> A second major problem facing Third World post-revolutionary states is the weight of conservative ideologies and practices; this is often subsumed in official literature under the categories of "traditionalism" or "feudal residues". The impact and nature of "traditionalism" is subject to considerable variation between countries but where it retains any force it may constitute an obstacle to economic and social development which has to be overcome in the formation of a new society. In some societies customary practices tend to bear especially heavily on women. Institutions such as polygyny, the brideprice, child marriages, seclusion, and forms of mutilation such as footbinding or female "circumcision" are woven into the very fabric of pre-capitalist societies. They often survive in Third World countries long after they have been made illegal and despite the overall changes that have occurred.[9]

Maxine Molyneux sees "systems of inheritance and arranged marriages" as being one of the central ways "by which forms of pre-capitalist property and social relations are maintained."

One immediate problem with this approach is that it is extraordinarily general. The level of generality applied to the "Third World" would be dismissed as too vague to be informative if applied to Western industrialized nations. However, Molyneux implies that since "Third World" women are outside of capitalist relations of production, entering capitalist relations is, necessarily, an emancipating move.

> There can be little doubt that on balance the position of women within imperialist, i.e. advanced capitalist societies is, for all its limitations, more advanced than in the less developed capitalist and non-capitalist societies. In this sense the changes brought by imperialism to Third World societies may, in some circumstances, have been historically progressive.[10]

This view of imperialism will be addressed in more detail later in the chapter. At this point we wish to indicate that the use of such theories reinforces the view that when black women enter Britain they are moving into a more liberated or enlightened or emancipated society than the one from which they have come. Nancy Foner saw the embodiment of West Indian women's increased freedom and liberation in Britain in the fact that they learned to drive cars![11] Different herstories, different struggles of black women against systems that oppress them are buried beneath Euro-centric conceptions of their position. Black family structures are seen as being produced by less advanced economic systems and their extended kinship networks are assumed to be more oppressive to women. The model of the white nuclear family, which rarely applies to black women's situation, is the measure by which they are pathologized and stands as a more progressive structure to the one in which they live.

It can be seen from this brief discussion of the use of the concept "the family" that the terms "patriarchy" and "reproduction" also become more complex in their application. It bears repetition that black men have not held the same patriarchal positions of power that the white males have established. Michèle Barrett argues that the term "patriarchy" has lost all analytic or explanatory power and has been reduced to a synonym for male dominance. She tries therefore to limit its use to a specific type of male dominance that could be located historically.

> I would not . . . want to argue that the concept of patriarchy should be jettisoned. I would favour retaining it for use in contexts where male domination is expressed through the power of the father over women and over younger men. . . . Hence I would argue for a more precise and specific use of the concept of patriarchy, rather than one which expands it to cover all expressions of male domination and thereby attempts to construe a descriptive term as a systematic explanatory theory.[12]

Barrett is not thinking of capitalist social organization. But if we try to apply this more "classic" and limited definition of patriarchy to the slave systems of the Americas and the Caribbean, we find that even this refined use of the concept cannot adequately account for the fact that both slaves and manumitted males did not have this type of patriarchal power. Alternatively, if we take patriarchy and apply it to various colonial situations, it is equally unsatisfactory because it is unable to explain why black males have not enjoyed the benefits of white patriarchy. There are very obvious power structures in both colonial and slave social formations and they are predominantly patriarchal. However, the historically specific forms of racism force us to modify or alter the application of the term "patri-archy" to black men. Black women have been dominated "patriarchally" in different ways by men of different "colors."

In questioning the application of the concepts of "the family" and "patriarchy" we also need to problematize the use of the concept of "reproduction." In using this concept in relation to the domestic labor of black women we find that in spite of its apparent simplicity it must be dismantled. What does the concept of reproduction mean in a situation where black women have done domestic labor outside of their own homes in the servicing of white families? In this example they lie outside of the industrial wage relation but in a situation where they are providing for the reproduction of black labor in their own domestic sphere, simultaneously ensuring the reproduction of white labor power in the "white" household. The concept, in fact, is unable to explain exactly what the relations are that need to be revealed. What needs to be understood is, first, precisely *how* the black woman's role in a rural, industrial or domestic labor force affects the construction of ideologies of black female sexuality, which are different from, and often constructed in opposition to, white female sexuality; and second, how this role relates to the black woman's struggle for control over her own sexuality.[13]

If we examine the recent herstory of women in postwar Britain we can see the ways in which the inclusion of black women creates problems for hasty generalization. In pointing to the contradiction between "home-making as a career" and the campaign to recruit women into the labor force during postwar reconstruction, Elizabeth Wilson fails to perceive migration of black women to Britain as the solution to these contradictory needs. The Economic Survey for 1947 is cited as an example of the ways in which women were seen to form "the only large reserve of labour left"; yet, as we know, there was a rather large pool of labor in the colonies that had been mobilized previously to fight in World War II. The industries that the survey listed as in dire need of labor included those that were filled by both male and female black workers, though Elizabeth Wilson does not differentiate them.

> The survey gave a list of the industries and services where labour was most urgently required. The boot and shoe industry, clothing, textiles, iron and steel, all required female workers, as did hospitals, domestic service, transport, and the women's land army. There was also a shortage of shorthand typists, and a dire shortage of nurses and midwives.[14]

This tells us nothing about why black women were recruited more heavily into some of these areas than others; perhaps we are given a clue when the author goes on to point out that women were welcomed into the labor force in a "circumscribed way"

> as temporary workers at a period of crisis, as part-time workers, and as not disturbing the traditional division of labour in industry along sex lines – the Survey reflected the view which was still dominant, that married women would not naturally wish to work.[15]

Not all black women were subject to this process: Afro-Caribbean women, for example, were encouraged and chose to come to Britain precisely to work. Ideologically they were seen as "naturally" suitable for the lowest paid, most menial jobs. Elizabeth Wilson goes on to explain that "work and marriage were still understood as alternatives . . . two kinds of women . . . a wife and a mother or a single career woman." Yet black women bridged this division. They were viewed simultaneously as workers and as wives and mothers. Elizabeth Wilson stresses that the postwar debate over the entry of women into the labor force occurred within the parameters of the question of possible effects on family life. She argues that "wives and mothers were granted entry into paid work only so long as this did not harm the family." Yet women from Britain's reserve army of labor in the colonies were recruited into the labor force far beyond any such considerations. Rather than a concern to protect or preserve the black family in Britain, the state reproduced common-sense notions of its inherent pathology: black women were seen to fail as mothers precisely because of their position as workers.

One important struggle, rooted in these different ideological mechanisms, which determine racially differentiated representations of gender, has been the black woman's battle to gain control over her own sexuality in the face of racist experimentation with the contraceptive Depo-Provera and enforced sterilizations.[16]

It is not just our herstory before we came to Britain that has been ignored by white feminists, our experiences and struggles here have also been ignored. These struggles and experiences, because they have been structured by racism, have been different to those of white women. Black feminists decry the non-recognition of the specificities of black women's sexuality and femininity, both in the ways these are constructed and also as they are addressed through practices which oppress black women in a gender-specific but none the less racist way.

This non-recognition is typified by a very interesting article on women in Third World manufacturing by Diane Elson and Ruth Pearson. In analyzing the employment of Third World women in world market factories they quote from an investment brochure designed to attract foreign firms:

The manual dexterity of the oriental female is famous the world over. Her hands are small and she works fast with extreme care. Who, therefore, could be better qualified by *nature and inheritance* to contribute to the efficiency of a bench-assembly production line than the oriental girl?[17]

The authors, however, analyze only the naturalization of gender and ignore the specificity signaled by the inclusion of the adjective "oriental," as if it didn't matter. The fact that the sexuality of the "oriental" woman is being differentiated is not commented upon and remains implicit rather than explicit as in the following remarks.

It is in the context of the subordination of women as a gender that we must analyse the supposed docility, subservience and consequent suitability for tedious, monotonous work of young women in the Third World.[18]

In concentrating an analysis upon gender only, Elson and Pearson do not see the relation between the situation they are examining in the periphery and the women who have migrated to the metropole. This last description is part of the common-sense racism that we have described as being applied to Asian women in Britain to channel them into "tedious, monotonous work." Elson and Pearson discuss this ascription of docility and passivity and compare it to Frantz Fanon's analysis of colonized people, without putting together the ways in which the women who are their objects of study have been oppressed not by gender subordination alone but also by colonization. The "oriental" sexuality referred to in the advertising brochure is one of many constructions of exotic sexual dexterity promised to Western male tourists to Southeast Asia. This ideology of "Eastern promise" links the material practice of the move from the bench – making microchips – to the bed, in which multinational corporate executives are serviced by prostitutes. This transition is described by Elson and Pearson but not understood as a process which illustrates an example of racially demarcated patriarchal power.

> If a woman loses her job in a world market factory after she has re-shaped her life on the basis of a wage income, the only way she may have of surviving is by selling her body. There are reports from South Korea, for instance, that many former electronics workers have no alternative but to become prostitutes. . . . A growing market for such services is provided by the way in which the tourist industry has developed, especially in South East Asia.[19]

The photographs accompanying the article are of anonymous black women. This anonymity and the tendency to generalize into meaninglessness the oppression of an amorphous category called "Third World women" are symptomatic of the ways in which the specificity of our experiences and oppression are subsumed under inapplicable concepts and theories. Black feminists in the US have complained of the ignorance, in the white women's movement, of black women's lives.

> The force that allows white feminist authors to make no reference to racial identity in their books about "women" that are in actuality about white women, is the same one that would compel any author writing exclusively on black women to refer explicitly to their racial identity. That force is racism. . . . It is the dominant race that can make it seem that their experience is representative.[20]

In Britain too it is as if we don't exist.

There is a growing body of black feminist criticism of white feminist theory and practice, for its incipient racism and lack of relevance to black women's lives.[21] The dialogues that have been attempted[22] have concentrated more upon visible, empirical differences that affect black and white women's lives than upon developing a feminist theoretical approach that would enable a feminist understanding of the basis of these differences. The accusation that racism in the women's movement acted so as to exclude the participation of black women has led to an explosion of debate in the USA.

... from a black female perspective, if white women are denying the existence of black women, writing "feminist" scholarship as if black women are not a part of the collective group American women, or discriminating against black women, then it matters less that North America was colonized by white patriarchal *men* who institutionalized a racially imperialist social order, than that white women who purport to be feminists support and actively perpetuate anti-black racism.[23]

What little reaction there has been in Britain has been more akin to lighting a damp squib than an explosion. US black feminist criticism has no more been listened to than indigenous black feminist criticism. Yet, bell hooks's powerful critique has considerable relevance to British feminists. White women in the British WLM are extraordinarily reluctant to see themselves in the situations of being oppressors, as they feel that this will be at the expense of concentrating upon being oppressed. Consequently the involvement of British women in imperialism and colonialism is repressed and the benefits that they – as whites – gained from the oppression of black people ignored. Forms of imperialism are simply identified as aspects of an all-embracing patriarchy rather than as sets of social relations in which white women hold positions of power by virtue of their "race."

Had feminists chosen to make explicit comparisons between ... the status of black women and white women, it would have been more than obvious that the two groups do not share an identical oppression. It would have been obvious that similarities between the status of women under patriarchy and that of any slave or colonized person do not necessarily exist in a society that is both racially and sexually imperialistic. In such a society, the woman who is seen as inferior because of her sex can also be seen as superior because of her race, even in relationship to men of another race.[24]

The benefits of a white skin did not just apply to a handful of cotton, tea or sugar plantation mistresses: all women in Britain benefited – in varying degrees – from the economic exploitation of the colonies. The pro-imperialist attitudes of many nineteenth- and early-twentieth-century feminists and suffragists have yet to be acknowledged for their racist implications. However, apart from this herstorical work, the exploration of contemporary racism within the white feminist movement in Britain has yet to begin.

Feminist theory in Britain is almost wholly Eurocentric and, when it is not ignoring the experience of black women "at home," it is trundling "Third World women" onto the stage only to perform as victims of "barbarous," "primitive" practices in "barbarous," "primitive" societies.

It should be noted that much feminist work suffers from the assumption that it is only through the development of a Western-style industrial capitalism and the resultant entry of women into waged labor that the potential for the liberation of women can increase. For example, foot-binding, clitoridectomy, female "circumcision" and other forms of mutilation of the female body have been described as "feudal residues," existing in economically "backward" or "underdeveloped" nations (i.e. not the industrialized West). Arranged marriages, polygamy and these forms of mutilation are linked in reductionist ways to a lack of technological development.

However, theories of "feudal residues" or of "traditionalism" cannot explain the appearance of female "circumcision" and clitoridectomy in the United States at the same moment as the growth and expansion of industrial capital. Between the establishment of industrial capitalism and the transformation to monopoly capitalism, the United States, under the influence of English biological science, saw the control of medical practice shift from the hands of women into the hands of men. This is normally regarded as a "progressive" technological advance, though this newly established medical science was founded on the control and manipulation of the female body. This was the period in which links were formed between hysteria and hysterectomy in the rationalization of the "psychology of the ovary."

> In the second half of the [nineteenth] century . . . fumbling experiments with the female interior gave way to the more decisive technique of surgery – aimed increasingly at the control of female personality disorders. . . . The last clitoridectomy we know of in the United States was performed in 1948 on a child of five, as a cure for masturbation.
>
> The most common form of surgical intervention in the female personality was ovariotomy, removal of the ovaries – or "female castration." In 1906 a leading gynecological surgeon estimated that there were 150,000 women in the United States who had lost their ovaries under the knife. Some doctors boasted that they had removed from fifteen hundred to two thousand ovaries apiece. . . . it should not be imagined that poor women were spared the gynecologist's exotic catalog of tortures simply because they couldn't pay. The pioneering work in gynecological surgery had been performed by Marion Sims on black female slaves he kept for the sole purpose of surgical experimentation. He operated on one of them thirty times in four years.[25]

These operations are hardly rituals left over from a pre-capitalist mode of production. On the contrary, they have to be seen as part of the "technological" advance in what is now commonly regarded as the most "advanced" capitalist economy in the world. Both in the USA and in Britain, black women still have a "role" – as in the use of Depo-Provera on them – in medical experimentation. Outside of the metropoles, black women are at the mercy of the multinational drug companies, whose quest for profit is second only to the cause of "advancing" Western science and medical knowledge.

The herstory of black women is interwoven with that of white women, but this does not mean that they are the same story. Nor do we need white feminists to write our herstory for us; we can and are doing that for ourselves. However, when they write their herstory and call it the story of women but ignore our lives and deny their relation to us, that is the moment in which they are acting within the relations of racism and writing *his*tory.

Constructing Alternatives

It should be an imperative for feminist herstory and theory to avoid reproducing the structural inequalities that exist between the "metropoles" and the "peripheries," and within the "metropoles" between black and white women, in the form of inappropriate polarizations between the "First" and "Third World," developed/underdeveloped or advanced/back-ward. We have already argued that the generalizations made about women's lives across societies in the African and Asian continents would be thought intolerable if applied to the lives of white women in Europe or North America. These are some of the reasons why concepts which allow for specificity, whilst at the same time providing cross-cultural reference points – not based in assumptions of inferiority – are urgently needed in feminist work. The work of Gayle Rubin and her use of discrete "sex/gender systems" appears to provide such a potential, particularly in the possibility of applying the concept within as well as between societies. With regard to the problems with the concept of patriarchy discussed above, she has made the following assessment:

> The term "patriarchy" was introduced to distinguish the forces maintaining sexism from other social forces, such as capitalism. But the use of "patriarchy" obscures other distinctions.[26]

In arguing for an alternative formulation, Gayle Rubin stresses the import-ance of maintaining

> a distinction between the human capacity and necessity to create a sexual world, and the empirically oppressive ways in which sexual worlds have been organized. Patriarchy subsumes both meanings into the same terms. Sex/gender system, on the other hand, is a neutral term which refers to the domain and indicates that oppression is not inevitable in that domain, but is the product of the specific social relations which organize it.[27]

This concept of sex/gender system offers the opportunity to be historically and culturally specific but also points to the position of relative autonomy of the sexual realm. It enables the subordination of women to be seen as a "product of the relationships by which sex and gender are organized and produced."[28] Thus, in order to account for the development of specific forms of sex/gender systems, reference must be made not only to the mode of production but also to the complex totality of specific social formations within which each system develops. Gayle Rubin argues that kinship relations are visible, empirical forms of sex/gender systems. Kinship relations here is not limited to biological relatives but is rather a "system of categories and statuses which often contradict actual genetic relationships."

What are commonly referred to as "arranged marriages" can, then, be viewed as the way in which a particular sex/gender system organizes the "exchange of women." Similarly, transformations of sex/gender systems brought about by colonial oppression, and the changes in kinship patterns which result from migration, must be assessed on their own terms, not just in comparative relation to other sex/gender systems. In this way patterns of subordination of women can be understood historically, rather than being dismissed as the inevitable product of pathological family structures.

At this point we can begin to make concrete the black feminist plea to white feminists to begin with our different herstories. Contact with white societies has not generally led to a more "progressive" change in African and Asian sex/gender systems. Colonialism attempted to destroy kinship patterns that were not modeled on nuclear family structures, disrupting, in the process, female organizations that were based upon kinship systems which allowed more power and autonomy to women than those of the colonizing nation. Events that occurred in the Calabar and Owerri provinces of Southern Nigeria in the winter months of 1929 bear witness to this disruption and to the consequent weakening of women's position. As Judith Van Allen points out, these events are known in Western social science literature as the "Aba Riots," a term which not only marginalizes the struggles themselves but which makes invisible the involvement of Igbo women. "Riots" implies unsystematic and mindless violence and is a perfect example of the constructions of *his*tory. The Igbo people, on the other hand, remember this conflict as Ogu Umuniwanyi (the "Women's War").[29]

> In November of 1929, thousands of Igbo women ... converged on the Native Administration centers. ... The women chanted, danced, sang songs of ridicule, and demanded the caps of office (the official insignia) of the Warrant Chiefs, the Igbo chosen from each village by the British to sit as members of the Native Court. At a few locations the women broke into prisons and released prisoners. Sixteen Native Courts were attacked, and most of these were broken up or burned. The "disturbed area" covered about 6000 square miles and contained about two million people. It is not known how many women were involved, but the figure was in tens of thousands. On two occasions, British District Officers called in police and troops, who fired on the women and left a total of more than 50 dead and 50 wounded. No one on the other side was seriously injured.[30]

Judith Van Allen examines in detail the women's organizations that ensured and regulated women's political, economic and religious role in traditional Igbo society. Although their role was not equal to that of men, they did have "a series of roles – despite the patrilineal organization of Igbo society."[31] Two of the associations that Judith Van Allen finds relevant were the *inyemedi*, or wives of a lineage, and the *umuada* – daughters of a lineage. Meetings of the *umuada* would "settle intralineage disputes among their 'brothers' as well as disputes between their natal and marital lineages." Since these gatherings were held in rotation among the villages into which members had married, "they formed an important part of the communication network of Igbo women." *Inyemedi*, on the other hand, came together in village-wide gatherings called *mikri*, gatherings of women who were in common residence rather than from a common place of birth (*ogbo*).

> The *mikri* appears to have performed the major role in the daily self-rule among women and to have articulated women's interests as opposed to those of men. *Mikri* provided women with a forum in which to develop their political talents and with a means for proecting their interests as traders, farmers, wives and mothers.[32]

Men recognized the legitimacy of the decisions and rules of the *mikri*, which not only settled disputes among women but also imposed rules and sanctions which directly affected men's behavior. The *mikri* could impose fines for violations of their decisions, and if these were ignored, women would "sit on" an offender or go on strike.

> To "sit on" or "make war on" a man involved gathering at his compound at a previously agreed upon time, dancing, singing scurrilous songs detailing the women's grievances against him (and often insulting him along the way by calling his manhood into question), banging on his hut with pestles for pounding yams, and in extreme cases, tearing up his hut (which usually meant pulling the roof off).[33]

A strike, on the other hand, "might involve refusing to cook, to take care of small children or to have sexual relations with their husbands."[34]

British colonizers in Nigeria dismissed all traditional forms of social organization that they found as "organized anarchy," and promptly imposed a system of administration that ignored female political structures and denied Igbo women any means of representation, leave alone any decision-making or rule-instituting power. Coming from sex/gender systems of Britain in the 1920s these colonial males could not conceive of the type of autonomy that Igbo women claimed. When the women demanded that they should serve on the Native Courts, be appointed to positions as District Officers, and further that "all white men should go to their own country," they were scoffed at by the British, who thought they acted under the influence of "savage passions." Their demands were viewed as totally irrational. The war waged by Igbo women against the British was a concerted organized mobilization of their political traditions. The fruits of colonialism were the imposition of class and gender relations which resulted in the concentration of national, economic and political power in the hands of a small, wealthy elite. We have quoted at length this example from the herstory of Igbo women in order to illustrate the ways in which an unquestioning application of liberal doses of Eurocentricity can completely distort and transform herstory into *his*tory. Colonialism was not limited to the imposition of economic, political and religious systems. More subtly, though just as effectively, it sedimented racist and sexist norms into traditional sex/gender systems. Far from introducing more "progressive" or liberating sex/gender social relations, the colonizing powers as

> class societies tend to socialize the work of men and domesticate that of women. This creates the material and organizational foundations for denying that women are adults and allows the ruling classes to define them as wards of men.[35]

Karen Sacks, in her essay "Engels Revisited," examines the ways in which these class societies have domesticated the field of activity for women to the extent that "through their labor men are social adults; women are domestic wards."[36] Although this work agrees with much white feminist theory, which has focused on the isolation of women within the nuclear family as a prime source of oppression in Western sex/gender systems, it does not necessarily follow that women living in kinship relations organized in different sex/gender systems are not oppressed. What it does mean is that analysis has to be specific and is not to be deduced from European systems. She goes on to explain that in India

> in Untouchable tenant-farming and village-service castes or classes, where women work today for village communities . . . they "have greater sexual freedom, power of divorce, authority to speak and witness in caste assemblies, authority over children, ability to dispose of their own belongings, rights to indemnity for wrongs done to them, rights to have disputes settled outside the domestic sphere, and representation in public rituals." In short, women who perform social labor have a higher status *vis-à-vis* men of their own class than do women who labor only in the domestic sphere or do no labor.[37]

Unfortunately feminist research has neglected to examine the basis of its Eurocentric (and often racist) framework. In the words of Achola O. Pala:

> Like the educational systems inherited from the colonial days, the research industry has continued to use the African environment as a testing ground for ideas and hypotheses the locus of which is to be found in Paris, London, New York or Amsterdam.[38]

Throughout much of this work, what is thought to be important is decided on the basis of what happens to be politically significant in the metropoles, not on what is important to the women who are under observation. Thus, from her own experience, Achola Pala relates how the major concerns of women are totally neglected by the researcher.

> I have visited villages where, at a time when the village women are asking for better health facilities and lower infant mortality rates, they are presented with questionnaires on family planning. In some instances, when the women would like to have piped water in the village, they may be at the same time faced with a researcher interested in investigating power and powerlessness in the household. In yet another situation, when women are asking for access to agricultural credit, a researcher on the scene may be conducting a study on female circumcision.[39]

The non-comprehension of the struggles and concerns of the African women, which Pala talks about, is indicative of the ways in which much Euro-American feminism has approached the lives of black women. It has attempted to force them into patterns which do not apply and in the process has labeled many of them deviant.

Another problem emerges from the frequently unqualified use of terms such as "pre-capitalist" and "feudal" to denote differences between the point of view of the researcher and her object of study. What is being indicated are differences in the modes of production. This distinction is subsequently used to explain observable differences in the position of women. However, the deployment of the concept "sex/gender system" interrupts this "logical progression" and reveals that the articulation of relations of production to sex/gender systems is much more complex. "Pre-capitalist" and "feudal" are often redundant and non-explanatory categories which rest on underestimations of the scope and power of capitalist economic systems. Immanuel Wallerstein, for example, has argued that the sixteenth century saw the creation of

> a world-embracing commerce and a world-embracing market . . . the emergence of capitalism as the dominant mode of social organization of the economy . . . the only mode in the sense that, once established, other "modes of production" survived in function of how they fitted into a politico-social framework deriving from capitalism.[40]

Wallerstein continues to dismiss the idea that feudal and capitalist forms of social organization could coexist by stressing that:

> The world economy has one form or another. Once it is capitalist, relationships that bear certain formal relationships to feudal relationships are necessarily redefined in terms of the governing principles of a capitalist system.[41]

There are ways in which this economic penetration has transformed social organization to the detriment of women in particular. Work on sexual economics by Lisa Leghorn and Katherine Parker demonstrates that the monetary system and heavy taxation that European nations imposed on their colonies directly eroded the status of women.

> In many nations the impact of the sudden need for cash was more devastating than the steep taxes themselves. Only two mechanisms for acquiring cash existed – producing the new export crops and working for wages – both of which were made available only to men. Men were forced to leave their villages and farms to work in mines, plantations or factories, at extremely low wages. Women were often left doing their own as well as the men's work, while most of the men's wages went to taxes and to support themselves at the higher standard of living in urban areas. As men who remained on the farms were taught how to cash crop, most technological aid and education went only to them, and women were left maintaining the subsistence agricultural economy that sustained themselves and their children. In Africa women still do 70% of the agricultural work while almost all the agricultural aid has gone to men.[42]

We need to counteract the tendency to reduce sex oppression to a mere "reflex of economic forces"[43] whilst at the same time recognizing that

> sexual systems cannot, in the final analysis, be understood in complete isolation. A full-bodied analysis of women in a single society, or throughout history, must take everything into account: the evolution of commodity forms in women, systems of land tenure, political arrangements, subsistence technology, etc.[44]

We can begin to see how these elements come together to affect the lives of black women under colonial oppression in ways that transform the sex/gender systems in which they live but that are also shaped by the sex/gender system of the colonizers. If we examine changes in land distribution we can see how capitalist notions of the private ownership of land (a primarily economic division) and ideas of male dominance (from the sex/gender system) work together against the colonized.

> Another problem affecting women's agricultural work is that as land ownership shifts from the collective "land-use rights" of traditional village life, in which women shared in the distribution of land, to the European concept of private ownership, it is usually only the men who have the necessary cash to pay for it (by virtue of their cash-cropping income). In addition, some men traditionally "owned" the land, while women "owned" the crops as in the Cameroons in West Africa. As land becomes increasingly scarce, men begin to rent and sell "their" land, leaving women with no recourse but to pay for land or stop their agricultural work.[45]

It is impossible to argue that colonialism left pre-capitalist or feudal forms of organization untouched. If we look at the West Indies we can see that patterns of migration, for both men and women, have followed the dictates of capital.

When men migrated from the islands for work in plantations or building the Panama Canal, women migrated from rural to urban areas. Both have migrated to labour in the "core" capitalist nations. Domestic, marginal or temporary service work has sometimes been viewed as a great "opportunity" for West Indian women to transform their lives. But as Shirley-Ann Hussein has shown,

Take the case of the domestic workers. A development institution should be involved in more than placing these women in domestic jobs as this makes no dent in the society. It merely rearranges the same order. Domestic labour will have to be done away with in any serious attempt at social and economic reorganisation.[46]

If, however, imperialism and colonialism have ensured the existence of a world market, it still remains necessary to explain how it is in the interests of capitalism to maintain social relations of production that are non-capitalist – that is, forms that could not be described as feudal because that means pre-capitalist, but which are also not organized around the wage relation. If we return to the example of changes in ownership of land and in agricultural production, outlined above, it can be argued that

the agricultural division of labor in the periphery – with male semi-proletarians and female agriculturalists – contributes to the maintenance of a low value of labor power for peripheral capital accumulation through the production of subsistence foodstuffs by the noncapitalist mode of production for the reproduction and maintenance of the labor force.[47]

In other words the work that the women do is a force which helps to keep wages low. To relegate "women of color" in the periphery to the position of being the victims of feudal relations is to aid in the masking of colonial relations of oppression. These relations of imperialism should not be denied. Truly feminist herstory should be able to acknowledge that:

Women's economic participation in the periphery of the world capitalist system, just as within center economies, has been conditioned by the requirements of capital accumulation . . . [but] the economic participation of women in the Third World differs significantly from women's economic participation within the center of the world capitalist system.[48]

Black women have been at the forefront of rebellions against land seizures and struggle over the rights of access to land in Africa, Latin America and the Caribbean. Adequate herstories of their roles in many of these uprisings remain to be written. The role of West Indian women in the rebellions preceding and during the disturbances in Jamaica in 1938, for example, though known to be significant, has still not been thoroughly described. White feminist herstorians are therefore mistaken when they portray black women as passive recipients of colonial oppression. As Gail Omvedt has shown in her book *We Will Smash This Prison*,[49] women in India have a long and complex herstory of fighting oppression both in and out of the wage relation. It is clear that many women coming from India to Britain have a shared herstory of struggle, whether in rural areas as agricultural laborers or in urban districts as municipal employees. The organized struggles of Asian women in Britain need to be viewed in the light of this herstory. Their industrial battles, and struggles against immigration policy and practice, articulate the triple oppression of race, gender and class that have been present since the dawn of imperialist domination.

In concentrating solely upon the isolated position of white women in the Western nuclear family structure, feminist theory has necessarily neglected the very strong female support networks that exist in many black sex/gender systems. These have often been transformed by the march of technological "progress" intended to relieve black women from aspects of their labor.

> Throughout Africa, the digging of village wells has saved women enormous amounts of time which they formerly spent trekking long distances to obtain water. But it has often simultaneously destroyed their only chance to get together and share information and experiences. Technological advances such as household appliances do not free women from domestic drudgery in any society.[50]

Leghorn and Parker, in *Women's Worth*, attempt to create new categories to describe, in general terms, the diversity of male power across societies. Whilst they warn against the rigid application of these categories – few countries fit exactly the category applied to them – the work does represent an attempt to move away from Euro-American racist assumptions of superiority, whether political, cultural or economic. The three classifications that they introduce are "minimal," "token" and "negotiating power" societies. Interestingly, from the black women's point of view, the most salient factor in the categorization of a country has

> usually been that of women's networks, because it is the existence, building or dissolution of these networks that determines women's status and potential for change in all areas of their lives.[51]

These categories cut through the usual divisions of First/Third World, advanced/dependent, industrial/non-industrial in an attempt to find a mechanism that would "free" thinking from these definitions. Space will not allow for a critical assessment of all three categories but it can be said that their application of "negotiating power" does recognize as important the "traditional" women's organizations to be found in West Africa, and described above in relation to the Igbo. Leghorn and Parker are careful to stress that "negotiating power" is limited to the possibilities of negotiating;

it is not an absolute category of power that is held *over* men by women. The two examples of societies given in their book where women hold this negotiating position are the Ewe, in West Africa, and the Iroquois. Both, of course, are also examples where contact with the whites has been for the worse. Many of the Ewe female institutions disintegrated under colonialism, whilst the institutions that afforded Iroquois women power were destroyed by European intrusion. In contrast to feminist work that focuses upon the lack of technology and household mechanical aids in the lives of these women, Leghorn and Parker concentrate upon the aspects of labor that bring women together. Of the Ewe they note:

> Women often work together in their own fields, or as family members preparing meals together, village women meeting at the stream to do the wash, or family, friends and neighbours, walking five to fifteen miles a day to market together, sitting near each other in the market, and setting a day's prices together. They share childcare, news, and looking after each other's market stalls. In addition to making the time more pleasant, this shared work enables women to share information and in fact serves as an integral and vital part of the village communications system. Consequently, they have a tremendous sense of solidarity when it comes to working in their collective interest.[52]

It is important not to romanticize the existence of such female support networks, but they do provide a startling contrast to the isolated position of women in the Euro-American nuclear family structure.

In Britain, strong female support networks continue in both West Indian and Asian sex/gender systems, though these are ignored by sociological studies of migrant black women. This is not to say that these systems remain unchanged with migration. New circumstances require adaptation and new survival strategies have to be found.

> Even childcare in a metropolitan area is a big problem. If you live in a village in an extended family, you know that if your child's outside somewhere, someone will be looking out for her. If your child is out on the street and your neighbour down the road sees your child in some mess, that woman is going to take responsibility of dealing with that child. But in Brooklyn or in London, you're stuck in that apartment. You're there with that kid, you can't expect that child to be out on the street and be taken care of. You know the day care situation is lousy, you're not in that extended family, so you have a big problem on your hands. So when they talk about the reduction of house-work, we know by now that that's a lie.[53]

However, the transformations that occur are not merely adaptive, neither is the black family destroyed in the process of change. Female networks mean that black women are key figures in the development of survival strategies, both in the past, through periods of slavery and colonialism, and now, facing a racist and authoritarian state.

There is considerable evidence that women – and families – do not . . . simply accept the isolation, loss of status, and cultural devaluation involved in the migration. Networks are re-formed, if need be with non-kin or on the basis of an extended definition of kinship, by strong, active, and resourceful women. . . . Cultures of resistance are not simple adaptive mechanisms; they embody important alternative ways of organizing production and reproduction and value systems critical of the oppressor. Recognition of the special position of families in these cultures and social structures can lead to new forms of struggle, new goals.[54]

In arguing that feminism must take account of the lives, herstories and experiences of black women, we are not advocating that teams of white feminists should descend upon Brixton, Southall, Bristol or Liverpool to take black women as objects of study in modes of resistance. We don't need that kind of intrusion on top of all the other information-gathering forces that the state has mobilized in the interest of "race relations." White women have been used against black women in this way before and feminists must learn from history. After the Igbo riots described above, two women anthropologists were sent by the British to "study the causes of the riot and to uncover the organisational base that permitted such spontaneity and solidarity among the women."[55] The WLM, however, does need to listen to the work of black feminists and to take account of autonomous organizations like OWAAD (Organization of Women of Asian and African Descent) who are helping to articulate the ways in which we are oppressed as black women.

In addition to this it is very important that white women in the women's movement examine the ways in which racism excludes many black women and prevents them from unconditionally aligning themselves with white women. Instead of taking black women as the objects of their research, white feminist researchers should try to uncover the gender-specific mechanisms of racism amongst white women. This, more than any other factor, disrupts the recognition of common interests of sisterhood.

In *Finding a Voice*, by Amrit Wilson, Asian women describe many instances of racial oppression at work from white women. Asian women

are paid low salaries and everything is worse for them, they have to face the insults of supervisors. These supervisors are all English women. The trouble is that in Britain our women are expected to behave like servants and we are not used to behaving like servants and we can't. But if we behave normally . . . the supervisors start shouting and harassing us. . . . They complain about us Indians to the manager.[56]

Black women do not want to be grafted onto "feminism" in a tokenistic manner as colorful diversions to "real" problems. Feminism has to be transformed if it is to address us. Neither do we wish our words to be misused in generalities as if what each one of us utters represents the total experience of all black women. Audre Lorde's address to Mary Daly is perhaps the best conclusion.

> I ask that you be aware of how this serves the destructive forces of racism and separation between women – the assumption that the herstory and myth of white women is the legitimate and sole herstory and myth of all women to call for power and background, and that non-white women and our herstories are note-worthy only as decorations, or examples of female victimization. I ask that you be aware of the effect that this dismissal has upon the community of black women, and how it devalues your own words. . . . When patriarchy dismisses us, it encourages our murders. When radical lesbian feminist theory dismisses us, it encourages its own demise. This dismissal stands as a real block to communication between us. This block makes it far easier to turn away from you completely than attempt to understand the thinking behind your choices. Should the next step be war between us, or separation? Assimilation within a sole Western-European herstory is not acceptable.[57]

In other words, of white feminists we must ask, what exactly do you mean when you say 'WE'??

1982

Acknowledgments

The debt I owe to my sisters, Valerie Amos and Pratibha Parmar, is enormous for the many hours we have spent discussing our experiences as black women and as feminists. Both contributed to the ideas in this chapter but any criticisms for inadequacies should be directed at me. To Paul, John and Errol, thank you for those transatlantic calls – support and brotherly affection was regularly transmitted. To Susan Willis I owe especial thanks for her support and friendship in a new job and a new country. To faculty, staff and students at the African American Studies Program at Yale and the Birmingham Centre for Contemporary Cultural Studies, thank you for your encouragement and enthusiasm for my work.

Notes

1. Gayl Jones, *Corregidora*, New York: Random House, 1975, pp. 14, 72.
2. Winthrop Jordan, *White Over Black*, London: Penguin, 1969, pp. 238, 495, 500.
3. My thanks to Michèle Barrett, who, in a talk given at the Social Science Research Council's Unit on Ethnic Relations, helped to clarify many of these attempted parallels.
4. Combahee River Collective, "A Black Feminist Statement," in Cherrie Moraga

and Gloria Anzaldúa, eds, *This Bridge Called My Back: Writings by Radical Women of Color*, Watertown, MA: Persephone Press, 1981, p. 213.

5. Michèle Barrett, *Women's Oppression Today*, London: Verso, 1980, p. 214.
6. Bert James Loewenberg and Rush Bogin, eds, *Black Women in Nineteenth-Century American Life*, University Park: Pennsylvania State University Press, 1978, p. 235. This speech has been erroneously attributed. See Nell Painter, *Sojourner Truth: A Life, A Symbol*, New York: W. W. Norton, 1996.
7. Pratibha Parmar and Nadira Mirza, "Growing Angry, Growing Strong," *Spare Rib*, no. 111, October 1981.
8. Ibid.
9. Maxine Molyneux, "Socialist Societies Old and New: Progress Towards Women's Emancipation?," *Feminist Review*, no. 8, Summer 1981, p. 3.
10. Ibid., p. 4.
11. Nancy Foner, *Jamaica Farewell*, London: Routledge & Kegan Paul, 1979. She also argues that:

> In rural Jamaica, most women do not smoke cigarettes; in London, many of the women I interviewed smoked, and when I commented on this they noted that such behaviour would not have been approved in Jamaica. Thus in England there is an enlargement of the women's world. (pp. 69–70)

12. Barrett, *Women's Oppression Today*.
13. See Centre for Contemporary Cultural Studies, *The Empire Strikes Back: Race and Racism in Seventies Britain*, London: Hutchinson, 1982, Chapter 7, for an elaboration of this point.
14. Elizabeth Wilson, *Only Halfway to Paradise: Women in Postwar Britain 1945–1968*, London: Tavistock, 1980, pp. 43–4.
15. Ibid.
16. *Fowaad, Newsletter of the Organisation of Women of Asian and African Descent*, no. 2, London: OWAAD, 1979.
17. Diane Elson and Ruth Pearson, "Nimble Fingers Make Cheap Workers: An Analysis of Women's Employment in Third World Export Manufacturing," *Feminist Review*, no. 7, Spring 1981, p. 93. Original emphasis.
18. Ibid., p. 95.
19. Ibid.
20. bell hooks, *Ain't I a Woman*, Boston: South End Press, 1981, p. 138.
21. Much of this critical work has been written in America but is applicable to the WLM in Britain. Apart from the books cited in this chapter, interested readers should look out for essays and articles by Gloria Joseph, Audre Lourde, Barbara Smith and Gloria Watkins that represent a range of black feminist thought. In Britain, the very existence of the feminist Organization of Women of Asian and African Descent (OWAAD) is a concrete expression of black feminists' critical distance from "white" feminism. See also Valerie Amos and Pratibha Parmar, "Resistances and Responses: Black Girls in Britain," in Angela McRobbie and Trisha McCabe, eds, *Feminism for Girls: An Adventure Story*, London: Routledge & Kegan Paul, 1982, who criticize the WLM for its irrelevance to the lives of black girls in Britain.
22. See Gloria Joseph and Jill Lewis, *Common Differences: Conflicts in Black and White Feminist Perspectives*, New York: Anchor, 1981, for an attempt at a dialogue that shows just how difficult it is to maintain.

23. hooks, *Ain't I a Woman*, pp. 123–4.
24. Ibid., p. 141.
25. Barbara Ehrenreich and Dierdre English, *For Her Own Good*, New York: Doubleday Anchor 1979.
26. Gayle Rubin, "The Traffic in Women," in Rayna R. Reiter, ed., *Toward an Anthropology of Women*, New York: Monthly Review Press, 1975, p. 167.
27. Ibid., p. 168.
28. Ibid., p. 177.
29. Judith Van Allen, "'Aba Riots' or Igbo 'Women's War'? Ideology, Stratification and the Invisibility of Women," in Nancy Hafkin and Edna Bay, eds, *Women in Africa: Studies in Social and Economic Change*, Palo Alto, CA: Stanford University Press, 1976, p. 59.
30. Ibid., p. 60.
31. Ibid., p. 62.
32. Ibid., p. 69.
33. Ibid., p. 61.
34. Ibid., p. 69.
35. Karen Sacks, "Engels Revisited: Women, the Organization of Production, and Private Property," in Reiter, ed. *Toward an Anthropology of Women*.
36. Ibid., p. 231.
37. Ibid., p. 233.
38. Achola O. Pala, "Definitions of Women and Development: An African Perspective," *Signs: Journal of Women in Culture and Society*, vol. 3, no. 1, Autumn 1977.
39. Ibid., p. 10.
40. Immanuel Wallerstein, *The Modern World System 1*, New York: Academic Press, 1974, p. 77.
41. Ibid., p. 92.
42. Lisa Leghorn and Katherine Parker, *Women's Worth: Sexual Economics and the World of Women*, London: Routledge & Kegan Paul, 1981, p. 44.
43. Rubin, p. 203.
44. Ibid., p. 209.
45. Leghorn and Parker, *Women's Worth*, p. 45.
46. Shirley-Ann Hussein, "Four Views on Women in the Struggle," in *Caribbean Women in the Struggle*, p. 29: quoted in Leghorn and Parker, *Women's Worth*, p. 52.
47. Carmen Diane Deere, "Rural Women's Subsistence Production," in Robin Cohen, Peter Gutkind and Phyllis Brazier, eds, *Peasants and Proletarians: The Struggles of Third World Workers*, New York: Monthly Review Press, 1979, p. 143.
48. Ibid., p. 133.
49. Gail Omvedt, *We Will Smash This Prison*, London: Zed Press, 1980.
50. Leghorn and Parker, *Women's Worth*, p. 55.
51. Ibid., p. 60.
52. Ibid., p. 88.
53. Margaret Prescod-Roberts and Norma Steele, *Black Women: Bringing it all Back Home*, London: Falling Wall Press, 1980, p. 28.
54. Mina Davis Caufield, "Cultures of Resistance," *Socialist Revolution*, 20, vol. 4, no. 2, October 1974, pp. 81, 84.
55. Leis, "Women in Groups," quoted in Caufield, "Cultures of Resistance."

56. Amrit Wilson, *Finding a Voice: Asian Women in Britain*, London: Virago, 1978, p. 122.
57. Audre Lorde, "An Open Letter to Mary Daly," in Moraga and Anzaldúa, eds, *This Bridge Called My Back*, p. 96.

6

Race and the Academy: Feminism and the Politics of Difference

The title of my essay, "Race and the Academy: Feminism and the Politics of Difference," indicates that I have two particular but closely interrelated concerns to address. It would seem that, in the United States, we are at a historical moment when issues of race have become absorbed within, or subsumed under, frameworks of critical thinking that organize themselves around concepts of difference and otherness. At the end of the eighties it was possible to see that feminist debate had become more concerned to focus on a pluralist concept of women rather than a unitary concept of woman and was increasingly evoking the experiences of multiple identities and subjectivities rather than assuming the formation of a single identity and subjectivity. Of course, we are still, all too frequently, confronted by colleagues who assume that the subjects of feminist work are the minority of women in the world who are white, European or North American, and middle or upper middle class, but perhaps now their assumptions do not so easily pass unchallenged. I had a request from someone whose publisher would not let the anthology she was editing go to press because there were no essays in the volume on, or by, women of color. This woman was clearly desperately telephoning all the women she could think of who had "color" asking if they could "write something in a month." While I was particularly outraged by this call and have earnestly wished that this particular anthology disintegrate into dust (the politically correct response would be to wish it recycled), the incident is instructive about a shift in some publishing practices in North America. It would appear as if a gesture toward diversity is now a required element of marketing to a Women's Studies audience. I want to use what I am calling "the politics of difference" – and could also be described as the politics of diversity – within contemporary feminist critical thinking and practice as an example of the ways in which issues of race are actually being avoided, displaced, and even abandoned, while it appears as if racism is being directly challenged and confronted.

But before I directly address issues of difference and diversity within feminism I would like to speak more generally about this particular historical moment in the United States. As a black intellectual I am both intrigued and horrified by the contradictory nature of the black presence in North American universities. We are, as peoples and as cultural producers, simultaneously visibly present in, and starkly absent from, university life. Of course, the academy is not a subject of much popular concern, being marginal to the lives of most people. Academics, in particular, are not figures who generate much general interest and are usually only visible in the media of the United States as the shadowy presences of "experts" in the fields of foreign relations, or national and international finance, on Public Broadcasting System news programs. I cannot resist, therefore, making a comment about the unusual event of the presence of a professor, let alone a black professor, on the cover of the April 1 1990 *New York Times Magazine*.[1]

The main subject of the story was Professor Henry Louis Gates, Jr, a prominent critic of African American literature and culture, but an important secondary subject was the field of African American Studies. Both the man and his field of knowledge were repeatedly referred to as controversial, and I was particularly struck by the number of times that the word "controversial" was used. I have been screening the 1959 Douglas Sirk movie *Imitation of Life* recently with my students and we had all been commenting on the use of the words "controversy" and "controversial" in that film to both signal and marginalize the historical moment of unrest in which the film was made. The history of an increasingly assertive and aggressive demand for black civil rights was a history outside of the story of the film but was also a history that kept threatening to erupt into the film in ways that the plot couldn't contain except through these repeated references to "controversy." The *New York Times Magazine* article was equally contradictory and ambiguous about exactly what is supposed to be controversial about a black professor and Black Studies.

However, the story about Professor Gates is an instructive occasion for thinking about the ambiguous and contradictory nature of the positions that we, as black intellectuals, occupy in universities and about the ambiguities and contradictions that are embedded in our work.

On the surface we appear to have "made it." Some would say that we appear to be gaining a voice, that the syllabi of some university courses in the United States have changed, or are changing, that there is at least debate about what should be taught and about which subjects. My response would be to dive beneath this surface and to question for whom and on whose terms are these changes happening? To extend the analogy between our existence as black subjects in universities and within the pages of the *New York Times Magazine*, we clearly have to temper any enthusiasm about being taken seriously, at long last, with the recognition that we are being paid attention to for what we have long been considered to be good at in the history of the United States. We are being seriously considered as higher educational entertainment. Lest we start believing, as black professors, that we have been allowed to evacuate our place on the outside of the real work of academia, the words of Stanley Fish, Chair of the Department of English at Duke University, are at the center of the *New York Times Magazine* article characterizing Henry Louis Gates as the P.T. Barnum of African American Studies. If Gates is being characterized as a twentieth-century reincarnation of the nineteenth-century P.T. Barnum (master manipulator of popular culture and founder of the circus), then, presumably, African American Studies itself is the circus arena and, as practitioners in that arena, I guess that black intellectuals are the performing animals and trapeze artists.

As a black cultural critic, I consistently try to broaden the use of terms like "intellectual" and "cultural producer" to include other cultural practices like music and film to disrupt the ways in which the description of intellectuals is often limited to practices based on writing and/or to people employed as professors. But, of course, institutions like universities and the *New York Times* are more concerned than I am with setting and policing the boundaries of cultural acceptability and with limiting what should be considered legitimate intellectual work. So, to be seriously considered as entertainment within the sacred halls of academe is not a political triumph. As Malcolm X always warned us, to the dominant social order a black Ph.D is a "nigger." Stanley Fish's characterization, of course, also acts to reassure the vigorous defenders of the canon that allowing the black folks to play the April Fool is a side show and not threatening to the main event.

There is, I would argue, a very important distinction that needs to be made between an apparent black cultural presence in the academy and the presence of black peoples. If there seems to be a vocal commitment to diversifying university campuses in the United States, I would like to remind you that more than 90 percent of all faculty members across the nation are white. In the most recent years for which I have figures, 1985–86, the presence of minority regular faculty was as follows: 3.8 percent Asian; 4.1 percent black; 0.4 percent Native American; and 1.3 percent Latino. In the previous decade the percentage of minority faculty members who were black decreased relative to the members of other minority groups. The percentage of black students in college populations has also steadily decreased and, as the number of bachelor's degrees awarded has been increasing nationally, the number of BAs awarded to black students has declined.

In graduate schools the proportion of American graduate students who are black is decreasing and the proportion of doctorates awarded to black people is in steady decline. At the professorial level, while it is possible to see that the number of tenured black faculty members has increased slightly, the number of black people holding untenured appointments has declined. What should be the subject of so-called "controversy," then, is not our presence but our increasing disappearance from university popu-lations in the United States. An African American intellectual presence in the academy is not at this moment being reproduced, in striking contrast, for example, to the presence of white women, who have been steadily increasing their numbers as students and as faculty in universities during the same period. In North America it is clearly easier to integrate a syllabus in a course than to recruit black faculty to teach it or black students to engage with it.

Should we regard it as paradoxical, then, that so much energy is being directed toward a black presence in the curriculum of universities in the United States and so little to the material conditions that exclude our actual bodies? The National Research Council's recent publication *A Common Destiny: Blacks and American Society*[2] argues that while there exists support for national policies promoting equality of opportunity through social institutions and governmental policy, there is significantly less sup-port for the actual practice of equality of treatment. Of course, it is obvious that at the national level such support is gradually being eroded, but there is a marked difference between the apparent national commitment to rectify the existence of a separate but unequal society and the apartheid nature of residential neighborhoods and schools. The residential segrega-tion of whites and blacks in large metropolitan areas in the United States was as high in the 1980s as it was in the 1960s. We now have a white population that has been raised on the celebration of the theme of diversity in the television program *Sesame Street* but refuses to integrate its public school systems, condemns apartheid in South Africa but supports it in all major urban areas. High school drop-out rates for black school children are double those for whites, and blacks account for half of the prison population. Surely, prison must be the only institution where we are overrepresented – four times our representation in the population. Increas-ingly, the poor are the working poor. In 1987, 20 percent of children under eighteen in the United States were being raised in families with incomes below the poverty line; 45 percent of all black children and 39 percent of all Hispanic children live and will remain living in poverty.

We live, in the United States, in a society structured in dominance by race and in which the practice of apartheid, particularly in housing and education, is strong and not, as far as I can see, in danger of being eroded. This is the set of material conditions to which, I would argue, a commit-ment to the language of diversity and difference is a totally inadequate response. What, for example, does the debate about the opening up of the canon mean in relation to these material conditions of existence? And what has been the role of feminist theory in trying to come to terms with the meaning of race as it has attempted to diversify the concept of women?

Elizabeth Weed, in her collection *Coming to Terms,*[3] has recently chal-lenged us to interrogate and reveal the politics of the theories that we use as feminists. I would like to, briefly, focus your attention on the politics of difference because this is, perhaps, the most usual way now that feminists in North America try to signal their concern to develop concepts of women and womanhood that are plural rather than unitary in their effects. I wonder if theories of difference, as they are currently being formulated, are leading to a further ghettoization of our cultural and political presence within academic work in the United States. The category of difference is often used as if it were an absolute social, cultural and political division. As a black British cultural critic has recently argued, "where black art and aesthetics are debated in conference after conference it is becoming harder to dislodge the belief that ethnic differences constitute an absolute break in history and humanity."[4] In practice, the politics of difference can censor the complexity of a black cultural presence and also censor who can speak. If ethnic differences are absolute, then the response from many liberal, white students is that they won't speak because they are of the dominant group. The political effect of this position is indistinguishable from not having to take any political position whatsoever in relation to the culture of the other. If one does not have to take a position, then difference does not actually have to be confronted. Indeed, difference has been preserved as absolute and so has the dominant social order.

On the other hand, if we try to recognize that we live in a social formation which is structured in dominance by race, then, theoretically, we can argue that everyone has been constructed as a racialized subject. In this sense it is important to recognize the historical invention of the category of whiteness in the United States as well as the category of blackness and, consequently, to make visible what is usually rendered invisible because it is viewed as being the normative state of existence. The political practice that should come from this theoretical position would situate everyone as being a racialized subject and would argue that processes of racialization should be a central conceptual category in all our work. But, because the politics of difference work with concepts of diversity rather than structures of dominance, race is a marginalized concept that is wheeled on only when the subjects are black. However, I want to distinguish my argument for the importance and centrality of the concept of race from positions from within a framework of the politics of difference which argue that everyone has an ethnicity. I am not arguing for pluralism, the result of much work on ethnicity in North America, but for revealing the structures of power relations that are at work in the racialization of a social order.

We can see a further marginalization of the concept of race in the current use of the phrase "women of color" in North American universities. In the need to find a common ground among non-dominant groups of women and in a desire to establish a system of alliances among exploited groups of women, this phrase has been lifted from its ground of origins and reinserted into the language of difference in feminist theory. What does "women of color" come to mean when taken up by feminist theories of difference? In practice we are all familiar with the use of the term as a referent, but do some people lack color? Do white women have no color? What does it mean to not have color? Does it mean that somehow those without color are not implicated in a society structured in dominance by race? Are those without colour outside of the hierarchy of social relations and not racialized? Are only the so-called "colored" to be the subjects of this specialized discourse and therefore effectively marginalized yet again? Do existing power relations remain intact? Are the politics of difference here apparently effective in making visible women of color while rendering invisible the politics of race?

It would seem important to ask these questions before we can start to think about the disparity between the fascination for black women as subjects on a syllabus in many universities in the United States and the total disregard for the material conditions of most black people in those same universities. Often it seems that black women appear as romantic anthropological subjects or primitive presences in the university curriculum. For whom are they there? If black students and faculty agitated for the existence of African American Studies, has feminism created the need for a black female subject that is compatible with the politics of diversity? Feminism in many universities in the United States has created an essential black female subject for its own consumption; it is a figure that can be used as an example of the most victimized of the victims of patriarchal oppression, or as an example of the most noble of noble womanhood that endured: Faulkner's Dilsey reborn. Certainly, this black female subject seems to be needed to embody an essential black female experience, whatever that may be. But, above all, this new black woman subject, of women's studies in particular, acts to berate the white woman for her racism, acts as a mechanism to cleanse her soul, becomes the hair-shirt which she can wear and can then feel self-satisfied and politically correct. Does this fantasized black female subject exist, primarily, to make the white middle class feel better about itself?

What we need to do is to teach ourselves to recognize the existence of historically specific forms of racism: to think in terms of racisms instead of an idea of racism that doesn't change through history; to think in terms of racial formations rather than eternal or essential races. Then, perhaps, we can begin to see how an apparent commitment to diversity in a university can be engaged very intimately in a new form of racism. The important thing to remember about racism is that it promotes a transformation of the whole ideological field in which it operates, and this is what I would argue has happened in relation to changes in the curriculum.

As Elizabeth Weed concludes: "Identity, as feminism's compulsion, speaks compulsively of the problem of difference."[5] I would add to this observation that it speaks not at all of structures of power. The category of woman may have become women, difference may now be differences, and the question of identity now be the problem of multiple identities, but the politics behind the theories of identity and difference are pluralist and little concerned with establishing the complexity of racialized structures of dominance. The political consequences of this thinking are evident in the language of diversity. For example, we hear a lot about oppression but nothing at all about systems of exploitation; the concept of resistance is frequently used but the concept of revolution has disappeared. Oppression and resistance are terms more easily applied to individualist and pluralist ideals of political change. But as Barbara Harlow has asked, where is the liberationist agenda?[6] Where is the collective emancipatory project? Theories of difference and diversity in practice leave us fragmented and divided but equal in an inability to conceive of radical social change. Of course, we are not supposed to need or to use revolutionary theories of history, the so-called "master narratives," because they are regarded as the master's tools. It is my contention that the master appropriated those tools along with the labor of those he exploited and that it is high time that they were reclaimed.

1994

Notes

1. Adam Begley, "Henry Louis Gates Jr.: Black Studies' New Star," *New York Times Magazine,* April 1 1990, pp. 24–7.
2. National Research Council, *A Common Destiny: Blacks and American Society,* Washington, DC: National Academy Press, 1989.
3. Elizabeth Weed, ed., *Coming to Terms: Feminism, Theory, Politics,* New York: Routledge, 1989.
4. Paul Gilroy, "Cruciality and the Frog's Perspective," *Third Text,* vol. 5, Winter 1988/89, pp. 33–44.
5. Elizabeth Weed, "Introduction: Terms of Reference," in Weed, ed., *Coming to Terms.*
6. Barbara Harlow, *Resistance Literature,* New York: Methuen, 1987.

National Nightmares:
The Liberal Bourgeoisie and
Racial Anxiety

This is an age of the world when nations are trembling and
convulsed. A mighty influence is abroad, surging and heaving the
world, as with an earthquake. And is America safe? Every nation that
carries in its bosom great and unredressed injustice has in it the
elements of this last convulsion. . . . Not by combining together, to
protect injustice and cruelty, and making a common capital of sin,
is this Union to be saved, – but by repentance, justice and mercy;
for, not surer is the eternal law by which the millstone sinks in the
ocean, than that stronger law, by which injustice and cruelty shall
bring on nations the wrath of Almighty God!

Harriet Beecher Stowe, *Uncle Tom's Cabin*

We live in chaos. . . . Everyone is trying to control their fear.

"Davies" in *Grand Canyon*

. . . the destruction of the racist complex presupposes not only the
revolt of its victims, but the transformation of the racists themselves
and, consequently, *the internal decomposition of the community created by
racism.*

Etienne Balibar, *Race, Nation, Class*[1]

For a hundred and thirty years, Harriet Beecher Stowe's novel *Uncle Tom's
Cabin* has been closely associated in the North American cultural and
political imagination with the Civil War that followed on the heels of the
book's publication in 1852. Indeed the association is now so close that
Stowe's words appear prophetic of the bloody conflagration that was to
come. In the same way, Lawrence Kasdan's film *Grand Canyon* has become
haunted by the specter of the rebellion in the streets of Los Angeles that
began on the night of April 29 1992.

My general concern is with the role of narrative in the production of what Etienne Balibar has called "genealogies" of race and nation, what Toni Morrison has referred to as the inscription of national issues on black bodies, and what Michael Rogin has described as "the surplus symbolic value of blacks, the power to make African Americans stand for something beside themselves."[2] My particular examples are narratives that both evoke and provoke a number of apparently contradictory racialized and gendered anxieties, fears and desires. These narrative genealogies, in their production of symbolic power, have significant political resonance when they are produced in response to a perceived crisis in the social formation of a society. I believe that the process of inscribing national issues on all black bodies accomplishes the ideological work which is necessary for the everyday maintenance of systems of racial injustice and inequality, but in this essay I wish to focus attention on and raise questions about the surplus symbolic power of black male bodies.

I am particularly drawn to popular narratives that exhibit an explicit and self-conscious didacticism in their production, reproduction or reconstruction of the meanings of race in order to create new genealogies, new surplus symbolic value and new inscriptions of national concerns specific to a particular historical moment. Harriet Beecher Stowe's *Uncle Tom's Cabin* and Lawrence Kasdan's *Grand Canyon* are texts that self-consciously address the historical moment of their production and are explicitly didactic. But, of course, these texts are each specific to their time: Stowe invents her genealogy of race and nation within a crisis of modernity, while Kasdan is reimagining relations between race and nation in ways that are symptomatic of a crisis in what is now frequently referred to as our postmodern moment.

A basic assumption of *Grand Canyon* is that we are living through a national crisis, a moment in history when the nation, as Harriet Beecher Stowe described it in 1852, "is trembling and convulsed" with its people on the brink of civil war. Indeed, the possibility of an imminent descent into chaos is a consistent visual and verbal motif of the film. Juxtaposing Stowe's description of the national tensions of the 1850s to Kasdan's filmic response to the social and political conditions of the 1990s is not a superficial gesture. The relation between these two cultural producers, even though they are separated by history and by ideological belief, is deeper than their shared premonitions of national disaster. Both *Grand Canyon* and *Uncle Tom's Cabin* are cultural texts that fear for the continued secure existence of the white and middle-class America to which they and their authors belong. Kasdan and Stowe each construct a racially defined and class-specific worldview, a worldview which is also, and not incidentally, the same class-specific and racially specific context that enables and secures the cultural production of their text; both are motivated by a desire to expose injustice and inequality; and each actively tries to construct a radical, political and interventionist narrative of protest.

Grand Canyon and *Uncle Tom's Cabin* are texts which display a Dickensian urge to modify the existing social order through moral and ethical exhortation. Both appeal to the hearts and minds of the privileged to intervene in the lives of those less fortunate than themselves. However, what appear to be appeals to undertake acts of selfless charity must also be identified as *selfish* acts: acts motivated by a desire to preserve both individual and class privilege. While stark inequalities of wealth, power and privilege are identified in each text as being a threat to the continued existence of the social fabric, neither Stowe nor Kasdan calls for a dramatic change in the social organization of power and powerlessness, nor do they argue for a redistribution of wealth to end economic injustice. Neither text imagines the "destruction of the racist complex" which, Balibar asserts, "presupposes not only the revolt of its victims, but the transformation of the racists themselves and, consequently, *the internal decomposition of the community created by racism.*"[3] While the narrative structures of both *Grand Canyon* and *Uncle Tom's Cabin* are haunted by the fear that the victims of injustice will rebel, they are blind to the necessity for social and economic transformation. Rather, both texts seek to preserve the powers and privileges of the white middle class by attempting to demonstrate why it is in the self-interest of that class to become the patrons of the underprivileged. Acts of patronage, far from transforming or destroying institutionalized inequality, actually reinforce such inequality, because the power of the patron is secured at the same moment that those subjected to patronage are confirmed in their powerlessness. Further, Stowe and Kasdan each construct the terms and conditions of a national crisis in their texts, so that the representation of the acts of white individuals, acts which are enacted upon black bodies, serve not only the self-interest of the white middle class, but are simultaneously interpreted as acts that serve the national interest. In the face of imminent chaos, then, Stowe and Kasdan construct racialized and gendered genealogies that attempt to secure and confirm racialized national identities and, in so doing, attempt to bring narrative coherence and cohesion to the incoherence and fragmentation of their own historical time. Before turning to Kasdan's *Grand Canyon*, I want to consider, briefly, the general terms of Stowe's creation of a narrative genealogy, an inscription of national concerns onto black bodies, in *Uncle Tom's Cabin*.

Planter paternalism was founded through the doctrines and practices of Anglicanism in the British mainland colonies, and by the antebellum period was the dominant ideology that both justified and resolved the social contradictions that arose from the enslavement of African peoples in North America. Harriet Beecher Stowe directly confronted and, indeed, utilized the glaring contradictions between a doctrinal emphasis on sentiment, charity and love within the Christian ethical system and the simultaneous blindness of Christians to the everyday acts of violence which were perpetrated upon black bodies.[4]

Stowe became an Anglican as an adult. In 1851 she said that, while she was taking communion, she had a vision of "a saintly black man being mercilessly flogged and praying for his torturers as he died."[5] This vision and the novel which subsequently grew from it speak to the heart of one of the major contradictions in the ideology of planter paternalism. Stowe mobilized sentiment, charity and love explicitly against two forms of social violence: against the violence of the slave system and against the potential violence of concerted acts of African rebellion. To enable her fictional act of dissent from the discourse of the dominant ideology of planter paternalism, Stowe actually had to reinscribe major portions of it: paternalism is not so much undermined in her text as revised and reinforced. The creation of the character of Uncle Tom, the figure who can pray for his torturers while they torture him, is crucial to this process of revision.

Tom is consciously constructed as a de-Africanized figure; he is an embodiment of what Jon Butler describes as an African spiritual holocaust accomplished through the process of Christianization.[6] The surplus symbolic value of the figure of Uncle Tom consists of a fictive ethnicity which has the power to dislodge blackness from its association with perpetual disobedience and rebelliousness. At the same time, Tom's restraint, his refusal to take revenge on those who abuse him, epitomizes absolute obedience to the Christian ethical system and subordination to the will of his persecutors. In other words, the figure of Tom is granted moral authority and occupies the ground of moral superiority only because he complies with the central doctrine of absolute obedience. The mechanism of his submission is Christianity, which, while it separates Tom from those despised traits of African degeneracy, confirms the existence of African degeneracy in the un-Christianized. In this genealogy of race and nation, Tom has an ideal existence in the category of humanity. The resolution of Stowe's grand narrative simultaneously asserts the necessity for the Christianization of Africans and the necessity to exclude them from the national entity, and this reinforces the insurmountable racial difference of their social existence. At the end of the novel, George, his family and Topsy are re-Africanized outside the boundaries of America, and returned to Africa as Christian zealots and African patriots – a fictive ethnicity which denies the possibility that they could be imagined as American patriots.[7]

In the face of the institutional crisis and antagonistic social relations of the antebellum period, Stowe's narrative accomplishes the ideological work necessary for a realignment of the national hegemonic structures of her time.[8] *Uncle Tom's Cabin* reconstructs a past, an alternative narrative of the meaning of slavery, in order to imagine an alternative national future: a future in which a paternalistic racial formation can be maintained under the hegemonic control of the white, Northern, middle class. This reimagining of the past, this new genealogy, is produced in conjunction with the production of fear: a fear of supernatural retribution and a fear of the chaos that would inevitably result from the dissolution of the social order.

It is this fear of what will happen in the present as a consequence of the slavery of the past that provides the motivation for action. Fear is Stowe's tool of persuasion, it inspires the white middle class to act in the interest of its own class security and, for Stowe, these class interests are synonymous with the national interest.

As *Grand Canyon* opens, a blank screen is all that can be seen. Within the darkness the audience can gradually hear the unmistakable pulsating sound of chopper blades. My mind, like so many others of my generation, is conditioned to make an immediate connection between this sound and a particular social and geographic space. For more than twenty years the noise made by a low-flying helicopter was used by film and television studios to signify the presence of Americans in the war zones of Southeast Asia, but I am unable to remember exactly when, in the last few years, I stopped associating the rhythmic sweep of these blades with Vietnam or Korea, and started, instead, to link the sound to Los Angeles.[9] Thus, although I knew nothing about the subject of the film, when I started to watch it I knew, because of this sound, that the blank screen would be replaced by the symbolic landscape of a black urban neighborhood.

For Hollywood filmmakers, the black neighborhoods of Los Angeles are important sites not just for the representation of death and destruction but for the enactment of social and political confrontations that constitute a threat to national stability. These neighborhoods are as fascinating in their exoticism, potential danger and commercial marketability as Vietnam. In the United States, until quite recently, Southeast Asia has been culturally produced as the primary site of a national nightmare: a landscape through which North Americans moved under constant surveillance by a subhuman population of menacing "gooks." The "enemy" masqueraded as ordinary men, women and children but, within the heart of the nightmare, these people were never ordinary and never innocent. This haunting vision has been supplanted in the popular cultural and political imagination by images of black inner-city neighborhoods: neighborhoods that are spaces in which to enact the current national nightmares of the white, suburban, middle class; nightmares which are inscribed upon the bodies of young, urban, black males and patrolled by the "Bloods" and the "Cripps."

Lawrence Kasdan's film exemplifies the fascination of Hollywood with the black inner city as the symbolic space of suburban anxiety. The film conceals its role in the actual production of white fear of black aggression under the guise of merely confirming the already existing material reality of the threat which underlies the nation's anxieties. As the promotional material describes this process, "*Grand Canyon* is director Lawrence Kasdan's powerful and uplifting film about real life and real miracles . . . and about how, after the millions of choices we make in life, one chance encounter can change it all."[10]

At the beginning of the film, Mack, an immigration lawyer played by

Kevin Kline, searches for a way of avoiding the heavy traffic leaving the Forum after a Lakers' game. He strays into a black neighborhood that is so alien to him that he will later categorically assure his family, "You have never been where I broke down." What happens to Mack is evocative of the modernist journey into the "heart of darkness," a journey originally conceived in the context of European imperialism in Joseph Conrad's novel of that name, and re-created by Hollywood in Francis Ford Coppola's postmodern fantasy of war in Southeast Asia, *Apocalypse Now*. As Mack peers anxiously out of his windscreen at the unfamiliar and, to him, menacing aspect of a black residential neighborhood, Warren Zevon's music plays in his car.

Music is very significant for Kasdan, and he selects the Warren Zevon sound track "Lawyers, Guns, and Money" to establish a genealogy for his protagonist. Clearly, the plea to "send lawyers, guns and money" strengthens the visual evidence that Mack is in physical danger, but the song also acts to situate Mack in history. Zevon's music is a product of seventies, white, yuppie, Southern California culture. Mack's familiarity with the words and apparent nostalgia for the song locate him within this culture and provide him with a history of who he is and where he comes from, a history that is otherwise absent from the film.[11] But Kasdan also uses music to signal the distance between the modernist conceptions of history and subjectivity at work in Conrad's novel and his own postmodern recognition of the fragmentation of social and political positionality. In Kasdan's editing room the Zevon sound track was dubbed to the film not only in order to register cultural and political conflict, but also to become the very ground of social and political contestation.

The words of "Lawyers, Guns, and Money" evoke, with a wry liberal irony, memories of the Cold War, of danger to Americans trespassing in exotic locales, and of covert US intervention in other countries. The song establishes the liberal credentials of the protagonist, creates a mood of empathy for his mistake, and alerts the audience to the gravity of Mack's situation. As Mack's anxiety grows, Kasdan multiplies his visual and aural strategies for creating tension in the minds of the audience, who watch with an increasing sense of helplessness and panic if they identify with the plight of the protagonist. Mack switches off Warren Zevon in order to concentrate more effectively on finding his way home and, like a mouse in a laboratory maze, he turns his car around in a futile effort to escape. As Mack drives ever deeper toward the "horror" that awaits, he passes the shells of cars and the skeltons of abandoned buildings. As the landscape increasingly resembles a war zone, he begins to sing the words of the song himself in order to seek comfort in their familiarity and to raise the hope of summoning help. But as Mack mutters "send lawyers, guns, and money," his words are overwhelmed by the taunting voice of Ice Cube, "ruthless, plenty of that and much more," emanating from what looks like a white BMW that slows down and drives beside him for a while. At this moment music becomes the prime vehicle for a cultural war which has encoded within it the political potential of a larger civil war. Ice Cube's band, NWA, is polarized against Warren Zevon in a symbolic confrontation which is central to the narrative genealogy of race and nation that is about to pit a liberal, white, suburban male against Kasdan's creation of a "gang" of young, black, urban males. The musical battle both produces and is the conduit for the wider class and racialized meanings of the scene; meanings which confirm ideological beliefs about what is currently characterized as the problem of the inner city and about what is imagined to be wrong with America.

However, the process of representing this war is structurally as well as ideologically unjust, and this is clear if we analyze the unequal editing of the musical battle. In contrast to the verbal and musical fragments of NWA's "Quiet on the Set," the audience is presented with coherent narrative selections from the Zevon lyrics. We are not played sequential sections of a verse or even complete sentences of the NWA lyrics, and, unlike "Lawyers, Guns, and Money," the narrative coherence of "Quiet on the Set" was abandoned to the cutting-room floor. The voice of Ice Cube fades in and out in the cat-and-mouse game being played out on the screen, and the words that can be clearly distinguished, "ruthless, plenty of that and much more," are intended only to confirm the menacing intentions of the occupants of the BMW, five young, black males who take careful note of the existence of an interloper in their territory. Mack responds to his surveillence by singing:

> I'm an innocent bystander . . .
> Send lawyers, guns and money
> The shit has hit the fan.

His car coughs, splutters, stalls and finally breaks down, and Mack becomes a man under siege. He uses his car phone in an attempt to get help but on being asked for his location Mack suddenly hesitates: "I dunno . . . let's say . . . Inglewood," he decides, without conviction, as the car phone also crackles and then dies. Apparently having run to a convenience store to find a public telephone, Mack continues to find it difficult, if not impossible, to describe exactly where he is, or, to continue the military analogy, to give his coordinates: "Buckingham, yes," he pants, "but remember it's about half a mile west, I guess, of there." Mack is not only lost, he is in alien territory, and his very survival is at stake. On being told by roadside assistance that it will take forty-five minutes to get to him, Mack replies that he understands but states, "if it takes that long I might be like, ah, dead." He remains under surveillance and the NWA sound track changes to include fragments of "F—— tha Police," signifying, presumably, the imminence of the moment of confrontation. Mack returns to his car to wait for help, and the BMW pulls up behind him.

What follows is a filmic moment in which the entire gamut of language, sound and image used up until this point to symbolize danger and to produce fear in the audience coalesce into an intense evocation of an American soldier coming down in enemy territory. Mack vocalizes his own personal distress and simultaneously gives voice to the anxieties of a constituency of the white, suburban, middle class, whose greatest fear is being stranded in a black urban neighborhood at night. The young black men advance toward Mack's car framed through its rear windscreen. Mack's face is at the center of the screen; as his eyes flicker with recognition at the rearview mirror, his voice quietly but clearly calls to the audience: "Mayday, Mayday. We're coming down."

There is a great irony in what Kasdan excludes from his audience in this scene that only those who know the lyrics of "Quiet on the Set" and "F——tha Police" would perceive. In fact, I would argue that Kasdan depends upon the ignorance of his target audience for this film. Those who know the album *Straight Outta Compton* would be aware that "Quiet on the Set" is actually about the power of performance and, specifically, about the potential power that a successful rap artist can gain over an audience. Power is, quite explicitly, the power of words over the body. For example, "ruthless, plenty of that and much more" is about controlling the movements of people on a dance floor and about the power to create "a look that keeps you staring and wondering why I'm invincible." But the invicibility is entirely the result of being able to persuade with words, "when you hear my rhyme it's convinceable." Kasdan, however, disrupts NWA's intended narrative structure, and lines like "I'm a walking threat" and "I wanna earn respect" are transformed into a filmic representation of the contemporary figure of the disobedient and dangerous black male who believes that respect is only gained through the possesssion of a gun. Perhaps the greatest irony of all is that the NWA song, in fact, predicts the misuse of their words. Near the end of the rap an interesting dialogue occurs between Ice Cube and an unidentified voice that mimics the supposedly dispassionate, analytic tone of the sociologist or ethnographer. Ice Cube asserts that he can create "lyrics to make everybody say," and the voice responds: "They can be cold and ruthless, there's no doubt about that but, sometimes, it's more complicated." And Ice Cube concludes: "You think I'm committing a crime, instead of making a rhyme."

A tow truck driver, Simon, played by Danny Glover, comes to Mack's rescue at the height of his confrontation with the "gang." Mack has been forced out of the safety of his car when a blaze of oncoming headlights announces his imminent rescue. However, the camera tantalizes the audience as it hesitates to reveal the identity of the man who climbs out of the truck. The camera swings from the truck to Mack flanked by the gang and then back again to the tow truck driver's boots, and then slowly pans upwards. What Kasdan does here is to reproduce the same low-angled shot that he used moments before to stress the menacing nature of the black male faces that lean toward Mack in his car. The rescuer is revealed to be black and to be armed with an enormous steel crowbar, the size of which is exaggerated by the camera angle, but before we can completely see his face, the tow truck driver bends into the cab to reach for a cap. This second of uncertainty about his identity is a cinematically produced hesitancy about the possible allegiance of the tow truck driver: is he a rescuer, as implied by the change to music evocative of the cavalry coming over the hill, or is he an additional figure of menace, as implied by the filming of his body? However, the hesitation is only momentary. Once the face is revealed to be that of Danny Glover, his filmic persona as LAPD's heroic cop Sergeant Murtaugh from a series of three *Lethal Weapon* films so well established in our popular cultural imagination, assures the audience that he is Mack's savior.

The ideology that Kasdan reproduces in his genealogy of race and nation works in a structurally similar way to the ideology that was reasserted by Harriet Beecher Stowe, in which the imagining of the good black is dependent upon a rejection of an alien black presence. Though Africa no longer functions, as it did for Stowe, as a possible metaphoric and material place for disposing of the alien element that threatens to disrupt the formation of national unity, I would argue that prisons function in our political imaginations as an equivalent site. Kasdan produces a visual narrative of what happens when disobedient, disaffected and aggressive black males are pitted against a lone, liberal and well-meaning white male who made an innocent, if foolish, mistake.

For Kasdan, the figure of Simon is an important mechanism for solving the dilemma at the center of his visual reconstruction of our contemporary racial national narrative, a dilemma captured in the cinematic hesitation I have already described: how, exactly, can the white middle class distinguish between the good and the bad black male? It is precisely at the moment of Mack's rescue that it is possible to speculate about the significance of Kasdan's manipulation of a specific performance of black masculinity in his selection of the actor Danny Glover to play Simon.[12]

In *Lethal Weapon III* there is one particular scene, which I will discuss in a moment, that acts as a climax to the relationship between two LAPD homicide detectives, Martin Riggs, played by Mel Gibson, and Roger Murtaugh: a relationship which has gradually matured throughout the two previous films in the series. Considered together, the three films document the development of a close and increasingly intimate partnership between an older black and a younger white male. It is interesting that it is not the history of the movement to gain civil rights that is the means for imagining a relationship of equality between Riggs and Murtaugh, but an evocation of the history of the desegregation of the United States Armed Forces in the "policing" of Southeast Asia that enables us, in the terms of the film, to imagine the possibility and conditions of their partnership. This filmic selection of history is important, as it establishes the possibility of their friendship as external, not internal, to the continental United States. What Riggs and Murtaugh share is not an internal political or historical condition, but the experience of Vietnam. This experience is the ground of their apparent equality and the basis for their mutual respect.

Lethal Weapon, the first in the series, forges Riggs and Murtaugh into an unbeatable fighting team as they defeat a rogue group of Special Forces mercenaries against a Los Angeles landscape that increasingly resembles Vietnam as the film progresses. In *Lethal Weapon II*, the national significance of their partnership is established in the narrative of a battle to save the nation from a drug cartel run by South African diplomats. Riggs's and Murtaugh's partnership and friendship also advance in this film when Riggs's antiracist credentials are secured, and he is declared by the diplomats to be a "Kaffir-lover." In *Lethal Weapon III*, Los Angeles and Vietnam are again fused in the landscape as they wage war against a homegrown enemy who has declared war on the entire Los Angeles Police Department, a police force which, at this stage of the series, has become a national entity.

The relationship between Riggs and Murtaugh also has an explicit homoerotic character which Richard Donner, the director, plays for laughs. Homoeroticism appears gradually, from a single question in the first film – "What are you, a fag?" shouts Riggs, in response to Murtaugh jumping on top of him in an attempt to extinguish the flames that threaten to consume his body – to a series of running jokes in the second film that stems from Riggs jumping with Murtaugh into a bath as he rescues him from a toilet wired to a bomb. In *Lethal Weapon III* the homoeroticism is somewhat more mature and less directly inspired by anal humor.

In the scene which provides a climax to the terms and conditions of the friendship between Riggs and Murtaugh, Donner attempts through his two cops to rewrite the mythical dimensions of the relationship between Huck and Jim on the raft.[13] Riggs and Murtaugh face a crisis as partners and as friends, a crisis as serious as that faced by Huck and Jim when they missed the entry into the Ohio river and sailed ever deeper into the slave states of the South. In Mark Twain's novel *The Adventures of Huckleberry Finn*, this mistake secured the historical terms and conditions of Jim's existence and his dependence on Huck Finn: as a black male, in order to survive he had to "belong" to someone. In *Lethal Weapon III*, in a similar fashion, Donner reworks the contemporary terms and conditions of the relationship between his white male and black male protagonists. The crisis has been precipitated by two events: Murtaugh is agonizing over the fact that, in an armed confrontation, he shot and killed a fifteen-year-old black male, whom he discovered to be his son's best friend. Riggs is distraught because their partnership is about to be dissolved when Murtaugh retires from the force in just three days.

This long, eight-minute segment explores the complex and contradictory possibilities for expressing interracial male intimacy, and while the scene is, at times, intensely homoerotic, it simultaneously effects a series of closures, both visual and verbal, on the possibility that this intimacy could encompass a homosexual relation. As Huck and Jim's navigational error determined the public nature of their relation to each other, Donner likewise opens this scene in a way that determines the possibilities for interpreting what follows.

Riggs goes to find Murtaugh, who is hiding out on his boat, drinking whiskey. He finds Murtaugh drunk and apparently out of control. Murtaugh holds a gun to Riggs's head and, in clichéd terms, threatens to harm the best friend he ever had. What has to be explored, therefore, is not the basis for their equality but the issue of how, in a relationship of partners, Murtaugh could possibly betray his friend, his "brother," who has clearly demonstrated his loyalty to him. The moment is fraught with the tension arising from the political anxiety evident in Riggs's agony and accusation of betrayal that Murtaugh's imminent retirement precipitates. This tension creates and reproduces on the screen a contemporary political anxiety, a common-sense understanding, that black America, having demanded and gained equality, has somehow betrayed the white and middle-class America that graciously acceded to these demands. The political effect is such that when Riggs shouts at Murtaugh, "You selfish bastard," a large segment of white male America makes the same accusation.

The accusation of the betrayal of white America by an aggressive black American informs and shapes the work of a number of contemporary liberal political analysts. Andrew Hacker, in *Two Nations: Black and White, Separate, Hostile, Unequal,* addresses this anxiety, and argues that the processes of racialization and nationalization imagined to be inherent in the social consensus to grant civil rights was, indeed, only imaginary. He concludes that such a consensus no longer exists, and that America must be regarded as two separate nations confronting each other. Hacker situates his discussion of the liberal anxiety evident in this political crisis in the context of the black urban rebellions of the late 1960s. He states:

> After those disturbances, race relations never returned to their former plane. Whites ceased to identify black protests with a civil rights movement led by students and ministers. Rather, they saw a resentful and rebellious multitude, intent on imposing its presence on the rest of society. Blacks were seen as trying to force themselves into places and positions where they were not wanted or for which they lacked the competence. As the 1970s started, so came a rise in crimes, all too many of them with black perpetrators. By that point, many white Americans felt they had been betrayed. Worsening relations between the races were seen as largely due to the behavior of blacks, who had abused the invitations to equal citizenship white American had been tendering.[14]

Hacker's belief that white Americans have lost all sympathy for black Americans shapes his political agenda. This political belief in this apparent lack of sympathy also influences Donner's decision to imagine the source for black male and white male mutual respect as being in Southeast Asia rather than in the history of the struggle for civil rights. Hacker's genealogy of race and nation attempts to regain this lost sympathy through an extraordinary performance of intellectual black-face. In a chapter called "Being Black in America," in which Hacker provides an account of what he imagines it would be like to be black, he reveals an intense masculine anxiety about black male bodies.

Hacker is only one of many political critics who are busily constructing genealogies of race and nation that are centrally concerned with white male anxiety, particularly liberal anxiety, about relationships with black men. For example, Hacker's argument that white men feel betrayed by actually or potentially rebellious black men is echoed in Thomas Edsall's very influential book *Chain Reaction: The Impact of Race, Rights, and Taxes on American Politics*, in which such betrayal is used by Edsall as an explanation for what he describes as the alienation of white, Democratic (male) voters from the special interest politics of racial injustice.[15] In the popular cultural imagination, this political anxiety is most frequently being reproduced against a nightmarish landscape of urban crisis.

What *Grand Canyon*, the *Lethal Weapon* series and a number of other contemporary Hollywood films have in common is that they attempt to resolve what is presented as a national, racialized crisis through an intimate male partnership. What Danny Glover can bring to directors like Kasdan is his close association with a filmic performance of black manhood which has money, is the law, and which embodies all the ethical codes of middle-class white America. In other words, what Kasdan can incorporate into *Grand Canyon* from the *Lethal Weapon* series is the national embodiment of the perfect black male, a sensitive black father and relentless seeker of justice. Danny Glover's persona is the lethal weapon that is used to eliminate representations of other black men that Hollywood creates as dangerous. The cultural construction of such a figure is a direct political response to the national bourgeois dilemma: how to distinguish the good from the bad black men.

Kasdan grants Simon the moral authority to exclude the five young men who constitute his rebellious "gang" from all acceptable definitions of what it means to be human. This moral authority is acquired gradually and in a number of ways. First, Simon manages to extract Mack and himself from the clutches of the young men without resorting to violence. He establishes who made the call and then continues to talk to Mack about the problem with the car as if the others are not there. This behavior is quickly identified by the young men as a sign of disrespect. Next, Simon tries to persuade them that he is just doing his job. As the young men are unresponsive to the terms of the work ethic, Simon tries another tactic: he identifies the young man he supposes is the leader and takes him aside. He explains that he is responsible for the truck, Mack's car and Mack himself, and asks a favor, to be allowed to go on his way. This exchange is a very important moment, because it establishes the ground upon which Simon's role as a mouthpiece for the philosophy of the film will be built. The young man asks: "Are you askin' me a favor as a sign of respect, or are you askin' me a favor 'cos I got the gun?" Simon pauses and then replies:

> Man, the world ain't supposed to work like this, maybe you don't know that but this ain't the way it's supposed to be. I'm supposed to be able to do my job without asking you if I can. That dude is supposed to be able to wait with his car without you ripping him off. Everything is supposed to be different than what it is.

The young man is clearly puzzled by this response, and says, "So, what's your answer?" To which Simon states, "You don't have the gun, we ain't having this conversation," which gets the response, "That's what I thought, no gun, no respect. That's why I always carry the gun."

Having confirmed that Simon can vocalize the moral codes and ethics of the middle class and can, simultaneously, be streetwise, Simon is also used to dehumanize the young men. In a conversation with Mack that takes place back at the service station while waiting for the car to be fixed, Simon adopts a folksy persona, a persona from which many Americans seem to draw comfort, and compares the young men to predatory sharks. Simon explains to Mack that what happened to him was a matter of chance, that

> one day, just one particular day you bump into the big shark. Now the big shark don't hate you, he has no feelings for you at all, you look like food to him.... Those boys back there, they got nothing to lose. If you just happen to be swimming along and bump into them, well.... It might not be worth worrying about; it's like being in a plane crash.

Having dismissed these boys from the realm of humanity, they can be conveniently forgotten. They do not appear again in the film, and presumably they can disappear into jail, say, or be absorbed into statistical evidence of urban homicides, for do we really care or even think about what happens to sharks as long as they are contained and prevented from preying upon us? What is to be feared has been identified, given a body, but no name. The young black men presented as "gang" have served their purpose, and the conversation of Mack and Simon can shift to a more general level and establish the wider concerns of the film. For the confrontation of Mack and the five young black men is a metaphor, a means to address what ails this nation.

However, Kasdan deliberately distances his male characters from the homoeroticism that permeates the *Lethal Weapon* series. When the noise of the helicopter which opens the film fades, a basketball net appears, surrounded by black hands reaching upward. In a black-and-white opening sequence on an urban basketball court, the camera strays over sections of the bodies of the black players, torsos, legs, hands and feet. There is a clear visual analogy with the second half of the credit sequence, which takes place in the forum and is filmed in color. However, the force of the analogy is not established in the black–white communality of the basketball court, a site which is reserved for the safe portrayal of intimacy between men; rather, the analogy works through the similarities between the strayed gaze of the camera over black male bodies in the first sequence, and the sexually desiring gaze of Mack across the court at the women who walk by. In this part of the credit sequence, again the camera lingers over sections of bodies, particularly torsos and breasts of the walking women.

Certainly the blatantly sexual and somewhat predatory stare of Mack at these passing female bodies is intended to lock him into heterosexuality, and to act as an early closure on the possibility of interpreting his later desire for Simon as homosexual. But these opening sequences, and the scene of black–white urban confrontation that follows, and that I have already discussed, do establish the cultural spaces designated by the film as safe. Safe spaces are sites in which whites can be in close proximity to and gaze at black bodies. Both opening sequences prefigure the establishment of a close relationship between Simon and Mack; a friendship that comes to a cinematic climax when they play basketball with each other in Mack's driveway.

What we are witnessing in the creation of these intimate black and white male partnerships is a performance of black masculinity that meets the desires of the white male liberal imagination for a perfect partner and partnership. Together, we are promised, these men can annihilate what ails this nation and resolve our contemporary crisis of race, of nation and of manhood. In the face of the institutional crisis of the last decade of the twentieth century, these popular narratives accomplish the ideological work necessary for the realignment of the national hegemonic structures of our time. All we need to do is relax and place our faith in the LAPD.

1995

Notes

1. Harriet Beecher Stowe, *Uncle Tom's Cabin, Or, Life Among the Lowly* (1852), New York: Penguin, 1981, p. 629. *Grand Canyon*, written, produced, and directed by Lawrence Kasdan, Twentieth Century-Fox, 1991. Etienne Balibar and Immanuel Wallerstein, *Race, Nation, Class: Ambiguous Identities*, London: Verso, 1991, p. 18.
2. See Balibar, "The Nation Form," in Balibar and Wallerstein, *Race, Nation, Class*, pp. 86–106; Toni Morrison's introductory essay to *Race-ing, Justice, Engendering Power: Essays on Anita Hill, Clarence Thomas and the Construction of Social Reality*, New York: Pantheon, 1992; and Michael Rogin, "Blackface, White Noise: The Jewish Jazz Singer Finds His Voice," *Critical Inquiry*, vol. 18, no. 3, 1991, pp. 417–44.

3. Balibar and Wallerstein, *Race, Nation, Class*, p. 18.
4. In an historical account of the process of the "Christianizing of the American People," Jon Butler dramatically describes how, in the eighteenth century, Christianity directly shaped the system of slaveholding, and led to what he calls an African spiritual holocaust in North America: "a spiritual holocaust that effectively destroyed traditional African religious *systems*, [if] not all particular or religious practices." An "emerging Anglican understanding of slavery," Butler argues, "fitted with uncanny precision the elaboration of slave codes and social behavior that increasingly specified the degraded condition of captive Africans after 1680 ... the law that guaranteed liberty to English men and women became the seal of slavery for Africans." It was Anglican concepts of authority that "shaped a paternalistic ethic among planters," an ethic

> that not only coalesced with the doctrine of absolute obedience but made it all the more palatable and attractive.... [Anglican] clergymen helped planters explain slave "misbehavior" in ways that solidified the masters' prejudices about slave degradation.... [and] transformed planter views about laziness, lust, and lying among slaves into powerfully detailed pictures of African depravity.

This paternalistic ethic, continues Butler, rooted as it was in the doctrine of absolute obedience,

> reinforced the growing violence of eighteenth-century slaveholding. It encouraged owners to excuse nearly all discrete instances of violence toward slaves. Ironically, paternalism loaded owners with obligations that were difficult to fulfill in a competitive, erratic economy where there were few effective restraints on the owner's treatment of their labor. Even "ethical" owners mistreated slaves. Worse, both "ethical" and unethical owners could readily agree that slaves disobeyed. A rigid doctrine fostered rigid responses. The stress on absolute obedience turned minor infractions of planter authority into major confrontations, and the result brought forth the first fixing of an indelible image in American race relations – the perpetually disobedient black ... the meanings of blackness and disobedience had already begun to converge. ...
>
> The emergence of absolutist, paternalistic, and violent slavery gave Christianity as thoroughly a different cast as Christianity had given to slaveholding. Christianity's interpretation of social behavior and religious ethics produced a distended emphasis on sentiment, charity, and love utterly uncharacteristic of the society in which it was propounded.

See Jon Butler, *Awash in a Sea of Faith: Christianizing the American People*, Cambridge, MA: Harvard University Press, 1990, pp. 153, 144, 146, 147.
5. Ann Douglass, "Introduction: The Art of Controversy," Stowe, *Uncle Tom's Cabin*, p. 8.
6. Butler, *Awash in a Sea of Faith*.
7. The concepts of "fictive ethnicity" and genealogies of race and nation are drawn from Balibar and Wallerstein, *Race, Nation, Class*.
8. See Wallerstein, "Construction of Peoplehood: Racism, Nationalism, Ethnicity," ibid., p. 78. "Pastness is a mode by which persons are persuaded to act in the present in ways they might not otherwise act. Pastness is a tool persons use against each other."

9. It is clear that this association between the war zones of Southeast Asia and Los Angeles has been progressively established. Of particular importance to this process are the three *Lethal Weapon* films, which will be discussed toward the end of this essay and which, like *Grand Canyon*, starred Danny Glover. *Lethal Weapon III* is a culmination of the themes of the previous two: policing is indistinguishable from military intervention, and the burning of a housing complex is visually evocative of the burning of villages in Vietnam. My reading of this scene of fire is, of course, directly influenced by *Apocalypse Now*, which reinforces my sense that Hollywood has mediated and informed this process of transition in the political imagination of the culture industry, and continues to do so.

10. Promotional description, *Grand Canyon*, Fox Video, 1992.

11. This superficial way of locating Mack is of course a postmodern substitute for history. See Fredric Jameson, *Postmodernism and the Cultural Logic of Late Capitalism*, Durham: Duke University Press, pp. 6, 67–8.

12. Perhaps it is crass to point to the biblical resonance of the choice of Simon as a name for Mack's rescuer, but it gains significance through the consistent references to the religious in the film, particularly the concern with spiritual and miraculous transformation. Kasdan's "gang" take pleasure not only in threatening physical harm but in taunting and mocking Mack:

> And they spit upon him, and took the reed, and smote him on the head.
>   And after that they had mocked him, they took the robe off from him, and put his own raiment on him, and led him away to crucify him.
>   And as they came out they found a man of Cyrene, Simon by name: him they compelled to bear his cross. (Matthew 27, 30–2)

As Gary Wills has recently argued, even if it works only at a subliminal level, it is important to recognize that Mack (and the white middle class) are being rescued from a possible crucifixion, a metaphor which has political and ideological meanings. Mack (and the white middle class) are only innocent victims in such a scenario, and the subjects, therefore, of unjust persecution.

13. I am grateful to Michael Denning for pointing out this literary parallel.

14. Andrew Hacker, *Two Nations: Black and White, Separate, Hostile, Unequal*, New York: Macmillan, 1992, p. 19.

15. Thomas Byrne Edsall with Mary D. Edsall, *Chain Reaction: The Impact of Race, Rights, and Taxes on American Politics*, New York: Norton, 1992.

8

America Inc. – The Crisis at Yale: A Tale of Two Women

At Columbia, on February 6 1996, students occupied the office of the Dean of Columbia College in protest at the lack of Ethnic Studies in the undergraduate curriculum. Similar protests, if dissimilar actions, have been lodged against the office of the Dean of Yale College at the university where I teach and, of course, at many universities across the country. Indeed, in the face of attempts by university administrations to bury history by pretending that there is no relation between social movements and curricular innovation and transformation, we must not only insist that this history be kept alive – there would be no African American Studies programs, for example, without the Civil Rights movement – but also struggle to ensure that the history and cultures of the working peoples of the Americas are the absolute heart of any curriculum that dares call itself American Studies.

Yet, I also want to sound a warning lest anyone imagine that the mere establishment of courses or programs labeled Ethnic Studies, or African American Studies, or Women's Studies, or Cultural Studies, or Post-Colonial Studies automatically resolves the problem of the absence of the history and cultures of working peoples, be they African Americans, Latinos and Latinas, Chicanos and Chicanas, Asian Americans, women, the previously colonized or whatever, once they are named on a syllabus.

Gaining a set of courses or a program entitled Ethnic Studies, for example, is only the beginning of another set of struggles to define exactly what this will mean and whom it will include, and requires constant vigilance over the historical constitution of the field. As students, you have to make yourself aware of the distance between the existence of so-called "minority" fields of study and what an academic institution feels is its central educational endeavor or mission. My advice to you would be that you study very carefully the daily practices of the educational institutions that do presently offer some or all of these fields and that you interrogate not only the work but the practice of intellectuals in the field to see if they are, in fact, committed to provide a truly inclusive, democratic history of all the peoples in their field.

The first problem that concerns me is the problem of ghettoization. You need to ask if an established program exists in isolation from the rest of the programs in the humanities and social sciences, for example. The effective ghettoization of these "minority" fields of study serves two, inter-dependent, purposes for university administrations: to apparently satisfy the political demand for that program, while sufficing merely to contain the force of those demands which threaten to transform the structure and organization of traditional fields of knowledge. But there is a third import-ant aspect to ghettoization that it is important to consider: do university administrators and traditional departments, in their practice, reduce human bodies to fields of knowledge? While departments of English or American Studies feel no apparent need to seek for reincarnations of seventeenth- or eighteenth-century men and women to teach the literatures of that period, or demand that only an Irish republican male be employed to teach the work of James Joyce or of W.B. Yeats, we constantly see universities addressing absences in the fields of knowledge as if they were the same problem as a lack of diversity in the faculty and student body and then devising schemes to address these completely different issues in the same way. Fields of knowledge are reduced to specific imaginings of bodies in particularly insidious ways; if one is a person subject to the historical and political processes of ethnicization or racialization, then one is desig-nated as appropriately existing within the boundaries of what are deemed to be ethnic or racialized studies. Of course, what this achieves is not only the ghettoization of certain specified fields of knowledge but the ghetto-ization of the handful of so-called "minority" faculties as well. The problem of ghettoization, then, is one very important reason for creating a strong system of alliances, but alliances can only be created when a historical and cultural vision of inclusion is shared across the various groups involved, and I do not want to imply that such solidarity is easily won. However, achieving such is absolutely essential in the face of the new corporate America and its handmaiden, the corporate university.

This is why I feel that what is happening at Yale in the late nineties is important. The current struggles over terms and conditions of employment there are of national importance to the future shape of universities and higher education in general. For some years I have been decrying the distance that exists between the attempts to institute curricular and progra-matic reform to achieve greater diversity under labels like multiculturalism and the complete lack of regard for the continually deteriorating material conditions of exploitation and oppression under which increasing numbers of our diverse population actually live. In particular, as an African Ameri-canist I have been distressed by the fetishization of African American cultural forms in syllabi while the increasing segregation of our society is ignored. Much supposed multicultural curricular reform, reduced to ques-tions of what black writers to include on a syllabus, for example, completely ignores the relationship between the university and the black and Latino(a) communities that not only surround it, but serve it and clean up its mess. I would like to symbolize this relationship in the two tales I wish to tell, tales which embody a symbolic relation that is starkly absent in Yale's overwhelmingly lily-white senior faculty, administration and board of trustees. Thus I am going to approach the issue of America Incorporated through a narrative of the private American university as capitalist corporation.

Scene I

Vivienne Whyte, an African American woman, has worked for Yale University for four years: two years as a casual worker and two years as what is characterized as a "below-benefit-worker." Yale classifies Vivienne Whyte as a "17.5 hour per week worker," which means that she does not qualify for benefits. Vivienne Whyte particularly worries about the lack of health care because if she or any of her children get sick they have to go to the ER.

At Yale you have to be *classified* as working for a minimum of twenty hours a week to qualify for benefits. This classification, you may think, is automatic if someone is *actually* working twenty or more hours a week, but this isn't the case. In fact, Vivienne Whyte's working hours average twenty-eight hours per week and she regularly works between thirty and forty hours a week, way above the minimum of twenty hours. As far as Yale is concerned this is a perfectly fair system: the terms of its contract, it says, are absolutely clear, and workers like Vivienne Whyte are absolutely "free" to accept or turn down the extra shifts that they are regularly offered.[1] Perfectly "free," that is, to choose to say no to the hours of work over and above 17.5, and perfectly "free" to say no to the extra money earned during these hours, money which pays for rent and heat and which enables Vivienne Whyte to buy food and clothes for her kids. But it's a free system so it's her choice . . . right? Yale denies insurance to more than a thousand of its workers in this way, workers who are disproportionately black and Latino(a) residents of New Haven.[2]

Yale University is the fourth richest university in the United States and it is located in New Haven, Connecticut, the fourth poorest large city in the nation.[3] Yale's endowment alone is currently worth over $4.1 billion, but its economic worth far exceeds that figure. In 1995 the stock market rose in value by approximately 30 percent, meaning that Yale's stock and bond holdings alone rose in value by approximately $1 billion in one year and the value of the university's vast holdings of land and buildings, the value of its substantial art collections, books, and so on, rose by millions more.[4] In other words, Yale University is an extraordinarily wealthy American institution that can afford to pay its workers well and to provide them with decent benefits. But the university is governed by a corporation, a corporation led by its board of trustees, a board overwhelmingly consisting of corporate CEOs, predominantly men, who are currently overseeing what is now euphemistically called "the downsizing" of America.[5] I wonder, however, why the non-corporate, so-called "liberal" elements in the faculty and the administration are so reluctant to speak out against what I would non-euphemistically call the dehumanization of Yale.

Vivienne Whyte likes working at Yale. She says she likes the people she works with, but she, like other Yale workers who do not qualify for benefits, is constantly anxious about the lack of medical insurance and the fact that her wages, though better than the minimum wage or below-minimum wage so many service workers receive, cannot come close to covering the exorbitant costs of seeing doctors and buying medicine.[6] What does the future look like for Vivienne Whyte, as a casual worker, and for the permanent workers who may join Yale's workforce in the future? Indeed, what does Yale imagine its workforce to look like in the future? The trend in the nation is that women with children are having their welfare benefits cut drastically or are increasingly being pushed off the welfare rolls, or being refused welfare assistance entirely, and forced into service-sector jobs with below-poverty wages and no benefits. Yale University and its board of CEO trustees seek to exploit and to profit from this national trend in a number of ways. It has made proposals to offer its future dining hall workers lower wages than it presently offers, but in addition to a two-tier wage system, Yale also seeks to subcontract for any work it wishes under the claim that it needs more flexibility in its relations with its workforce.

The attitude of the Yale trustees can be aptly summarized by a statement made by Thomas G. Labrecque, CEO of Chase Manhattan after he cut 10,000 jobs and looked toward cutting thousands more: "If you're doing what you think is right for everyone involved," he said, "then you're fine. So, I'm fine."[7] Labrecque's self-satisfaction comes in the wake of the growth of Chase's assets by 38 percent over the past decade and the shrinking of its workforce by 28 percent. Yale University administrators seek the same satisfaction from the protection of its vast profits (except that, of course, Yale University is a non-profit organization so let's just call its profits a "healthy return on its investments"). What does it mean when CEOs like Labrecque say they're fine. According to an article in the *New York Times*, the median increase in total compensation for the CEOs of America's largest corporations rose 31 percent in 1995 alone. This increase was double the increase in compensation for 1994 and triple the increase for 1993. The rise for the nation's workers over the same period of time has been under 3 percent.[8] The increase in CEO compensation has been achieved by corporate "downsizing," the euphemism for throwing people out of work, and has also been the reward for busting unions. Donald V. Fites, chairman of Caterpillar, received a total package in 1995 of $4.07 million, a 53 percent increase on his previous year's compensation.[9]

Yale's initial proposals would have established a two-tier wage system where all future hires would be earning $3.00 per hour less than current employees. This contract also contained a proposal to cut the work year from fifty-two weeks to thirty weeks, laying off its dining hall staff for remaining weeks, thus forcing them onto New Haven's city welfare rolls. Thus, the starting salary for future dining hall workers would have dropped from $22,000 per year to just under $10,000 per year with a maximum lifetime ceiling of approximately $12,000. Not a living wage in any conceivable terms. The Yale administration has since modified these proposals somewhat but now seeks to achieve the same outcome through subcontracting. It proposes protecting the wages and benefits of present workers but preserving the right to subcontract whenever an employee leaves. This will effectively de-unionize the university in the long term. A subcontractor like McDonald's, for example, will not employ union labor, will not offer the same benefits and retirement packages and will not employ dining hall workers during the summer.[10]

Yale's current administration, under the leadership of President Richard Levin, a member of Yale's faculty, has a liberal reputation. At a recent faculty meeting to discuss the present strike, I asked President Levin about the much publicized series of strategies for improving the university's relationship to its host city. I questioned whether it was essential to this improved relationship that Yale have a policy of social responsibility to its workers as citizens of the city of New Haven. The administration's proposals will severely compromise, if not totally undermine any plans to help New Haven because low future wages will impoverish a sector of its future workforce. Rick Levin replied that social responsibility was not the relevant issue in the current negotiations, that all Yale's proposals to its unions were market-driven and set by the condition of the local economy. As we all know, the economy of the North East has been slow to pull out of the recession, if it is pulling out at all, and Yale's trustees recognize that they can take advantage of this weak local economy while protecting the healthy return on Yale's investments. In addition, Yale is New Haven's largest employer: it can, in fact, *set* the trend for wages; it does not have to follow a trend. With ever-increasing subcontracting, Yale will eventually be able to shift all responsibility for its future workforce on to subcontractors. Although the future workforce will work on Yale property, it will have no recourse against Yale for its impoverished conditions of employment. This denial of social responsibility on the part of the Yale administration threatens to plunge a poverty-stricken city into even deeper poverty in the future. But, one has to ask, does anyone in the Yale administration or on Yale's board of trustees really care about the future prosperity of the people of New Haven, a population that is substantially black and Latino? Certainly the response of the majority of Yale's supposedly liberal faculty is total apathy toward the condition of New Haven's citizens.

In 1984, many of Yale's faculty were supportive of a strike by Yale's Clerical and Technical Employees Union, Local 34 of the Federation of University Employees, a strike to gain union recognition. In sharp contrast it has been extremely difficult to elicit the support of those same faculty for this current strike. While graduate student support for the strike is strong and undergraduate support growing, faculty are apathetic or hostile. Although only a small percentage of Yale's faculty are women, in 1984 many of these women faculty said that they were supportive of the strikers because they saw the issues behind the strike as an issue of women gaining equality.[11] (The majority of clerical and technical employees at Yale are women.) In particular, I am very struck by the contrast between the strong presence of female faculty, many of them associated with Women's Studies, in support of Yale's striking workers in 1984 and the lack of support from those same female faculty and, indeed, liberal progressive and pro-feminist male faculty now. Some of these faculty hold administrative positions and many have influence in administrative circles but they are not using this influence to support the strikers. Indeed, many feminist faculty and faculty who would consider themselves sympathetic to feminist causes will point to the job actions of 1984 as a women's cause and justify their lack of support for the current striking workers by characterizing the current job actions as not women's issues at all but labor actions – as if, somehow, that meant that they are mutually exclusive causes.

Scene II

Cynthia (Cindy) Young is an African American graduate student in the American Studies Program at Yale curently writing a dissertation entitled "Soul Power: Cultural Radicalism and the Formation of a U.S. Third World Left." I serve as a member of Cindy Young's dissertation committee and think, like many of my colleagues, that she is an extraordinarily brilliant young scholar and teacher, a rising star in the academy. You would think that Cindy Young's future in academia was assured as she is, already, such a powerful intellectual presence in the university, but that is not the case. Cindy Young was one of three female graduate students who were subject to *ad hoc* disciplinary hearings.

Diana Paton, Nilanjana Dasgupta and Cindy Young were charged by Thomas Appelquist, Dean of the Yale Graduate School, with the following offenses:

- Failure to adhere to a code of conduct that respects the values and integrity of the academic community.
- Coercion, harassment or intimidation of members of the University community.
- Disruptions of University functions and business.
- Defiance of legitimate authority, such as refusal to comply with an order issued in the line of duty by a University police officer, faculty member, or other University official.[12]

These charges come from the "Regulations for Academic and Personal Conduct" laid out in a Yale University handbook called *Programs and Policies* and commonly referred to as the "Red Book." The first charge comes from the preamble, which states that "graduate students are expected to adhere to a code of conduct that respects the values and integrity of the academic community." The second charge is selected from rule 4, which deals with cases of assault, including "the use of a teaching position to harass or intimidate another student." The third charge is taken from rule 5, which specifies "disrupting classes and meetings, blocking entrances and exits to University buildings, and unauthorized occupation of any space on the Yale campus." The final charge is a complete statement of rule 6. These violations of academic conduct carry severe penalties, including fines, probation, suspension and expulsion.

In politically charged language many faculty declared that graduate students were holding the university hostage, that they had betrayed them. One leading post-colonial critic, supposed defender of the subaltern, complained of being "accosted." What crime was it that these three young women committed? Did they harass the students in their sections or classes, did they block access to university buildings, storm the President's office, threaten violence? No, they, along with 250 other graduate teachers, participated in a grade strike at the end of last semester and the university turned to punishment and reprisal. Two of these three women were punished as students for participating in a labor action as employees; the charges against the third were subsequently dropped.

Cindy Young is an active member of GESO, the Graduate Employee and Students' Organization, an organization that seeks recognition from the Yale University administration to act as a collective bargaining unit for graduate students in the humanities and social sciences. The grade strike was an attempt to persuade the administration to regularize its relationship with its graduate student teachers through the establishment of contractual relations. For the past twenty-five years various graduate student organizations have emerged that have tried to persuade various Yale administrations and the faculty to address issues arising from the terms and conditions of their employment.[13] GESO was formed in 1990 from an earlier organization called T.A. Solidarity, and for six years it has sought to persuade the administration to enter negotiations. However, the university absolutely refuses to recognize GESO.

The major characteristic of the response of Yale administrations and most of the faculty to graduate teachers' own assessment of their terms and conditions of employment has been to fail to take their views seriously. For example, in 1992 the Executive Committee of the Graduate School surveyed its graduate teachers and asked them how many hours they spent in class preparation. Having received the response, an average of 22.5 hours, the Committee ignored the results and wrote a job description of 17.5 hours anyway. This seems to be a magic number for Yale to determine its "casual" work! What this figure does is to support the contention of the administration that graduate teachers are not real employees. In a very recent example, although GESO has compiled an extraordinary amount of information about graduate teachers and teaching, even now the administration refuses to use it and has appointed new faculty committees to gather information. Even though GESO organized elections to select its representatives, Dean Appelquist still stubbornly insists on *appointing* student representatives to these committees. At Yale no-one is supposed to elect their representatives; only the administration can select and appoint those whom the administration will recognize as being representative by their measure. This is the Yale version of democracy in action.

It is not just the dining hall and custodial workers at Yale who have been subject to corporate "downsizing" during this period of a healthy return on Yale's investments. Despite the administration's denials, it is clear that as the Graduate School shrinks its intake of students, those same students bear an increasing load of the teaching responsibilities of Yale College. Indeed, according to *True Blue: An Investigation into Teaching at Yale*, a report produced by graduate students, in the spring semester of 1995 graduate teachers spent a total of 864 hours in the classroom per week while professors spent a total of 756.5 hours in the classroom each week.[14] Yale professors, of course, overwhelmingly deny that they depend upon graduate student labor in any way. The truth of the situation, however, is that Yale offers its faculty a low teaching load and generous research time because it employs graduate students to undertake much of the undergraduate teaching at a fraction of the cost of faculty salaries. The administration and the faculty, and it is important to remember here that the current President and his triumvirate, the Provost, the Dean of Yale College and the Dean of the Graduate School, are Yale faculty, refuse to recognize that graduate teachers are employees. Instead the favored term at Yale is to refer to the relation between graduate teachers and professors as an apprenticeship. It is not just the buildings at Yale that imitate the Gothic style. Yale faculty want to preserve the most patrician, paternalistic and exploitative aspects of the relation they have with the graduate students who teach for them under the guise of preserving a *mentoring* relationship. Apprentices, remember, had very few rights, if any, in the relation with their master. Yale faculty are deeply suspicious of any changes in this "mentoring" relationship and are deeply resentful that graduate teachers seek to have some say in their conditions of graduate existence at Yale. As I said at a faculty meeting in December 1995, graduate students are only recognized as our teaching colleagues at Yale as long as they say exactly what their so-called "mentors" want them to say.

Scene III

In 1983, the Secretary-General of the OECD (the Organization for Economic Cooperation and Development) made an acute observation. He said:

> At a particularly neuralgic level, one of the results [of mass unemployment] could be the progressive alienation from the rest of society of the young who, according to contemporary surveys, still *want* jobs, however difficult they may be to obtain, and still *hope* for meaningful careers. More broadly, there must be some danger that the coming decade will be a society in which not merely are "we" progressively divided from "they" (the two divisions representing, very roughly, the labor force and management), but in which the majority groups are increasingly splintered, with the young and the relatively unprotected at odds with the better protected and more experienced members of the workforce.[15]

I regard this observation as a particularly apt description of current divisions at Yale. The privileged senior faculty deny outright the extent to which their privilege is gained at the expense of graduate teachers. In addition, faculty deny the extent to which clerical and technical workers and service and maintenance workers perform the domestic labor of the university, labor which enables us to function as intellectuals.

One of the most shocking, if not absolutely appalling, spectacles of the crisis at Yale has been watching female members of the senior faculty accomplishing the work of the old boy corporate network by publicly accusing, denouncing and condemning their graduate teachers for attempting to unionize. Sara Suleri Goodyear, Margaret Homans, Annabel Patterson, Linda Peterson and Ruth Yeazell have not only been active and vocal as apologists in defense of the punitive actions of the university but, in the case of Homans, Patterson, Peterson and Yeazell, have also publicly, and, in my opinion, unethically, denounced their own students in letters distributed to all members of the Modern Language Association.

But what is also very revealing is the open contempt of many senior faculty for the alliance between GESO and the other two unions at Yale which are affiliated with HERE, the Hotel Employees' and Restaurant Employees' International Union. This contempt has been openly expressed at meetings of the faculty of Yale College and can be aptly figured through the example of a supreme act of class snobbery and condescension exhibited by Annabel Patterson in her letter where she states with an almost audible sniff that GESO "has always been a wing [of a union] that draws its membership from the dining workers in the colleges and other support staff." And she continues:

> Yale is not prepared to negotiate academic policy, such as the structure of the teaching program or class size, with the Hotel Employees and Restaurant Employees International Union. Yale administrators have made it perfectly clear

that they have no objections to working with an elected graduate student organization other than GESO, one that is not tied to the non-academic unions on campus.

Of course it is absolutely clear from the history of graduate student
organizing at Yale that the administration is *not* willing to negotiate with
any elected group that graduate students themselves collectively organize.
And an offer from GESO to negotiate without the administration having to
recognize them as a union was peremptorily rejected.

The building of alliances at Yale, however, between primarily blue-collar,
maintenance and service workers, pink-collar, technical and clerical workers, and white-collar graduate teachers is an extremely interesting and
hopeful development within the university community. The turn to increasing part-time and casual work is endemic and an experience shared by
graduate teachers, clerical workers and dining hall workers alike and forms
the basis for a new democratic alliance within the university. This alliance
aggressively challenges the narrow boundaries of who counts as being a
member of the university community and also provides us with a model for
rethinking the responsibilities of a university toward the community in
which it is located. But also in this crisis, the better protected, led by the
privileged women in the profession, are in the front lines of the defense of
management as the Secretary of the OECD predicted, while the young and
less protected are at odds with their selfish, privileged mentors and turning
to find support from working-class unionism. In the view of many law
professors, the faculty are not only unethically but illegally exercising the
extensive authority they have over graduate students to threaten and
punish them.

This is an alliance that we need to consider very seriously for it should
make us question the limits of middle-class academic feminism and the
limits of support for peoples of color as long as those peoples are
represented only by a novel on the syllabus and not through their own
voices on a picket-line. As the actions of the Yale administration against
graduate students were swift and punitive, so the employment of an outside
security firm, Professional Law Enforcement Inc., to police the present
strikers speaks volumes about Yale's intentions. PLE deploys private guards
during labor disputes and has a dubious reputation and a history of
provocation.[16] Unions at Yale have always been law-abiding and there is no
history of violence arising from labor actions, but does Yale intend to
change this peaceful history of labor relations? Is this another threat of
punitive action over workers?

The strikes at Yale, of GESO in December 1995 and in Spring 1996 of
Locals 34 and 35 are extremely important to consider in relation to our
national condition. The faculty at Yale are not only denying their students
the right to form a union and denying them their right to collectively
bargain about the conditions of their own employment, but are also
immersed in a battle to preserve their own privileged existence at the

expense of those they seek to relegate to the position of apprenticeship. The faculty are struggling to retain positions of unquestioned authority as masters and mistresses over all the graduate students they survey; the Yale Corporation fights to preserve the healthy return on its endowment at the expense of the well-being of its future workforce while the present work-force is engaged in strike action to protect future workers from such exploitation. The possible futures of America Inc. are embedded in these struggles in New Haven.

1996

Notes

1. See Andrew Julien, "Under Yale's Hours Policy, Worker Loses," *Hartford Courant*, October 25, 1995, pp. F1–2, and the pamphlet published by the Federation of University Employees Local 34, Local 35, GESO, "Good Employer? Yale Denies Insurance to 1000+ Workers," n.d.
2. See FUE, "Good Employer?"
3. As cited in "Why Provoke This Strike? Yale and the US Economy," a presentation by Rick Wolff, Professor of Economics at University of Massachusetts, Amherst, at Yale University, February 28 1996, unpublished, p. 1.
4. Ibid.
5. See Louis Unchitelle and N.R. Kleinfield, "On the Battlefields of Business, Millions of Casualties," *New York Times*, March 3, 1996, pp. 1, 26–9.
6. Julien, "Under Yale's Hours Policy," p. F2.
7. As quoted in N.R. Kleinfield, "The Company as Family, No More," *New York Times*, March 4 1996, pp. A1, A12–14.
8. Louis Uchitelle, "1995 Was Good for Companies, and Better for a Lot of C.E.O.'s," *New York Times*, March 29 1996, pp. A1, D8.
9. Ibid., D8.
10. See Adolph Reed, Jr, "New Voice, Old School?," *Village Voice*, March 19 1996, p. 19, for a good analysis of this situation.
11. For a superb account of the 1984 strike, see Toni Gilpin, Gary Isaac, Dan Letwin and Jack McKivigan, *On Strike for Respect: The Yale Strike of 1984–5*, Chicago: Charles H. Kerr, 1987.
12. Letter to Cynthia Young from Thomas Appelquist, December 18 1995.
13. For an excellent history of this organizing, see Cynthia Young, "On Strike at Yale," *the minnesota review*, 45/46, Fall 1995–Spring 1996, pp. 179–95.
14. As cited in ibid. I would like to thank Cynthia Young for allowing me to read her superb account of the events leading up to and during the grade strike before its publication. I am indebted to her acute analysis and to the many insights that this essay contains.
15. As quoted in Eric Hobsbawm, *The Age of Extremes*, London: Michael Joseph, 1994, p. 433.
16. See *The New Face of Security at Yale: A Report to the Yale Community by the Federation of University Employees*, 1996.

Fictions of the Folk

9

Reinventing History/
Imagining the Future

> History gives topic and substance to black women's writing. No one
> can read a novel by Toni Morrison or Alice Walker or Paule Marshall
> without confronting history, feeling its influence and experiencing
> the changes wrought by history.
>
> Susan Willis, *Specifying*[1]

The opening sentences of Susan Willis's materialist–feminist analysis of five
twentieth-century black women writers challenge the contemporary critical
reader to confront history. Willis is one of the leading Marxist critics of
black culture, and *Specifying* now situates her as an outstanding feminist
critic of twentieth-century women's writing.

Much of the critical attention paid to the contribution of black women
to the formation of contemporary culture, whether as writers, entertainers
or filmmakers, appears slight and superficial as if they were a passing
phenomenon. But there is nothing faddish about the critical response of
Willis to black women as cultural producers in the contemporary marketplace. First, there is nothing "new" about Willis's historicism: it grounds
itself in a tradition of Marxist theory that has been shaped and transformed
by a serious engagement with the social constructions of race and gender
as ways in which experiences of class are lived. And second, she insists that
economic, patriarchal and racial forms of social domination are necessarily
interdependent modes of exploitation. Within this theoretical framework
Willis situates issues of race, gender and class as the key to an understanding of North American history and the black female as the central not the
marginalized American subject.

Willis begins by arguing that the transition from a predominantly
agrarian to a predominantly urban society "defines the entire modern
history of the Americas" (pp. 3–4). This is the historical context for the
discussion of American black women writers whose narratives document
this massive social upheaval and whose protagonists become the central
figures in the American landscape. Willis refuses the usual characterization

of black people as an underclass, for it is urbanization not proletarianiza-
tion that for her marks the shift from a land-based to an industrial-based
economy. "Thus," she states, "American history might be better understood
from a point of view that has traditionally been seen as a minority position
and an economics traditionally defined as marginal or aberrant" (p. 5). In
the tradition of Immanuel Wallerstein and Cedric Robinson,[2] Willis not
only utilizes the generalized insights of "world systems" theory, but elaborates their theoretical models, extending them to encompass gender and
applying them to cultural production.

"Histories, Communities, and Sometimes Utopia" is Willis's sophisticated
mapping of the field. She sets up a historical paradigm in which the first
level of black women's relation to history is "a relationship to mother and
grandmother" (p. 5): the relation of generations is a means of access to
the past and to the geography of migration. Willis emphasizes that the
history of black women is the history of a labor force; because black
foremothers are producers and workers, their representation enables
black women writers to reconstruct history as both period and as process.
The fictional representation of the geographical spaces across which migration has occurred are the means for conceptualizing history. The narrative
journey is, therefore, a central analytic category of her analysis.

> The relationship that obtains in black women's fiction between South and North,
> or between Caribbean island and Northern metropolis, or between Africa and
> the United States defines history as economic modes. The portrayal of the South
> is not backdrop, local color, or nostalgia, but precise delineation of the agrarian
> mode of production. Similarly, the Northern metropolis is depicted as the site of
> wage labor and the politics of class. Journey North is felt as the transition between
> two modes existing simultaneously within capitalism, but the one – the agrarian
> mode – is destined to pass out of existence. (p. 8)

The metaphoric use of the economic, however, Willis argues, is not merely
a nostalgic rendering of a lost community but is politically radical: in Toni
Morrison's *The Bluest Eye* metaphoric memory can produce utopian fantasy,
and in Paule Marshall's *Brown Girl, Brownstones* migrating to the metropolis
is "a metaphor for the transformation from peonage to worker alienation"
(p. 11).

The narrative form that reproduces this intense sensitivity to history is
derived from the black story-telling tradition, which Willis distinguishes
both from mainstream bourgeois contemporary fictional forms and from
postmodernism. What is important to Willis is that the teller–listener
relationship, as it evolved in the oral agrarian culture, embodies the
"rhythm of daily life" and a unified consciousness: "the speaking subject is
at one with the narrative, as are the listeners" (p. 15). "Specifying," as it is
taken from Zora Neale Hurston's *Dust Tracks on a Road*, is an integral
linguistic unit within the narrative form of story-telling which is interpreted

by Willis as speaking for what was, historically, a "non-commodified relationship to language" inherently antagonistic to the "schism between signified and signifier that . . . typifies . . . narratives and theories generated under capitalism', (p. 16). But Willis is careful not to romanticize folk cultural forms or their representation for, as she aptly demonstrates with examples from Morrison and Marshall, "the transition to the urban involves the erasure of the speaking subject" (p. 19) and leads to the representation of a plurality of stories seemingly autonomous from speaking subjects.

Willis treats the texts of black women writers as embodiments of their communities' relationship to history, a history which can be represented as complex and contradictory because their metaphoric structures are, in Freudian terms, condensed. The central figures in this fiction, which are historical in all the ways described above, are protagonists who are typical, in Lukács's theory of typicality, precisely because of their marginality. But in Willis's use of the marginal, protagonists like Morrison's Sula, Alice Walker's Meridian and Marshall's Selina move beyond the limitations of Lukácsian theories and simultaneously embody both the history and the future of the American experience.

Willis's close readings of particular texts start with Zora Neale Hurston. Unlike many critics of African American literature who situate Hurston in the generalized position of being foremother to contemporary black women writers, Willis characterizes Hurston as the precursor of modernist writers Morrison and Marshall, and distinct from realists like Ann Petry. Hurston's work is placed in "the incipient stages of modernism" and is described as using a language that incorporates the colloquialisms of "specifying" into a metaphorical structure simpler than "the highly condensed, multireferential figures . . . of Morrison's writing" (p. 32). Willis argues that Hurston's journey North and her subsequent education at Barnard created a distance between the author and the people she was to represent in her fiction, autobiography and anthropological writing. Hurston herself described this distance in schizophrenic terms: as being able to see herself "like somebody else," which Willis identifies as the process of alienation (p. 33). However, she does not discuss in any detail how Hurston's own move from a rural to an urban space and into the position of intellectual participates in the metaphorical construction of the figure of the "folk" which emerges in the work of African American intellectuals during the twenties and thirties. This is a pity because contemporary African American cultural history and criticism is re-creating a romantic discourse of a rural black folk in which to situate the source of an African American culture. Indeed, much current critical work that is concerned with the construction, reconstruction and revision of an African American literary canon has expanded the discursive category of the folk to mythic proportions, and romantic readings of Hurston's *Their Eyes Were Watching God* are an integral part of that mythology. Mary Helen Washington in *Invented Lives* has warned of the patriarchal nature of romantic readings of *Their Eyes* and analyzed the romantic limitations of the novel itself.[3] Willis adds another dimension to this work by acknowledging the importance of Hurston's decision to represent a rural people rather than a people in the process of becoming an urban working class.

> In describing Janie's relationship to her third husband, Hurston offers a utopian betrayal of history's dialectic. She chooses not to depict the Northern migration of black people, which brought Hurston herself to New York and a college degree and brought thousands of other rural blacks to the metropolis and wage labor. . . . By their absence from her novel, industrialization, the city, the black working class are not shown to represent the future for black people. (p. 48)

Willis argues that "the muck" on which Janie and Tea Cake live and work is Hurston's creation of a mythic space. I think that this argument could be extended to see Hurston's representation of "the muck" itself as a displacement of the urban and issues of black American migration. Florida is used as a geographic space that is outside of the present migration patterns to the northern United States but an integral part of migration patterns of the Caribbean: many of the workers on "the muck" are migrants from the islands.[4]

Hurston's mythic space is defined by Willis as a "utopian fantasy"; a far more radical response to male domination is, she argues, the killing of Tea Cake. In *Their Eyes*, she concludes, it is a vision of sisterhood that is opposed to images of a "backward, oppressed, exclusionary community," and Pheobe's recognition that relations between men and women might be transformed is "the book's most radical statement."

Specifying is structured throughout by the pattern of analysis used to explicate Hurston's work. The importance of the journey and the possibility of imagining radically alternative futures are the conceptual cornerstones of the book. Hurston's journeying is characterized in the chapter title as "Wandering"; journeys in Marshall's *Brown Girl, Brownstones, The Chosen Place, the Timeless People* and *Praisesong for the Widow* as "Arcs of Recovery." Marshall, Willis maintains, is an example of how contemporary black women writers "define themselves against the urban while at the same time [recognizing] the significant contribution city culture . . . made to their development" (p. 56). The culture of a previous generation is recovered in journeys that reconstruct the history of black people in the New World. But Marshall's work is also seen as symptomatic of a major problem facing black writers today, a problem that Willis describes as "how to preserve the black cultural heritage in the face of the homogenizing functions of bourgeois society" (p. 72). Marshall's tracing of the arc of recovery, Willis argues, results in an imaginative set of possibilities for the future that transcends Hurston's vision of sisterhood because Marshall's women are figures for the African American community as a whole.

Willis's penetrating analysis of Marshall is followed by "Eruptions of

Funk," a powerful and persuasive reading of the fiction of Toni Morrison, an earlier version of which originally appeared in *Black American Literature Forum.*[5] This chapter not only offers an original argument about the relations between the representation of history and sexuality and between the representation of geographic space and history, but it also utilizes Willis's knowledge of Latin American literature. She makes a brief but intriguing comparison between *Song of Solomon* and Mario Vargas Llosa's *La Casa Verde*, and concludes that Morrison's narrative methods in the former novel can be thought of "as a North American variant of the magical realism . . . [of] Gabriel García Márquez" (pp. 96, 108). The footnotes to the chapter elaborate these comparisons and add a detailed explication of the relations to and differences between Morrison's metaphorical structure and the structure of the metaphors of the surrealist poets.

For Willis the importance of acute critical analyses lies not only in how literary texts use and embody history but how they envision social transformation. In Alice Walker's *The Color Purple* Willis sees "a suggestion of what a nonsexist, nonracist community might be" (p. 119), and in *Meridian* she finds a protagonist who can be defined as a revolutionary woman. However, out of the climate of political conservatism in the eighties, Willis argues, has also come a much more problematic representation of political activism. Willis reads Toni Cade Bambara's *The Salt Eaters* as indicative of the recognition that "the political movements organized around minority oppression . . . which led the challenge against state capitalism during the late sixties, have failed to achieve the radical transformation of society" (p. 129). *The Salt Eaters* is described as a postmodern novel in which revolution seems inevitable and imminent but in which revolution or even a prescription for social change cannot be represented.

Nevertheless, Willis feels that the "most compelling aspect of black women's writing today is its ability to envision transformed human relationships and the alternative futures these might shape" (p. 159). The fiction of Walker and Morrison enables a redefinition of the family and community, Hurston uses childhood as a mode of utopian realization, and Morrison transforms images of domestic life through her varieties of a three-woman household. It is this fiction, Willis asserts, that represents the future in the present, produces utopian visions out of a transformation of daily life, and makes it possible for the reader to imagine the radical reconstitution of his or her daily life and space.

It is unusual for a reviewer to discuss the footnotes of a book under review, but what is evident from the footnotes to all Willis's chapters is that she is interested not just in the relations between black women writers but in situating their work in the broad context of the fiction of Latin America, the Caribbean and Africa, in making connections across literary movements and moments, and in making the politics of various modernisms explicit. Reading the footnotes carefully allows the reader to see another critical project; one that would enable black women's writing to move out from the ghetto of marginalization and into a comparative framework of a world literature constituted in and by anti-colonial and anti-imperialist politics. Willis offers a unique critical perspective to African American cultural criticism for she seeks for the utopian and politically transformative moments in American fiction. *Specifying* is a landmark text, for while its subject is how writers have reinvented history and imagined alternative futures, its form challenges us, as literary and cultural critics, to examine our own theoretical practices and premises and to imagine, perhaps, a radically transformed literary criticism.

1989

Notes

1. Susan Willis, *Specifying: Black Women Writing the American Experience*, Madison: University of Wisconsin Press, 1987, p. 3; hereafter page references given in the main text.
2. Immanuel Wallerstein, *The Modern World System*, New York: Academic Press, 1974; Cedric Robinson, *Black Marxism*, London: Zed Press, 1982.
3. Mary Helen Washington, *Invented Lives: Narratives of Black Women 1860–1960*, New York: Doubleday, 1987, pp. 237–54.
4. See Joel Garreau, *The Nine Nations of North America*, New York: Avon, 1981, pp. 167–206.
5. Susan Willis, "Eruptions of Funk: Historicizing Toni Morrison," *Black American Literature Forum*, no. 16, Spring 1982, pp. 34–42.

Proletarian or Revolutionary Literature?
C.L.R. James and the Politics of
the Trinidadian Renaissance

This essay addresses the inadequacies of our current attempts to consider issues of cultural production across national boundaries: in particular, relations between literary movements in the "Third" and the "First" Worlds. Teaching about "Third World" culture in the context of "First World" universities presents both students and teachers with some fundamental political dilemmas. Our teaching needs to make connections with, as well as provide a critique of, dominant ideologies and meanings of culture which, for example, structure the curricula of departments of English and American Studies. Teaching "Third World" culture must involve a constant and consistent critique of the forms of knowledge production that maintain the European and American cultural hegemony in which our students are embedded; either that or we remain politically marginal. If we are not in a state of constant political confrontation with the imperialist discourse that structures "First World" education systems, then we merely confirm our exoticism. Approaches to culture offered by programs in comparative literature provide no satisfactory alternative to English or American Studies, for historically they too are overwhelmingly Eurocentric. If we are to develop any sort of challenge to the ways in which educational institutions organize and structure forms of knowledge about the "Third World", then we have to be able to offer a coherent alternative political vision: a way of thinking critically across relations of cultural production in the "Third," "Second" and "First" Worlds. In what follows I try to situate what has been called the "Trinidadian Renaissance" in an international context, but in a more general way I hope the essay is regarded as a contribution to and a criticism of contemporary debate about constructing a "World Literature."[1]

In *Beyond a Boundary*, a cultural history of cricket, C.L.R. James tells us that the two major political and social influences in his life have been literature and cricket; indeed, literature and cricket are the two recurring motifs that figure the emergence of his political consciousness.[2]

His scholastic career as a scholarship boy in Trinidad forced upon him the contradictions of the intellectual in the colonies. James's assiduous study and practice of the art of fiction resulted in two convictions: a recognition of his alienation, which he expressed as an awareness that "intellectually [he] lived abroad, chiefly in England"; and a deep commitment to literature as an instrument of social reform.[3] It was in the practice of cricket (what James calls "the clash of race, caste and class") that the particular politics of colonization, of class and race rivalries were confronted: "the cricket field was a stage on which selected individuals played representative roles which were charged with social significance."[4]

When James left for England in 1932, he took with him two manuscripts that he describes as representative of the interrelation of cricket and politics in his life: a history of West Indian cricket and Learie Constantine, and a political history of the West Indies and Captain Cipriani.[5] His work with Constantine established a partnership that had West Indian self-government as its goal and led James directly into socialist and Marxist politics. Both these projects are recognizably the initiation of James's career as a political and cultural theorist whose work for the past fifty-seven years has engaged African, North American, Caribbean, European and Soviet politics. But besides these two manuscripts, James also carried with him a completed novel, *Minty Alley*, published in 1936, which provides important insights into the formation of James as a cultural and political theorist.[6] *Minty Alley* can also be regarded, more generally, as an exploration of the contradictions of colonial intellectual practice and as a contribution to a world debate about proletarian and revolutionary literature.

James had contributed short fiction to two Trinidadian journals: the *Trinidad*, of which only two issues were published, Christmas 1929 and Easter 1930; and the *Beacon*, which produced twenty-eight issues between March 1931 and November 1933.[7] James edited the *Trinidad* with Alfred Mendes and was a regular contributor to the *Beacon*, edited by Alfred Gomes, until 1932. He was part of a group of young intellectuals that used to meet and discuss each other's writings and who hoped that the *Trinidad* would be the first step in the establishment of an indigenous West Indian literary tradition. Alfred Mendes has stressed that two events "drove us into writing about our islands": the first was "the first world war where a large number of us had been abroad, and indeed, even those of us who had not been abroad were influenced considerably by what was happening in the world, and the second event was the Russian Revolution."[8] Reinhard Sander, in his introduction to a collection of four volumes of the *Beacon*, has argued that the occupation of the group "with the Russian experiment became an important ideological framework from which to criticize colonial society in Trinidad and to attack the Crown Colony system."[9]

When Albert Gomes returned to Trinidad in 1930 he sought out the editors of the *Trinidad*, copies of which he had read while in the United States, but he found that no more issues of the *Trinidad* were planned because the group who produced it were on the point of disbanding.[10] Gomes's decision to found and edit the *Beacon* is generally considered to be the moment of the integration of the political struggle to achieve independence and the creation of a national literature in Trinidad. Working for and writing in the *Beacon* shifted the concerns of a group of intellectuals from "armchair discussion" to the production of a journal dedicated to the achievement of drastic change in the Trinidadian social structure.[11]

The *Beacon* was a forum for the creation of a West Indian literature, a literature which was regarded primarily as a vehicle for the representation of the poor and dispossessed. But this fictional concern with oppression could not long be divorced from other more political modes of representation, and the *Beacon* group quickly retracted their initial apolitical stance and reluctance to write editorials and used the pages of the journal to attack Trinidadian politicians and political structures, to comment on world events, to openly support Soviet policies, to publish banned Soviet articles, and to develop a socialist and sometimes communist politics.[12]

It is an automatic reflex of literary and cultural criticism to consider literatures from the "Third World" as marginal to European or North American culture. It is usually the recognition of such literature as a product of a national culture and nationalist theories and movements that structurally marginalizes it. Though a socialist theory and practice of the teaching of world literatures cannot be an apology for nationalism, neither can it be limited to national "readings" of culture but should articulate the specificity of national culture with historical readings of the international significance of cultural production. The moment of the Trinidadian intellectual "renaissance" of the 1920s and 1930s is clearly of international significance, connected to both the Harlem Renaissance and intercontinental movements to create a proletarian literature. Each of these groups of cultural producers – Caribbean intellectuals, the writers of the Harlem Renaissance, and the writers of proletarian novels – has been treated as a discrete entity with a discrete history, as a literary movement that is marginal to the culture from which it springs. As a contribution to thinking across these categories, I would like to suggest ways in which an international perspective can question and counter this cultural marginalization.

The "Resolution of the First All-Union Conference of Proletarian Writers" (1925) recognized the important ideological role of literature in Soviet society.[13] The conference established many of the terms and conditions of proletarian literature that became influential in Europe, North America and, I will argue, the Caribbean. Arguing strongly against the tendency to make proletarian literature marginal to literature in general, the conference urged the principle of the hegemony of that literature. Among the resolutions was an acknowledgment of artistic literature as a powerful weapon in the class war and as an arena in which that conflict was unassuaged. The culture and literature of the bourgeoisie were said to be in crisis, in a state of decomposition; proletarian culture, in Lenin's terms, should become the natural continuation and development of reserves of knowledge developed under a capitalist society. In other words, a proletarian literature could take everything of value and all that was progressive from classical and contemporary bourgeois culture but go beyond it and "rework" it.[14] The conference intensely debated Trotsky's notion of "fellow travelers," writers who came from the intelligentsia, the lower middle classes and the peasantry, and questioned their possible contributions to the formation of a proletarian literature.[15]

Trotsky, on the other hand, argued that everyone needed to be freed from the "metaphysical concept of proletarian culture . . . and regard the question from the point of view of what the proletariat reads, what it needs, what absorbs it, what impels it to action, what elevates its cultural level and so prepares the ground for a new art . . . [a] literature vitally needed by an awakened people."[16] Against the concept of a proletarian literature, Trotsky posed the concept of a revolutionary literature: only literature that "promotes the consolidation of the workers in their struggle against the exploiters is necessary and progressive."[17] He also described the interrelation between class, individual and national characteristics of art "as it expresses definite demands which have a class character . . . [which] also means individual because a class speaks through an individual. It also means national, because the spirit of a nation is determined by the class which rules it and which subjects literature to itself."[18] Besides advocating an "artistic acceptance of reality," Trotsky acknowledged that "the new artist will need all the methods and processes evolved in the past . . . in order to grasp the new life."[19]

Katerina Clark has described how literature became a part of the general mobilization for industrialization in the Soviet Union and was integrated into the broad-based cultural revolution.[20] Literature had to be, she states, "of, by and for those 'little men' and their 'great deeds.' "[21] The demand for proximity meant that writers were expected to work in factories alongside the subjects of their fiction; in addition, writers were considered part of the national campaign to raise the cultural and educational level of the masses.[22] Clark maintains that it was never totally clear whether writers were molding the masses or were meant to be molded by them, but what was certain, she argues, was that writers had to abandon their position as independent observers of "the people."[23] In 1932 RAPP (The First All-Union Conference) was dissolved, and by the time of the international gathering of writers at the First Congress of Soviet Writers in 1934 a rigid adherence to the principles of proletarian authorship had disappeared. Nevertheless, the ideals of a proletarian literature had been disseminated internationally.[24]

I schematically outline this debate because it had a major influence on the literature that was being produced in the Caribbean. Many of the literary conventions of the Trinidadian Renaissance were shaped in response to both the proletarian literary movement and the Harlem Renaissance in the United States. A formal concern with the nature and function of realism was combined with the demand that a writer be directly involved with the subject(s) of his or her fiction. William Phillips and Philip Rahv, in their influential essay "Recent Problems of Revolutionary Literature" published in the United States, emphasized the importance of the replacement of the writer as external observer with the writer as direct participant in the life of "the people."[25] It was the critic's duty, they claimed, to point out to writers the dangers of the attitude of the spectator. Both Rahv and Phillips adapted the Soviet debate about realism and the direct representation of the class struggle into their own terms. They saw literature as a "medium" shaped in sensory experience which did not easily lend itself to the conceptual forms of the social-political content of the class struggle. Indeed, they concluded that "the transition of this content into images of *physical life* determines – in the aesthetic sense – the extent of the writer's achievement."[26]

Many of the Trinidadian intellectuals who contributed to the *Beacon* felt the necessity of "the cultural upheaval that must come" that Mike Gold heralded in his essay "Towards Proletarian Art."[27] And many shared his early and romantic evocation of "life at its fullest and noblest" in the representation of the masses. For in Trinidad the fictional representation of "the people" and the maturation of a socialist politics occurred together as writers translated their admiration for the Soviet experiment and the proletarian movement in North America into engagement with the specific conditions of the Caribbean and of colonialism. As James has insisted in his essay "Discovering Literature in Trinidad: The 1930s," the origins of his work and his thoughts were "to be found in Western European literature, Western European history and Western European thought." He reflects that the contradictions of his intellectual and class position were embodied in the atmosphere in which he came to maturity: "In my youth we lived according to the tenets of Matthew Arnold; we spread sweetness and light, and we studied the best that there was in literature in order to transmit it to the people – as we thought, the poor, backward West Indian people."[28] But James reinterpreted and redefined his Eurocentric education. As "a Man of the Caribbean" he considered himself also a man of the West who recognized the necessity of addressing the one world in which everyone lived.[29] He maintained that the political, social and cultural issues of the West Indies, of African exploitation, of underdevelopment and of colonialism in general were not marginal but central to the formation of Western civilization. The move toward Marxism, the education that Marxism provided, the joining of the Communist Party by Césaire and Padmore, and James's particular orientation to Trotskyism are situated by James as steps in a natural progression from the contradictions of each of their positions as colonial intellectuals and from their sense of intellectual and moral responsibility toward the communities in which they grew up.[30]

This sense of intellectual and moral responsibility toward a community was shared by left-wing writers in the United States and by the intellectuals of the Harlem Renaissance. But historians of the Harlem Renaissance have little to say about the relation between left-wing literary circles and the Harlem intellectuals, even though people like Langston Hughes and Claude McKay were important figures in both movements. Even less has been said about the links between these left-wing literary circles and Trinidadian intellectuals, although the involvement of Isidor and Nathan Schneider in the North American left and in the production of the *Beacon* would confirm that these links existed.

Melvin Dixon, however, has recognized the ways in which the Harlem Renaissance was a part of an international development of negritude which he defines as "the celebration of a black consciousness through literature."[31] He situates Harlem intellectuals in relation to colonized intellectuals. "Writers from the Harlem Renaissance in the United States, the *Revue Indigène* in Haiti and *La Revue du Monde Noir* in Paris gave birth to literatures that, although established along lines of national language and culture, created an arena wherein blacks throughout the world could articulate their presence and condition."[32] I would venture that the Trinidadian Renaissance and the birth of indigenous literature in the Caribbean could be considered a part of this wider movement. Claude McKay was originally from Jamaica; like James, he left to write and be published. Langston Hughes translated a Haitian novel, *Masters of the Dew* by Jacques Roumain, for an American readership. But Dixon's attempt to establish "a world black literature and community" can be extended even further if we consider the textual evidence of the fiction of the *Beacon* and of James.

Alfred Mendes has described how the group of intellectuals around the *Trinidad* and the *Beacon* were regarded in Trinidad: "We had come to be known as the Communist group, and indeed in those years we were very sympathetic towards what was occurring in the Soviet Union."[33] The group can be easily characterized in Trotsky's terms as "fellow travelers," for it was the revolutionary spirit and example of Soviet society that provided the conceptual framework from which they criticized colonial structures. Ideologically, the emergent working-class movement in Trinidad and the desire to establish an indigenous literature found their inspiration in the Russian Revolution. The struggle for political independence and artistic movements to establish an autonomous cultural presence were and would remain interdependent throughout the Caribbean.

The most politically interesting aspect of the encouragement of indigenous literature in the *Beacon* is the short fiction which was written mainly by members of the group, though an attempt was made to encourage the writing of short stories among its readership through a short story competition. The editorial of the January/February 1932 issue echoes the concerns of proletarian writers as it urges entrants to the competition to use the Trinidadian people as their characters, to utilize the speech forms of the people, and to make their social situation and their everyday conflicts the subject of the narrative.[34] The editorial rejected outright submissions which would be romantic or exotic, and encouraged its contributors to employ the techniques of narrative realism. The *Beacon*'s definition of realism and its desire to represent the Trinidadian "people" produced a fiction that drew upon life in the barrack-yards and the representation of an urban working class which was overwhelmingly of African and East Indian origin. The short fiction by Mendes and James, in particular, raised the issue of proximity in proletarian writing. Mendes lived in a barrack-yard for six months in order to be able to reproduce the language, the atmosphere and the incidents that he witnessed for his fiction.

James's first short story, "Triumph," was published in *Trinidad*; he described in detail a barrack-yard, the residents of which were "the porters, the prostitutes, carter-men, washerwomen and domestic servants."[35] "Triumph" focuses on three women whose precarious existence and whose financial and sexual dependence on men means that a loss of a boyfriend could result in starvation. At the beginning of the story, what triumphs is squalid adversity; what remains at the end of the story is a triumph of spirit.

In "Triumph" James reproduces the painstaking details of poverty but with an unmistakable distancing of tone if not of sympathy. The issues of proximity and intellectual rejection of the role of observer were not as easily resolved as Mendes's brief sojourn in a barrack-yard implied. Hence the problem of becoming an involved writer and the question of the extent to which the class barrier could be successfully bridged became the subject of Trinidadian fiction. In Ralph De Boissiere's "The Woman on the Pavement," published in the *Beacon*, a middle-class man finds himself an impotent observer when a black peasant woman has a fit. Unable to do what he knew he "should have done" to help, he is ashamed to watch while a black porter acts. He is unable to move "because of the people looking on, people of the middle classes like himself," and is able only to mouth the meaningless words, "It's hell to be poor." It occurs to him that an acceptable act would be to hire a taxi to take the woman home, but he hesitates and concludes that money must be the answer though he is not "man enough to go up to the woman in the open street and put silver in her hand." The closing sentences are a bleak recognition of the capitalist economic relation which divides the classes: "All the clerks and managers of the stores were busy now, and none saw her as she passed. The clerks were all eager to satisfy the managers, that they might get more money. The managers were doing all that their little consciences would allow them to wring the utmost out of the clerks."[36] This problem of proximity and the paradigm of the writer as observer became the central motif for James's *Minty Alley*, but before discussing that novel it is important to describe another significant aspect of the class conflict explored in Trinidadian fiction.

West Indian literature contributes to our understanding of how the poor are represented in socialist literature in the Americas by its particular interweaving of racial conflict with class conflict, a conflict expressed through sexual relations. A wide spectrum of the *Beacon* stories used sexuality as a terrain of racial and class conflict. In one particular story, "Brotherly Love" by Alistair Scott, an intraracial, incestuous relationship is used to figure the state of the intellectual and cultural decay of the white bourgeoisie in Trinidad.[37] More frequently, however, it was interracial sexual relations that were used as a metaphor for a political struggle for power.

"Boodhoo," by Alfred Mendes, is about a white woman, Minnie, who becomes fascinated by and eventually has a sexual relationship with her Indian servant, the title character, even though, as a new mistress, she is appalled and disgusted by her discovery that white men frequently had sexual relationships with Indian women. But she discovers that instead of being a lover she is merely the means for Boodhoo's revenge. Boodhoo's Indian mother tells Minnie how she was seduced and then abandoned by Minnie's husband and that Boodhoo is his son. Minnie realizes as she listens to his mother's story that she had been used by Boodhoo in his exact reconstruction of his own conception. Minnie's subsequent pregnancy threatens to reveal her sexually compromised social position as she fears giving birth to a black child. The burden of guilt leads to her death at the moment that she delivers a blond, blue-eyed son.[38]

The white woman's body within colonial discourse was the preserve of a white patriarchal order. Colonial sexual ideologies and social conventions situated the white female body beyond the reach of the colonized male in an attempt to ensure that only white males be granted sexual access. The white woman was not only regarded as the private property of the colonial patriarch, but was the means of securing heirs to imperial and colonial power. At the nexus of imperial relations, the white woman's body became symbolic of colonial oppression and is thus often represented in colonial fiction as a central figure in the struggle between colonizing and colonized males.

In general, in this fiction, the sexual awareness and maturity of the colonized male is a sign of the growth and maturity of a political awareness. Women as lovers are objectified as the means for revenge, as in "Boodhoo," or as the means for the male to gain independence, or as a sign that a new order is to be established. But women are also to be found as subjects; representations of the ways in which the sexuality of poor women was commodified under colonial capitalism often formed sympathetic fictions of women's lives in Trinidad, most notably in Alfred Mendes's "Five Dollars Worth of Flesh."[39]

In James's novel *Minty Alley* the ambiguity of the allegiance felt by colonial intellectuals toward the colonial order is represented by a female figure: the mother as empire. As the novel opens, the protagonist, Haynes, has inherited a house from his mother. Although she's dead, her influence dominates. Haynes as a colonized male cannot be truly independent – his future is heavily mortgaged. Haynes, himself a figure of the middle-class intellectual, has to move from his bourgeois existence to the yard next door in an attempt to pay this mortgage. He had never before noticed the ordinary folk who lived so close to him, though all the inhabitants of the yard know and respect the class position of Haynes.

Minty Alley is a novel that takes as its subject the question of cultural representation. Its central paradigm is the problem of how the intellectual can represent, either politically or figuratively, the Trinidadian proletariat. The issue of proximity becomes a central mechanism of the narrative: Haynes goes to live among the people. The specific problem of the writer as observer of the people is centered on a narrative device of a hole in the wall through which Haynes views the residents of the yard and which, as the text progresses, becomes enlarged and more elaborate until it becomes no longer necessary as Haynes becomes involved in the lives he has watched.

The intellectual as cultural producer, as author, cannot be separated from the intellectual as member of the bourgeoisie that shaped him. Haynes's move into the yard achieves proximity, but to the extent that he is a figure analogous to that of the writer making a detailed observation of the people he also observes that they cannot read. So for whom is he writing/observing? Ultimately, James situates Haynes as a voyeur. Unhappy at first with living in the yard, Haynes yearns to leave but he stays because he is titillated by the sexual behavior of the residents. Indeed, as events become more dramatic, Haynes becomes increasingly involved in everyday life. The crack in the wall is a class barrier that divides the intellectual from the people and has to be overcome. Yet Haynes's class position renders him impotent in the first crisis that arises. He experiences a paralysis similar to that described in "Woman on the Pavement." He feels horror but is helpless; his reaction is to desire a retreat back into his own childhood, a retreat back to the assurance of his class position as it is constructed through the mother/empire metaphor.

As *Minty Alley* progresses, Haynes enlarges and camouflages his crack in his wall to obtain a wide and comprehensive and secret view; then he suddenly finds himself "in the thick" of involvement in the yard. Involvement means a threat to his class position, possible scandal, the loss of job, property and respectability. Involvement also means that Haynes has to confront the economic relation between himself and the other yard occupants and to recognize the permanent state of indebtedness of the poor. Haynes's political consciousness is raised and this political maturity is paralleled by a sexual maturity. Nevertheless, James was not able to resolve the problems of representation surrounding the production of proletarian literature and his text stands as a critique of the literary theory of proximity. The only meaningful changes are for Haynes; nothing changes for the poor. When Haynes leaves the yard, the occupants disappear; he never knows where.

James was centrally concerned with the political as well as the literary problems of "fellow travelers," and the progression of his work suggests a shift from a concern with proletarian literature to the writing of revolutionary literature. James joined the Trotskyists in London but did not write a revolutionary novel. Instead, his revolutionary text was *Black Jacobins* (1938), a history of Toussaint L'Ouverture and the Haitian Revolution which stands as a narrative exploration of the relation between a leader and a revolutionary party.[40] James was never to return to writing his own fiction as a form of radical intellectual cultural production; thus *Minty Alley* demonstrates the limits of what Caribbean intellectuals thought they might achieve in fiction in the 1930s. This decision to abandon fiction reminds us that, too often, fiction is regarded as the privileged mode of cultural intervention. To return to the text with which this essay opened, it was not fiction in James's life that synthesized his political and cultural critique of the struggle between colony and empire; that struggle was ultimately represented through cricket and the figure of Learie Constantine in one of the most outstanding works of cultural studies ever produced – James's *Beyond a Boundary*.

1988

Notes

1. See Fredric Jameson, "Third-World Literature in the Era of Multinational Capitalism," *Social Text*, no. 15, Fall 1986, pp. 65–88.
2. C.L.R. James, *Beyond a Boundary*, London: Stanley Paul, 1963.
3. Ibid., p. 71.
4. Ibid., p. 72. See, in particular, Chapter. 4, "The Light and the Dark," which describes how the various cricket clubs represented the class and racial divisions in Trinidad.
5. Ibid., p. 119.
6. C.L.R. James, *Minty Alley*, London: New Beacon Books, 1971.
7. See Reinhard W. Sander, *From Trinidad: An Anthology of Early West Indian Writing*, New York, 1978, and *The Beacon: Volumes I–IV, Number 1 Port of Spain, Trinidad 1931–1939*, New York: Africana Publishing Co., 1977.
8. Cited in Sander, "Introduction: The *Beacon* and the Emergence of West Indian Literature," *The Beacon*, p. xix.
9. Ibid.
10. See the autobiography of Albert Gomes, *Through a Maze of Colour*, Port of Spain: Key Caribbean Publications, 1974, pp. 16–18.
11. Brinsley Samaroo, "Introduction," in Sander, *The Beacon*, p. i.
12. Ibid., iv.
13. See "The Ideological Front and Literature: Resolution of the First All-Union Conference of Proletarian Writers," in William G. Rosenberg, ed., *Bolshevik Visions: First Phase of the Cultural Revolution in Soviet Russia*, Ann Arbor: Ardis, 1984, pp. 469–74.

14. Ibid., p. 472.
15. Ibid., p. 473.
16. Leon Trotsky, *Literature and Revolution*, 1925; reprint, Ann Arbor: University of Michigan Press, 1960, p. 214.
17. Ibid., p. 230.
18. Ibid., p. 234.
19. Ibid., p. 236.
20. Katerina Clark, "Little Heroes and Big Deeds," in Sheila Fitzpatrick, ed., *Cultural Revolution in Russia, 1928–31*, Bloomington: Indiana University Press, pp. 189–206.
21. Ibid., p. 194.
22. Ibid., pp. 195–6.
23. Ibid., p. 198.
24. Ibid., pp. 205–6.
25. William Phillips and Philip Rahv, "Recent Problems of Revolutionary Literature," in Granville Hicks, Joseph North, Michael Gold, Paul Peters, Isidor Schneider and Alan Calmer, eds, *Proletarian Literature in the United States*, New York: International Publihers, 1935, pp. 367–73.
26. Ibid., p. 373.
27. Mike Gold, "Towards Proletarian Art," in Michael Folsom, ed., *Mike Gold: A Literary Anthology*, New York: International Publishers, 1972, pp. 62–70.
28. James, "Discovering Literature in Trinidad: The 1930s," in *Spheres of Existence*, London: Allison & Busby, 1980, p. 237.
29. Ibid., p. 238.
30. Ibid., p. 240.
31. Melvin Dixon, "Rivers Remembering Their Source," in Dexter Fisher and Robert B. Stepto, eds, *Afro-American Literature: The Reconstruction of Instruction*, New York: Modern Language Association of America, pp. 25–43.
32. Ibid., p. 26. See also "Toward a World Black Literature and Community," in Michael S. Harper and Robert B. Stepto, eds, *Chant of Saints: A Gathering of Afro-American Literature, Art, and Scholarship*, Urbana: University of Illinois Press, 1979, pp. 175–94.
33. Interview with Alfred Mendes, cited in Sander, *The Beacon*, p. xix.
34. Editorial, *Beacon*, no. 1, January–February 1932, p. x.
35. C.L.R. James, "Triumph," in Sander, *From Trinidad*, pp. 86–103.
36. R.A.C. De Boissiere, "The Woman on the Pavement," *Beacon*, no. 1, November 1931, pp. 4–5.
37. Alistair Scott, "Brotherly Love," *Beacon*, no. 2, August 1932, pp. 10–12.
38. Alfred Mendes, "Boodhoo," *Beacon*, no. 1, March–April 1932, pp. 18–25 and 23–7; *Beacon*, no. 2, May 1932, pp. 9–11.
39. Mendes, "Five Dollars Worth of Flesh," *Beacon*, no. 1, September 1931, pp. 13–15.
40. James, *The Black Jacobins: Toussaint L'Ouverture and the San Domingo Revolution*, 1938; reprint, London: Allison & Busby, 1980.

Ideologies of Black Folk:
The Historical Novel of Slavery

The title "Slavery and the Literary Imagination" should generate reflection on the ways in which we, as literary critics, have constructed African American literary history. Slavery appears to be central to the African American literary imagination, but, as a mode of production and as a particular social order, slavery is rarely the focus of the imaginative physical and geographical terrain of African American novels. The occasion for this essay is, therefore, a paradox.

One might explain this paradox in three ways. First, there is the critical influence on African American literary history of the antebellum slave narrative. Henry Louis Gates, Jr, has argued in *The Slave's Narrative* that slave narratives have had a determining influence on African American literature. Gates's theoretical proposition is that critical practice needs to elaborate a "black intertextual or signifying relationship" in order to produce "any meaningful formal literary history of the African American tradition."[1] Narrative strategies repeated through two centuries of black writing are seen as the link that binds the slave narrative to texts as disparate as Booker T. Washington's *Up from Slavery*, *The Autobiography of Malcolm X*, Ralph Ellison's *Invisible Man*, Richard Wright's *Black Boy*, Zora Neale Hurston's *Their Eyes Were Watching God* and Ishmael Reed's *Flight to Canada*. As readers and as writers, then, we become receivers of a textual experience that creates the unity of an African American literary tradition, a tradition that, Gates concludes, "rests on the framework built, by fits and starts and for essentially polemical intentions, by the first-person narratives of black ex-slaves."[2] Contemporary African American literary discourse thus situates a form of cultural production that reconstructs the social conditions of slavery as the basis of the entire narrative tradition.

Second, slavery haunts the literary imagination because its material conditions and social relations are frequently reproduced in fiction as historically dynamic; they continue to influence society long after emancipation. The economic and social system of slavery is thus a prehistory (as well as a pre-text to all African American texts), a past social condition that can explain contemporary phenomena. In the late nineteenth century the novels of Frances E.W. Harper, Pauline Hopkins and Charles Chesnutt used slavery in this sense. For example, Hopkins's *Contending Forces* begins with an eighty-page slave story that acts as an overture to her tale of a black New England family at the turn of the century.[3] Her slave prehistory provides all the necessary elements for the fictional resolutions to the novel; once Hopkins's characters *know* their history, they can control their futures. In a formal sense slavery can thus be a most powerful "absent" presence, and this device was perhaps most effectively used by W.E.B. Du Bois in *The Souls of Black Folk*, in which the slave condition, if not the slave mode of production, permeates the text.[4]

Third, our ideas of an African American literary tradition are dominated by an ideology of the "folk" from fictional representations of sharecropping. These novels, which might be called "novels of sharecropping," are those texts, central to contemporary reconstructions of an African American canon, which are interpreted as representations of the Southern "folk" – a folk emerging from and still influenced by the slave condition. Indeed, I would argue that the critical project that situates the ex-slaves writing their "selfhood" or their "humanity" into being as the source of African American literature also reconstructs black culture as rooted in a "folk" culture. The ex-slave consciousness becomes an original "folk" consciousness. Critics like Gates and Houston A. Baker, Jr, argue that the means of expression of this consciousness is the vernacular – for Baker it is the blues that is the "always already" of African American culture – and the search for this vernacular structures and informs the intellectual projects of both critics. Intertextuality is the concept that makes the abstract theoretical proposition a material relation, which is characterized as a series of variations, or riffs, on an original theme to produce an African American discourse, or "blues matrix."[5]

But in the production of this discourse the critical vernacular itself dissolves historical difference. A mythology of the rural South conflates the nineteenth and twentieth centuries and two very distinct modes of production, slavery and sharecropping, into one mythical rural folk existence. Of course, the ideological function of a tradition is to create unity out of disunity and to resolve the social contradiction, or differences, between texts. Consequently, not only are the specificities of a slave existence as opposed to a sharecropping existence negated, but the urban imagination and urban histories are also repressed. Our twentieth-century vernacular (the blues, if you like) is reinterpreted as emerging from a shared rural heritage, not as the product of social displacement and migration of the city. The fact that imaginative re-creations of the "folk," including the ex-slave, are themselves produced and distributed primarily within the urban environment and for urban consumption is not critically examined. A few examples of general critical trends will suffice to illustrate the dominance of this concern with the "folk."

In Zora Neale Hurston's *Their Eyes Were Watching God*, the character of Janie seeks to establish her independence and selfhood by breaking away from the limited possibilities for female existence imagined by her grand-mother, a woman shaped by the slave condition.[6] Hurston's highly romanti-cized novel is read by many contemporary critics as the epitome of "folk" wisdom; one might recall that this representation of the "folk" was decried as "minstrelsy" by Richard Wright, Langston Hughes and Arna Bontemps, and condemned as being a result of Hurston's reactionary politics.[7] On the other hand, there is little critical assessment of the ways in which Richard Wright attempted to rewrite and restructure representations of the rural folk in terms influenced by proletarian fiction and his radical political commitments. And, finally, a large proportion of the criticism written about Ralph Ellison's *Invisible Man* focuses on a minor section of the text, the "Trueblood" episode, a representation of a "folk" figure that covers twenty pages out of a novel of 568 pages, most of which is set in an urban context. It is these twenty pages that Baker analyzes, for example, in his critical search for the vernacular tradition in *Blues, Ideology, and Afro-American Literature.*[8]

These romantic evocations of the African American folk motif are not only to be felt in African American critical work but, at the moment, dominate the few representations of the black community in mass American culture. A romanticized folk has recently been reproduced by the enter-tainment industry in the movie *The Color Purple*. It is a sobering thought that perhaps Steven Spielberg's film is as romanticized a response to black cul-ture in the eighties as David Selznick's *Gone with the Wind* was to black culture in the thirties.

The results of this conflation of slavery and sharecropping into a rural folk that is at the base of the creation of an African American canon is, however, another essay. The idea that the ex-slaves "wrote [their selves] into being" through an account of the condition of being a slave is woven into the very fabric of the African American literary imagination and its critical reconstruction. However, novelistic representations of slav-ery are critically neglected, and why this is so intrigues me. This essay will look at this minority tendency in African American literature, the historical novel of slavery, and in particular at Arna Bontemps's *Black Thunder* and Margaret Walker's *Jubilee*.[9] These texts have received little critical attention, but what interests me the most about these historical novels is the choice of slavery as a period in which to set historical fiction and how that choice itself is generated from particular cultural conditions. I want to distinguish my critical position from a preoccupation with a historically undifferen-tiated "folk," and I hope to reinsert a concern with history both at the level of formal analysis and in relation to the moment of cultural production.

I want to outline a number of different ways of thinking about the relation between history and historical fiction, but first I should state some general principles. As Warren Susman has argued, myth, memory and history are three alternative ways to capture and account for an allusive past. Each has its own persuasive claim.[10] I am going to concentrate upon the two latter approaches, memory and history, first by looking at the novel of memory and oral culture – curiously, both Walker's *Jubilee* and Margaret Mitchell's *Gone with the Wind*.[11] Then I will look at the novel of slave rebellion, *Black Thunder*, and its cultural context. Each represents particular ideologies of the folk which are shaped by the cultural context in which they are produced.

Margaret Walker's *Jubilee* has been heralded as a reaffirmation of "the critical importance of oral tradition in the creation of [African American] history" in a "work based on black memories."[12] Published in 1966, *Jubilee* was a novel that seemed to engage directly the concerns of the Civil Rights movement and the ideologies of the new Black Aesthetic. Its revisionist history, which utilized African American oral culture as well as years of painstaking research, was seen by the Institute for the Black World, which published Walker's essay *How I Wrote Jubilee*, as an important contribution to the "challenge of the White Western value system – especially in education."[13] Walker herself has emphasized that she drew upon family history, that throughout her childhood she heard "stories of slave life in Georgia" from her grandmother, who retold incidents from her mother's life. *Jubilee*, Walker maintains, is the result of a promise to her grandmother that she would write her mother's story.[14] The paperback cover calls Vyry, the protagonist, "a heroine to rival Scarlett O'Hara" and proclaims the "devastating truth" of the story as it is "steeped in knowledge of and feeling for . . . the people." The relation of oral history to the production of the fictional world was seen to be important not only in a general sense that it was history from the bottom up, the "people's version," but also as a particular response to the dominant ideologies of the popular imagination embodied in Mitchell's *Gone with the Wind*.

The recovery of an African American history embedded in an oral culture has formed a very important part of the challenge to dominant interpretations of American history. But in the twenties Margaret Mitchell also felt that she was writing a revisionist history, the story of the beaten but undefeated South. Like Walker, what she felt authenticated *her* historical "truth" against what she saw to be a dominant northern version of history was the fact that she was writing from family memories, an oral history retold. Mitchell too had spent her formative years listening to stories of her ancestors and can be regarded as being as involved as Walker in the preservation of an oral culture. In a letter, Mitchell described the relation of this oral history to *Gone with the Wind*: "I am writing about an upheaval I'd heard about when I was a small child. For I spent Sunday afternoons of my childhood sitting on the bony knees of Confederate veterans and the fat slick laps of old ladies who survived the war and reconstruction."[15]

Both Walker and Mitchell authenticate their texts through references to popular memory, and both could be said to be re-creating cultural meaning through the vernacular of their fictional and historical subjects. But as

Georg Lukács has argued, history has "not aesthetic, but social and historical causes." Clearly, *Gone with the Wind* and *Jubilee* express very different
historical "truths," particularly about the slave condition.[16]

Mitchell wrote *Gone with the Wind* in the twenties. Her novel epitomizes
what Susman has characterized as the "fear" that runs through much
writing of the twenties and thirties – the fear "whether any great industrial
and democratic mass society can maintain a significant level of civilization,
and whether mass education and mass communication will allow any
civilization to survive."[17] Susman's argument is that the concept of civilization that in the late nineteenth and early twentieth centuries was synonymous with social advance and progress became detached from, and indeed
opposed to, these terms to the extent that progress was considered to be at
the risk of the destruction of civilization. In *Gone with the Wind*, a multi-
plicity of the cultural meanings of civilization compete with each other.
The figure of Scarlett O'Hara is a representation of this conflict. Mitchell's
landscape is the destruction of one civilization and the possibilities offered
to build another. Scarlett is in many ways the new capitalist woman who
literally builds the new Atlanta, an industrializing city, with the wood from
her own lumberyard. The constant battle against rigid conventions that
govern female behavior rewrites Mitchell's own unconventional response
to ideologies of womanhood in the twenties. In these two important ways
Gone with the Wind is a text that recognizes the uneasy relationship between
elements of progress and civilization but ultimately confirms a future that
must inevitably bind the two. For my purposes here, however, what is most
important is that Mitchell's fears of a mass democracy are condensed into
her representations of the newly emancipated black folk.

The postwar chapters of *Gone with the Wind* are filled with long passages
that describe in horrified terms mass assemblies of black people on the
streets of Atlanta. Mitchell represents emancipation as chaos, and blacks
uncontrolled by white people as the force with the potential to destroy
civilization. What Mitchell describes as the class system that structured
black people into house servants and field hands before the war is turned
upside down; "the lowest and most ignorant ones were on the top." What
Mitchell fears are the "hordes of 'trashy free issue niggers' who like monkeys
or small children turned loose among treasured objects . . . ran wild."
Atlanta's streets are crowded with black people who are "lazy and dangerous"; the refusal to work is a threat to the future prosperity and growth of
the city; and uncontrolled black male sexuality, a threat to all white
womanhood. If uncontrolled or "free" blacks are the mass threat to civilization, what can preserve civilization is perpetual slavery. Mitchell's black folk
figures who are individually characterized are all personal servants devoted
to their mistresses. In the antebellum chapters they are of course slaves, but
the material conditions of this relation to the white people for whom they
work do not change: after emancipation they remain virtually slaves. While
most of *Gone with the Wind* is concerned with the representation of massive

social upheaval and turmoil – out of the ashes of one civilization has to rise another – both civilizations must be based on an ideology of black people bound to this form of servility. As Mitchell writes, the "better class" of blacks "scorn[ed] freedom," "loyal field hands . . . refused to avail themselves of the new freedom," and "abandoned negro children" were taken by "kind-hearted white people . . . into their kitchens to raise."[18]

It is crucially important to consider *Gone with the Wind* because as a novel and as a film it has become the dominant mass cultural mythology of the formation of the rural black folk. The novel was published in 1936 and the movie premièred in 1939. The titles that open the film establish the same conditions for black people as the novel: there are no "slaves" who are named such because all black characters are listed under the headings "The House Servants" and "In the Fields." Yet the film confirms the fact that all the major black characters are slaves, and they remain in the same social position after "emancipation." But the Hollywood version of the tale rewrites Mitchell's vision in some respects. First, there is no forceful presence of massed blacks about to destroy the very basis of civilization. Clearly this is a concession to the growing effectiveness of black pressure groups in the Hollywood of the thirties. Second, there is the presence of Hattie McDaniel. McDaniel's performance is important because she rewrites in terms of visual imaging Mitchell's main literary black folk/slave figure and occasionally breaks through the limits of the cinematic black folk/slave figure written by the Hollywood scriptwriters. Hattie McDaniel contests for the first time in a product of American mass culture the literary source of the archetypal slave figure, the "Mammy." In this respect it is crucial to be aware of the engagement of the literary with a wider cultural imagination, for McDaniel manages to reconstruct for mass consumption a product of the literary imagination.

Near the beginning of the film is a scene that illustrates the possibilities and limits of McDaniel's contestation of the figure of the "Mammy." In preparation for a ball, Hattie McDaniel dresses a willful Vivian Leigh. Whether "Mammy" can also persuade "Scarlett" to eat before the party and thus preserve the appearance of a birdlike appetite in public, which convention requires of a lady, provides the occasion for a confrontation between them in which the full range of the stereotypical behavior of the "Mammy" figure is mobilized. McDaniel cajoles, bullies and wheedles. But, at the climactic moment of the scene, the contradiction between the Hollywood construction of the black woman as "Mammy," and McDaniel's performance, is clear. In her face the audience recognizes not only the fictional triumph of "Mammy" over the willful mistress but the triumph of McDaniel as an actress over the limitations of her role. For one brief moment the text cannot contain the implications of McDaniel's expression of complete disdain, and expected filmic and social meanings are disrupted for the spectator. Perhaps the most enduring of the literary conventions of slavery to have emerged from the plantation novels, the "Mammy" figure becomes in McDaniel's performance a contradictory space through subtle changes of facial expression and body movement. Her performance reveals the ideological contradictions of both Mitchell's ideas of loyal servants who eschew freedom and Selznick's liberal gesture in portraying blacks as peasants rather than as slaves.[19]

Gone with the Wind cements the relation between the literary and filmic imaginations in the twentieth century, and both movie and novel re-create the historical romance of an American slave society. This romanticism, which Lukács describes as "history transformed into a series of moral lessons for the present," re-creates a mythological slave condition, a carefully controlled space for the black folk in the South that resolves the social conflicts arising from black migration to southern cities and to the North in the twenties and thirties.[20]

Margaret Walker's *Jubilee* is in many ways a direct response to this mythology and to the conditions that allowed the mythology to flourish. Though the original source of her tale was in memories and oral culture, Walker transforms these memories through the structure of the social realist novel. One of the most powerful influences on the formal structure of the text was Lukács's *The Historical Novel*. "I have Lukács to thank for an understanding of the popular character of the historical novel," she says. Walker uses the analysis of Lukács to fuse popular memory with her extensive historical research in order to represent the transformations of history as the transformations of popular life.

Walker's social commitment to realism tempers her approach to her folk material. She carefully documented folk sayings, beliefs, songs and folkways for inclusion in her text, but she deliberately avoids a romantic evocation of an undifferentiated rural folk. All her characters, major and minor, are actors in history and, at the same time, are produced and shaped by that history. Walker's main protagonist, Vyry, is described as a product of plantation life and culture who has been "shaped by the forces that dominated her life," forces that limit her vision of the potential for social change. Randall Ware, the man Vyry marries, on the other hand, is a militant. Ware believes in the possibility and, indeed, the inevitability of social transformation; as a member of an artisan class of free laborers, he has a limited amount of freedom to travel and therefore to be active in the underground railroad. Vyry wants freedom, but she finds it hard at first to believe in, and then to imagine, its possibilities; Ware determines that escape from the South is a political necessity to continue an effective fight against slavery once civil war seems inevitable. Both see their children as the future. Ware insists that the children must be left behind; Vyry cannot do that, tries to escape with them, and is caught and returned to the plantation for a brutal whipping. Vyry and Ware, permanently separated, come to represent two opposing responses to the Civil War and reconstruction. Because of her particular slave experience Vyry searches for a home that is secure from white terrorists and for work that will make her a valuable resource for a white community and thus secure for her and her children a degree of protection. Ware, more aggressive, is dissatisfied with any compromise on his freedom. But both survive to shape different communal responses to an oppressive white society. Though I have described only two of Walker's folk, their position as the bearers and shapers of history is characteristic of the whole text. Walker's ideology of a black folk forged from the social system of slavery is a fictional representation of Lukács's formulation of historical necessity. Historical necessity, he argues, "is no other-worldly fate divorced from men; it is the complex interaction of concrete historical circumstances in their process of transformation, in their interaction with the concrete human beings, who have grown up in these circumstances, have been variously influenced by them, and who act in an individual way according to personal passions."[21]

Hortense Spillers has characterized *Jubilee* as "theonomous," a novel that is "not only historical but also, and primarily, Historical. . . . a metaphor for the unfolding of the Divine Will." In consequence, Spillers asserts, "agents (or characters) are moving and are moved under the aegis of a Higher and Hidden Authority." The "heroic as transparent prophetic utterance" becomes the "privileged center of human response."

> If Walker's characters are ultimately seen as one-dimensional, either good or bad, speaking in a public rhetoric that assumes the heroic or its opposite, then such portrayal is apt to a fiction whose value is subsumed in a theonomous frame of moral reference. From this angle of advocacy and preservation the writer does not penetrate the core of experience, but encircles it. The heroic intention has no interest in fluctuations or transformations or palpitations of conscience . . . but monumentality, or fixedness, becomes its striving. Destiny is disclosed to the hero or the heroine as an already-fixed and named event, and this steady reference point is the secret of permanence.

Spillers concludes that the characters "embody historical symbols – a captive class and their captors," and that these symbols have been encoded into actors in a future, making them "types or valences," masks through which they speak. The characters in this "theonomous view of human reality . . . are overdrawn . . . their compelling agency and motivation are ahistorical, despite the novel's solid historical grounding."[22]

These are important criticisms that point to the limits of historical possibility represented in the text, especially in relation to Vyry. Vyry's inability to imagine freedom is compounded by her reluctance to attempt an escape without her children. While she hesitates by her cabin door, her toddler wakes and asks where she is going. Vyry's reply "Nowhere" is not just a mother's reassurance to a child but also foreshadows her abortive attempt to run. Spillers interprets Vyry's journey into the swamp carrying a baby and dragging a toddler as the replication of the "paralysis of nightmare," the articulation of which "dictates the crucial psychological boundaries of *Jubilee* and decides, accordingly, the aesthetic rule."[23]

But Vyry's dilemma is not merely discursive. The psychological and aesthetic boundaries are shaped by two histories: a fictional reconstruction of the eve of the Civil War and the moment of the cultural production of the text. As historical agent, Vyry acts within the conventional parameters of woman as mother. The presence of children in slave narratives made the slave woman's relation to escape more complex than that of slave men.[24] Walker is clearly historicizing the contradiction for slave women between being a "good" mother and being free. However, Spillers's critical charges accurately describe the paucity of imaginative possibilities. As *Jubilee* entered the cultural conditions of 1966, it offered a severely limited historical, psychological and aesthetic vision of the possibilities of a free black community. Vyry's search for security becomes synonymous with dependence on white patronage.

However, Walker's rewriting of a folk ideology appeared to speak directly to the social transformations of the sixties while, at the same time, it was rooted in her response to the thirties and proletarian literature. Walker's political consciousness was shaped in the thirties when she worked for the Works Progress Administration (WPA) and wrote about black migrants to the south side of Chicago. She worked on a novel about a Chicago ghetto called *Goose Island* for a couple of years, but it was never published.[25] In the many years it took to write *Jubilee* sporadically between the thirties and the sixties Walker remained committed to "showing the interrelationships of class as well as race and . . . how these interrelationships shape the political, economic, and social structure in the entire panorama of the novel."[26] Walker's representation of slavery is her philosophy of history, which is to be understood as the necessary prehistory of contemporary society. The Civil War, she argues, was a bloody revolution, an inevitable and "irrepressible conflict brought on by great economic, political, and social forces of change." The promise of liberty and freedom she views as being defeated by "a white Southern counter-revolution" in which black people remained as pawns, "a sub-culture unrecognized by the dominant culture."[27]

A very different appropriation of slave history was made by Arna Bontemps in *Black Thunder*, published the same year as *Gone with the Wind* (1936) and reprinted in 1968 as the American culture industry rediscovered the 1930s. In particular, "the literary marketplace . . . rediscover[ed] novels virtually unread and critically ignored in the period and now hailed as significant."[28] In his 1968 introduction to this fictional reconstruction of the revolt of Gabriel Prosser in Virginia in 1800, Bontemps wonders if a story of "black self-assertion," of "volcanic rumblings among angry blacks," would find a more understanding audience after the death of Martin Luther King and after the Watts rebellion.[29] But if the late sixties appeared ready for the distribution of a literary black revolution, Bontemps wrote *Black Thunder* at a moment when rebellion against oppression seemed imminent. Two stories "dominated the news" and the "daydreams of the people" that he met, he recounts, "the demonstrations of Mahatma Gandhi and his followers in India and the trials of the Scottsboro boys."[30] In this atmosphere of "bleak hostility" Bontemps visited Fisk University and discovered "a larger collection of slave narratives than I knew existed."[31] Out of his reading of these slave narratives came *Black Thunder*.

Bontemps's novel also prefigures African American historiography in the late sixties and seventies, which would focus on the slave through slave testimony. What Bontemps called his "frantic" reading of slave narratives for a historical novel was not the central concern of African American historians for another thirty years, when a "concern for demonstrating the nature and strengths of black culture became an important aspect of research dealing with black America."[32] The Slave Narrative Collection was compiled by the WPA between 1936 and 1938, but interviews with ex-slaves were collected during the twenties and kept at Fisk, and Bontemps must have read some of them. The narratives from interviews contain much more of the "informal folk aspects of [the] daily round of slave life" that, Norman Yetman has argued, make these narratives very different from the "highly formalized, even stylized" structure of the antebellum slave narratives now considered canonic.[33]

African American historians are divided about the merits of using either the informal interviews or the antebellum narratives. In the sixties, Bontemps edited a collection of the latter, but *Black Thunder* certainly appears to have been influenced by these less formal interviews. The novel recreates in the daily round of slave life a black culture that existed as a space away from the control of whites.

The approach of literary critics to the antebellum narratives has been rather different from that of the historians. Contemporary critics see the struggle to attain literacy in the antebellum narratives as a means of asserting humanity. But in *Black Thunder* Bontemps uses literacy as a means by which his characters realize the necessity of revolution. "Reading's bad for a nigger. You just reads and you reads and pretty soon you sees where it say, Brother, come and unite with us and let us combat for a common good; then you is plum done for. You ain't no mo' count for bowing and scraping and licking boots. Oh, it's bad when niggers get to holding out they arms, touching hands, saying Brother this, Brother that, they is about to meet the whirlwind then."[34] Bontemps's slave folk are like Richard Wright's rebellious peasantry but they are also represented as having a community and culture that is a source for their group resistance. It was not until the 1970s that African American historiography applied the same analysis to the ways in which the black community sustained itself under the slave system.

The novel is the history of a community of black people inspired by the successful revolution in San Domingo (Haiti) led by Toussaint L'Ouverture. A group of both slave and free blacks is represented as influenced by Jacobinism and, more important, by a reinterpretation of the Bible by those in the group who can read. "God don't like ugly" and "God's against them what oppresses the po'" are phrases constantly repeated throughout the narrative to authenticate the justice of revolutionary action and the right to seek revenge against oppression.

In a review of *Black Thunder*, Richard Wright asserted that the novel was the only one he knew "dealing forthrightly with the historical and revolutionary traditions of the Negro people," and he praised Bontemps for the creation of a protagonist who displayed "a quality of folk courage unparalleled in the proletarian literature of this country."[35] The recovery of revolutionary traditions not only was the concern of proletarian literature but was echoed in black historiography during the thirties. During this period – the Depression decade – the first substantial studies of slave rebellions were produced. Responding to black colonial oppression in ways similar to Bontemps's work, C.L.R. James's epic history *The Black Jacobins* was published in 1938, and in the following year the first version of Herbert Aptheker's pathbreaking *Negro Slave Revolts* was issued.[36]

James's narrative of the revolution of Toussaint L'Ouverture was written in direct response to representations of people of African descent "constantly being the object of other people's exploitation and ferocity." Instead, James portrayed black people "taking action on a grand scale and shaping other people to their own needs."[37] Aptheker's introduction to *Negro Slave Revolts* reflects his awareness of the ways in which historians' recreations of the past are directly engaged with other cultural representations of history. He wrote to revise a history that was a "wholly erroneous conception of life in the old South" which dominated "movies and novels and textbooks [and was] invented by the slaveholders themselves."[38] Like Aptheker and James, Bontemps made a claim to a revolutionary black tradition that directly opposed the historiography of Ulrich Bonnell Phillips in *Life and Labor in the Old South*, an interpretation of plantation life generally considered to be a definitive history and embodied in Mitchell's *Gone with the Wind*.[39] Like Mitchell, Phillips was a Georgian who also referenced a popular memory of an idyllic South.[40]

In formal terms, a narrative of slavery has three conventional conclusions: escape, emancipation or death. Antebellum slave narratives conventionally ended with escape to the North. In historical sagas like *Jubilee*, emancipation is central. In novels based on rebellions, death is the conclusion. In three contemporary novels of slavery these conventions are rewritten. In Ishmael Reed's *Flight to Canada*, a postmodernist revision of the antebellum slave narrative and a novelistic representation of intertextuality, the escaped slave, Raven, returns to the plantation from Canada. In Sherley Anne Williams's *Dessa Rose*, slaves escape not to the North but to the West. In perhaps the most interesting revision of the form of the historical novel, David Bradley's *The Chaneysville Incident*, escape leads to death, and death itself is also a form of escape.[41]

Black Thunder opens with the testimony of a planter who recounts the discovery of a planned insurrection of over eleven hundred slaves to the Virginia Court in September 1800, "a testimony that caused half the states to shudder." It concludes with a vision of "Gabriel's shining body [and the] arc inscribed by the executioner's ax." Death awaits not only the revolutionary heroes but also the traitors. Ben Sheppard, a slave who betrays the planned revolution to the authorities, turns from looking at the execution block to the scene of Gabriel's lover being sold on the auction block and knows that in every hedge there are knives waiting for him.[42] Death is not just a risk in the cause of freedom but is preferable to slavery. " 'A wild bird what's in a cage will die anyhow, sooner or later,' Gabriel said. 'He'll pine hisself to death. He just is well to break his neck trying to get out.' "[43]

Death, in a narrative of slave rebellion, offers a figure of future revolution. Narratives of escape are usually organized as individual biographies; they are unlike the narratives of sharecropping, which are usually family stories. The historical novel that uses emancipation is bound by history in a particular way – emancipation is final and the narrative has to move on in history. But a narrative of slave rebellion can be read as a figure for the revolutionary change that has not come. James, in the context of colonial politics, and Bontemps, in the context of American oppression, were representing the collective acts of a black community as signs for future collective acts of rebellion and liberation.

The critically neglected novels of Walker and Bontemps challenge ideologies of a romantic rural folk tradition. Both writers worked for the WPA Illinois Project and were closely involved with the migrants who came to form the black urban community in Chicago in the thirties. Walker's poetry in her collection *For My People* and Bontemps's collaboration with Jack Conroy on *They Seek a City* link them to traditions of proletarian literature and to the neglected tradition of African American urban writing as embodied in the work of Wright, Gwendolyn Brooks and Ann Petry. Zora Neale Hurston, on the other hand, worked for the WPA on the Florida Project. With her anthropological training, she concentrated her literary imagination on evoking a folk past that displaced the context of the rural/urban confrontation in which she wrote. Contemporary critical theory, it seems to me, has likewise produced a discourse that romanticizes the folk roots of African American culture and denies the transformative power of both historical and urban consciousness.

1988

Notes

1. Charles Davis and Henry Louis Gates, Jr, eds, *The Slave's Narrative*, New York: Oxford University Press, 1985, p. xiii.
2. Ibid., p. xxxiii.

3. Pauline Hopkins, *Contending Forces*, Boston: Colored Co-operative Publishing Co., 1900.

4. W.E.B. Du Bois, *The Souls of Black Folk*, Chicago: A.C. McClurg, 1903. This argument could also apply to the early chapters of Du Bois's first novel, *The Quest of the Silver Fleece*, 1911; reprint, New York: Arno Press, 1969, and to the figure of Janie's grandmother in Zora Neale Hurston's *Their Eyes Were Watching God*, Philadelphia: J.B. Lippincott, 1937.

5. Houston A. Baker, Jr, *Blues, Ideology, and Afro-American Literature*, Chicago: University of Chicago Press, 1984, pp. 4, 8–9.

6. Hurston, *Their Eyes Were Watching God*, pp. 31–7.

7. Charles H. Nichols, ed., *Arna Bontemps–Langston Hughes Letters, 1925–1967*, New York: Dodd, Mead, 1980, pp. 31, 44, 111, 128; Richard Wright, "Between Laughter and Tears," *New Masses*, no. 25, October 5 1937, pp. 22–5. See also Mary Helen Washington, " 'I Love the Way Janie Crawford Left Her Husbands': Zora Neale Hurston's Emergent Female Hero," in her *Invented Lives: Narratives of Black Women, 1860–1960*, Garden City, NY: Anchor Press, 1987, pp. 237–54.

8. Baker, *Blues, Ideology*, pp. 172–99.

9. Arna Bontemps, *Black Thunder*, 1936; reprint, Boston: Beacon Press, 1968; Margaret Walker, *Jubilee*, New York: Bantam, 1966. I make no reference to the following popular novels of slavery: Alex Haley's *Roots*, Frank Yerby's antebellum novels, and the Falconhurst sex and slavery series written by Kyle Onstott, Lance Horner and Harry Whittington, the best known of which is probably Onstott's *Mandingo*. See Frank Yerby, *The Foxes of Harrow*, New York: Dial Press, 1946, his first and most popular antebellum novel; Alex Haley, *Roots*, Garden City, NY: Doubleday, 1976; Kyle Onstott, *Mandingo*, 1957; reprint, Greenwich, CT: Fawcett Publications, 1963.

10. Warren I. Susman, *Culture as History*, New York: Pantheon, 1984, p. 151.

11. My theoretical perspective is influenced by Georg Lukács, *The Historical Novel*, London: Merlin Press, 1962.

12. Institute for the Black World, "Afterword," in Margaret Walker, *How I Wrote Jubilee*, Chicago: Third World Press, 1977, p. 29.

13. Ibid.

14. Ibid., pp. 11–12.

15. Richard Harwell, ed., *Margaret Mitchell's Gone with the Wind: Letters, 1936–1949*, New York: Macmillan, 1976, p. 13.

16. Lukács, *The Historical Novel*, p. 84.

17. Susman, *Culture as History*, pp. 106–7.

18. Margaret Mitchell, *Gone with the Wind*, London: Pan Books, 1974, pp. 638–9.

19. For an account of the reactions to McDaniel's performance, see Thomas Cripps, *Slow Fade to Black: The Negro in American Film, 1900–1942*, New York: Oxford University Press, 1977, pp. 359–66.

20 Lukács, *The Historical Novel*, p. 77.

21. Ibid., p. 58.

22. See Hortense J. Spillers, "A Hateful Passion, A Lost Love," *Feminist Studies*, no. 9, Summer 1983, pp. 293–323. This particular discussion of *Jubilee* is from pp. 298–305.

23. Ibid., p. 304.

24. See Harriet Jacobs, *Incidents in the Life of a Slave Girl*, ed. Jean Yellin, Cambridge, MA: Harvard University Press, 1987.

25. See Jerre Mangione, *The Dream and the Deal: The Federal Writers' Project, 1935–1943*, New York: Avon Books, 1972, p. 124.
26. Walker, *How I Wrote Jubilee*, p. 27.
27. Ibid., p. 26.
28. Susman, *Culture as History*, p. 152.
29. Bontemps, *Black Thunder*, pp. viii, ix, xv.
30. Ibid., pp. x–xi.
31. Ibid., p. xii.
32. Norman R. Yetman, "Ex-slave Interviews and the Historiography of Slavery," *American Quarterly*, no. 36, Summer 1984, p. 193.
33. Ibid., p. 195.
34. Bontemps, *Black Thunder*, pp. 148–9.
35. Richard Wright, "A Tale of Folk Courage," *Partisan Review and Anvil*, April 1936, p. 31.
36. C.L.R. James, *The Black Jacobins: Toussaint L'Ouverture and the San Domingo Revolution*, 1938; reprint, London: Allison & Busby, 1980; Herbert Aptheker, *Negro Slave Revolts in the United States, 1526–1860*, New York: International Publishers, 1939. Other revisionist histories published at this time include W.E.B. Du Bois's *Black Reconstruction*, in 1935; Bell Wiley's *Southern Negroes, 1861–1865*, Aptheker's *The Negro in the Civil War* and Joseph Cephas Carroll's *Slave Insurrections in the United States, 1800–1865*, in 1938; and Harvey Wish's "Slave Disloyalty Under the Confederacy," published in the *Journal of Negro History* in October 1938.
37. James, *The Black Jacobins*, p. v.
38. Aptheker, *Negro Slave Revolts*, p. 3.
39. Ulrich Bonnell Phillips, *Life and Labor in the Old South*, Boston: Little, Brown, 1929.
40. See William Van DeBurg, *Slavery and Race in American Popular Culture*, Madison: University of Wisconsin Press, 1984, pp. 82–5.
41. Ishmael Reed, *Flight to Canada*, New York: Avon Books, 1976; Sherley Anne Williams, *Dessa Rose*, New York: William Morrow, 1986; David Bradley, *The Chaneysville Incident*, New York: Avon Books, 1981. I would also argue that Toni Morrison's *Beloved* is a remarkable exploration and revisioning of the limits of conventional historical narrative strategies for representing slavery.
42. Bontemps, *Black Thunder*, pp. 9, 224.
43. Ibid., p. 69.

On Zora Neale Hurston's
Seraph on the Suwanee

On April 15 1947, Zora Neale Hurston signed a contract with the publishing house of Charles Scribner & Sons for a novel concerned with life in Florida and entitled *The Sign of the Sun*. She had finally decided to leave J.B. Lippincott, the publisher of all her previous books, because the company had firmly dismissed her last two projects. Hurston had become disillusioned after Lippincott turned down her proposal for a novel about the black middle class, and she was openly depressed when it subsequently rejected a manuscript set in Eatonville, the town in which Hurston had grown up and which had provided such rich source material for the writing of *Mules and Men* and *Their Eyes Were Watching God*. Hurston felt that the new contract promised a new beginning. The obvious enthusiasm of the Scribner editors for her new novel about a southern white family renewed her confidence in herself, and the $500 advance enabled Hurston, at last, to finance the trip to Honduras that she had been planning for two years. She left in May and settled into the Hotel Cosenza, in Puerto Cortés on the north coast of Honduras, to write her novel and to plan an expedition into the mountains. As Hurston described this expedition to her editor at Scribner, Burroughs Mitchell, she hoped "to find a lost city ... which travellers have heard about for two hundred years, but has not as yet been seen."[1] Hurston wanted her novel to be "good" so she could finance the journey that she felt was "burning [her] soul to attack."[2]

Between May and November Hurston wrote and revised the novel for which, at various times, she had a number of titles, including *Sang the Suwaanee in the Spring, The Queen of the Golden Hand, Angel in the Bed, Lady Angel with Her Man, Seraph with a Man on Hand, So Said the Sea, Good Morning Sun* and *Seraph on the Suwanee River*. In January 1948, after three months of editorial hesitation, Scribner finally decided to go ahead with the book and asked Hurston to come to New York to work on more revisions. Her dreams of the lost city were left behind when she returned to a cold New York in February 1948. Worried that she had "been in the bush so many months," Hurston warned Burroughs Mitchell "you might have to run me down and catch me and sort of tie me up in the shed until I get house-broke again."[3]

Hurston aimed to make *Seraph on the Suwanee* "a true picture of the South." She was delighted that Burroughs Mitchell was impressed with her use of southern vernacular and idiom. In her previous novels and in the collection of folklore, *Mules and Men*, Hurston had established a reputation for her representation of black language and rhythms of speech. Though contemporary critics of Hurston's work have granted her a privileged position in the African American literary canon because of her sensitive delineation of black folk culture and black folk consciousness, particularly through language, Hurston's own views are more complex and controversial. In writing about *Seraph on the Suwanee*, Hurston repudiated theories of the uniqueness of black linguistic structures.

> I think that it should be pointed out that what is known as Negro dialect in the South is no such thing. Bear in mind that the South is the purest English section of the United States. . . . What is actually the truth is, that the South, up until the 1930's was a relic of England. . . . and you find the retention of old English beliefs and customs, songs and ballads and Elizabethan figures of speech. They go for the simile and especially the metaphor. As in the bloom of Elizabethan literature, they love speech for the sake of speech. This is common to white and black. The invective is practiced as a folk art from earliest childhood. You have observed that when a southern Senator or Representative gets the floor, no Yankee can stand up to him so far as compelling language goes. . . . They did *not* get it from the Negroes. The Africans coming to America got it from them. If it were African, then why is it not in evidence among all Negroes in the western world? No, the agrarian system stabilized in the South by slavery slowed down change . . . and so the tendency to colorful language that characterized Shakespeare and his contemporaries and made possible the beautiful and poetic language of the King James Bible got left over to an extent in the rural South.[4]

Hurston's opinions of the formative influences acting on the linguistic structures of the black folk may cause some discomfort to critics who valorize Hurston for preserving and reproducing in her work cultural forms that they argue are essentially and uniquely black. In *Seraph on the Suwanee* there are many phrases and sentences that evoke the language of Hurston's black figures in her previous work. Occasionally, the language is identical – whole phrases are lifted from the mouth of a black character in an earlier novel and inserted into the mouth of a member of the white Meserve family. The rhythm and syntax of Hurston's black folk haunt the reader throughout the novel.

Moreover, Hurston was concerned with establishing more than linguistic similarities between white and black in the South; she was actively trying to demonstrate her ideas of cultural influence and fusion in her novel. Kenny Meserve, the second son of Jim and Arvay Meserve, is trained as a musician by black Joe Kelsey. Hurston wrote a chapter, which the publisher later removed, on Kenny's success in New York, to explain this cultural exchange:

> I felt I had to add a chapter on Kenny in New York to explain his success. Though no one to my knowledge has come right out and said it yet, we have had a revolution in national expression in music that is equivalent to Chaucer's use of the native idiom in England. Gershwin's *Porgy and Bess* brought to a head that which had been in the making for at least a decade. There is no more Negro music in the U.S. It has been fused and merged and become the national expression, and displaced the worship of European expression. In fact, it is now denied, (and with some truth) that it never was pure Negro music, but an adaptation of white music. . . . But the fact remains that what has evolved here is something American.[5]

As a white musician playing black music, Kenny was intended to represent Hurston's conviction that black music was no longer an expression of black culture but had become a form of national expression.

However, *Seraph on the Suwanee* is not just a vehicle for Hurston's theories of the relation between black and white culture. The novel was also an attempt to realize two ambitions that she had been working toward throughout the forties. Hurston wanted to sell a novel to Hollywood and to see her fiction transformed into film. In 1942 she felt optimistic. "I have a tiny wedge in Hollywood," she wrote with excitement in a letter to Carl Van Vechten, a patron of black art and black artists; she went on to tell him that she had joined the Paramount writing staff. But in 1947 Scribner tried and failed to interest Metro-Goldwyn-Mayer Pictures in the novel.

Hurston's second ambition involved a challenge to the literary conventions of the apartheid American society in which Hurston lived – conventions she felt dictated that black writers and artists should be concerned only with representing black subjects. In the same letter she described how she had "hopes of breaking that old silly rule about Negroes not writing about white people."[6] In the postwar 1940s Hurston was not the only black artist to confront the question of whether a racial art was also a segregated art, an art confined permanently within the limits of differences. For all black people, the Second World War embodied the acute contradictions in mobilizing against the ideology of fascism abroad, on the one hand, and, on the other, living with the fascist practices of racism and segregation at home. For many it was an unresolved question of whether being an American and being a Negro were compatible or incompatible categories. For intellectuals, making a decision "whether it was better to be a 'Negro Artist' and develop a racial art or to be an American artist who was a Negro" was complex and contradictory.[7] In literature these tensions are present in the conscious decisions made by some black writers to write for white magazines or to create white subjects in their fiction.

In the nine years between the publication of *Moses, Man of the Mountain* in 1939 and *Seraph on the Suwanee* Hurston concentrated her energies on writing nonfiction for white audiences. Her autobiography, *Dust Tracks on a Road*, was published in 1942 and won the Ainsfield–Wolf Award, sponsored by the *Saturday Review*, for its contribution to "the field of race relations." Throughout the forties Hurston was a regular contributor of essays and reviews to magazines with a predominantly white readership. Of course she ran the risk of being positioned by these magazines as a "representative Negro" expressing "representative opinions," and she also invited, and received, heavy criticism from other black intellectuals for ignoring serious aspects of black life in order to pander to a white readership. But despite the risks and the controversy that her articles generated, Hurston seems to have sought and enjoyed her position as a conservative black spokesperson.[8]

However, it is important to remember that Hurston was not alone in her direct engagement with a white readership. Some magazines, like the *Saturday Evening Post*, regularly published work from a variety of black writers, and a significant number of black novelists, including Hurston, eventually published postwar novels about white characters. In 1947, Ann Petry published *Country Place* and Willard Motley published *Knock on Any Door*. Between 1946 and 1950 Frank Yerby published five novels aimed at a mass-market audience: *The Foxes of Harrow*, *The Vixens*, *Pride's Castle*, *The Golden Hawk* and *Floodtide*. In 1954 Richard Wright published his controversial novel *Savage Holiday*.[9] White reviewers and critics often condemned black novels about black subjects for being narrowly conceived, for being overly political, and for being didactic. The term "protest fiction" was frequently used to describe novels by and about black people in order to suggest that somehow the practice of art had been compromised, if not contaminated, by the presence of political and ideological issues. The phrase "protest fiction" implied that fiction that was uncritical of the racialized structures of subordination at work in society somehow expressed universal, not partisan, values. When black authors created white characters in novels that were apparently not about racism or the suffering that resulted from a racist society, reviewers indirectly expressed their relief. A reviewer of *Country Place* in the *Atlantic Monthly* was glad that the novel "preaches no sermons, [and] waves no flags."[10] In the paperback edition of Petry's novel, the publishers inserted a page entitled "About This Book" which explained that taking "the folksy, nostalgic front off 'Our Town'" was "a much more difficult task" than dealing with "the life of the Negro in our big Northern cities," the subject of Petry's first novel, *The Street*. Potential readers could safely retain their political illusions about the existence of democracy, for they were assured that Ann Petry was "a powerful American writer, unhampered by any one theme or hobby horse."[11] Writing about white people was thought by many white critics, reviewers and publishers to require more literary skill, and more talent, than writing about black characters. In addition, being an author of a white novel could apparently resolve the contradiction of being both black and American.

Seraph on the Suwanee, a novel of a poor white family in Florida that gradually achieves upward economic and class mobility, was published in October 1948.[12] Reviews on the whole were favorable if not overly enthusiastic, but Scribner was unable to interest any book clubs in the novel's distribution. The initial sales of *Seraph on the Suwanee* were good, about three thousand in the first few weeks of publication, and because of the favorable reviews, Scribner ordered another two thousand to be printed. But the events that created controversy around the novel and shattered Hurston's optimism had nothing to do with the fact that Hurston was black and her characters white. On September 13, Hurston had been arrested on charges rising from allegations of sexual misconduct with a ten-year-old boy. She emphatically denied all charges, using her passport as evidence that she had been in Honduras at the time the immoral acts were supposed to have taken place. It must have absolutely astounded Hurston that *Seraph on the Suwanee* could become a tool in the publicity that was eventually generated from the allegations against her. On October 23 the national edition of the Baltimore *Afro-American* published a distorted and inaccurate version of the original allegations (allegations that were eventually proved to be totally false) under the banner headlines "Did She Want 'Knowing and Doing' Kind of Love?" and "Boys, 10, Accuse Zora." Above the article itself ran the two headlines "Novelist Arrested on Morals Charge," "Reviewer of Author's Latest Book Notes Character Is 'Hungry for Love.'" The story was salacious: it suggested that *Seraph on the Suwanee* advocated sexual aggressiveness in women and then used selected sentences from the novel as if they provided evidence of the author's immorality. Hurston's exploration of the sexual expectations and repressions of the novel's protagonists became, in the hands of the Baltimore *Afro-American*, the means for crucifying her. She was literally tried and found guilty in the widely syndicated story and in a subsequent editorial, which appeared in the November 6 *Afro-American*, in which the paper defended itself against criticism of the front-page publicity granted to the case by arguing that "a hush-hush attitude about perversion has permitted this menace to increase."[13]

Charges against Hurston were not dismissed until March 14 1949, and by then, as Robert Hemenway has argued, "the damage had been done."[14] Hurston felt betrayed by a fellow black person, a court reporter who had originally leaked the story to the press, and by a black newspaper that she referred to as "the *Afro-American* sluice of filth." This sense of betrayal led Hurston to contemplate and threaten suicide in a letter that she wrote to Carl and Fania Van Vechten:

> All that I have ever tried to do has proved useless. All that I have believed in has failed me. I have resolved to die. It will take a few days for me to set my affairs in order, and then I will go . . . no acquittal will persuade some people that I am innocent. I feel hurled down a filthy privy hole.[15]

The letter seems to have been written as much from a feeling of hope that it could generate the assurance and support from friends that she needed as it was from a feeling of fear and despair that no-one believed in her innocence. Hurston must have received the assurance that she sought for she did not kill herself, and she gradually recovered her enthusiasm for living and for writing. But, presumably because of the negative publicity generated by the Baltimore *Afro-American*, Hurston seems to have done little to publicly promote her novel herself. In many ways *Seraph on the Suwanee* was Hurston's most ambitious and most experimental novel to date. But while she regained her confidence and recovered her ambitions for her fiction in the manuscripts of three more novels, *Seraph on the Suwanee* was the last of her novels to be accepted for publication by any publishing house.

The relation between the themes of Petry's *Country Place* and Hurston's *Seraph on the Suwanee* are striking – both concentrate on complex questions of female sexuality and the sometimes violent conflict between men and women that arises from the existence of incompatible and gender-specific desires. Arvay Meserve grows up in a poor family in the turpentine town of Sawley at the turn of the century. As a young woman she is convinced that she isn't important to anyone, and she develops a secret fantasy life in which she feels that she lives in mental adultery with her sister's husband. At twenty-one Arvay turns her back on the "sins of the world," and uses religious devotion as a mask, an escape from the pressures of "spinster-hood" into a space that represents the only legitimate, autonomous exist-ence for a woman. Arvay successfully gets rid of all unwanted suitors by throwing so-called fits until Jim Meserve arrives and refuses to be so easily dismissed. In the first part of the novel, Jim establishes his power over Arvay through two acts of violence. He "cures" her fits by dropping turpentine in her eye and subsequently rapes her under the mulberry tree, a tree that is symbolic of Arvay's innocent childhood. As the novel pro-gresses, the successful gendering of each protagonist is dependent on the other. Arvay becomes "a slave" to her husband, Jim, while Jim measures and defines his masculinity entirely in relation to the extent to which he can take care of a woman. To Jim Meserve, all women are incapable of taking care of themselves, and, as they have no brains, a man, in order to become a true man, has to think for all women in his care. Readers of *Their Eyes Were Watching God* will be reminded of the pompous second husband of Janie, Jody Starks, who asserted that "Somebody got to think for women and chillun and cows," because they couldn't think for them-selves.[16] The difficulty for a feminist reading of *Seraph on the Suwanee* is that Jim Meserve, unlike Jody Starks, does not conveniently die so that his wife can get on with her life. In *Seraph* it is Arvay's expectations and desires that must be transformed to accommodate the demands of her husband.

Nevertheless, the sexual politics of *Seraph on the Suwanee* cannot be easily dismissed. The sexual ambiguity of Jim and Arvay's role is, at times, intriguing. It is clear from Hurston's letters to her editor when she was writing about Arvay's doubts, fears and lack of confidence that she was thinking about the men she had met who had been intimidated in their relationship with a woman who was a success in her own right. In response to her editor's unsympathetic response to the character of Arvay, Hurston admitted that, at times, she got sick of her herself and then she asked:

> Have you ever been tied in close contact with a person who had a strong sense of inferiority? I have and it is hell. . . . I took this man I cared for down to Carl Van Vechten's one night so that he could meet some of my literary friends, since he had complained that I was always off with them, and ignoring him. . . . What happened? He sat off in a corner and gloomed and uglied away, and we were hardly out on the street before he was accusing me of having dragged him down there to show off what a big shot I was and how far I was above him.[17]

Reviewers also became confused about whether Jim or Arvay was the seraph of the title – who exactly was the guardian angel, and whom was the angel looking after? Frank G. Slaughter, in the *New York Times Book Review*, was convinced that Arvay set out to be the *Webster's* definition of a seraph: "One of an order of celestial beings conceived as fiery and purifying ministers of Jehovah." Herschel Brickell, in the *Saturday Review*, argued that it was "the hero, Jim Meserve," who played "the part of a 'fiery and purifying minister of Jehovah,' with sufficient success to make him seraphic."[18]

Arvay's discovery that she needs to be a mother to her husband long after her own children have grown is a vision of female fulfillment that is very different from, and more controversial than, the vision of female autonomy that Hurston created in *Their Eyes Were Watching God*. But it is the very complexity and depth of Arvay's frustrated and unsatisfied desires that make *Seraph on the Suwanee* a very modern text, a text that speaks as eloquently to the contradictions and conflict of trying to live our lives as gendered beings in the 1990s as it did in 1948.

1991

Notes

1. Zora Neale Hurston to Burroughs Mitchell, September 3 1947, Charles Scribner's Sons Archives, Author's File 3, Department of Rare Books and Special Collections, Princeton University Libraries. I would like to thank Princeton University Libraries for permission to quote from the unpublished correspondence in this collection and to thank the library staff for their invaluable assistance.
2. Zora Neale Hurston to Burroughs Mitchell, July 31 1947, ibid.
3. Zora Neale Hurston to Burroughs Mitchell, February 14 [1948], ibid.
4. Zora Neale Hurston to Burroughs Mitchell, October 2 1947, ibid.
5. Zora Neale Hurston to Burroughs Mitchell, October, "Something Late," 1947, ibid.

6. Zora Neale Hurston to Carl Van Vechten, November 2 1942, Carl Van Vechten Papers, James Weldon Johnson Memorial Collection, Beinecke Rare Book and Manuscript Library, Yale University. I would like to thank the Beinecke Library for permission to quote from personal correspondence and to acknowledge the invaluable assistance of the library staff.

7. See Ann Gibson, "Norman Lewis in the Forties," in *Norman Lewis: From the Harlem Renaissance to Abstraction*, May 10 1989–June 25 1989, New York: Kenkeleba Gallery, 1989, pp. 9–23. Gibson argues, convincingly, that a number of black artists in the forties, including Romare Bearden, Harlan Jackson, Ronald Joseph, Norman Lewis and Hale Woodruff, "decided it was better to be an American artist who was a Negro."

8. Robert E. Hemenway, "Ambiguities of Self, Politics of Race," in *Zora Neale Hurston: A Literary Biography*, Urbana: University of Illinois Press, 1977, Chapter 11, particularly pp. 288–9.

9. Willard Motley, *Knock on Any Door*, New York: D. Appleton-Century Company, 1947; Ann Petry, *Country Place*, New York: Houghton Mifflin, 1947; Frank Yerby, *The Foxes of Harrow*, New York: Dial Press, 1946; *The Golden Hawk*, New York: Dial Press, 1947; *The Vixens*, New York: Dial Press, 1948; *Pride's Castle*, New York: Dial Press, 1949; *Floodtide*, New York: Dial Press, 1950; Richard Wright, *Savage Holiday*, New York: Avon, 1954.

10. John Caswell Smith, Jr, review of *Country Place*, *Atlantic Monthly*, November 1947, pp. 178, 180.

11. "About This Book," in Ann Petry, *Country Place*, New York: New American Library, 1949.

12. Zora Neale Hurston, *Seraph on the Suwanee*, 1948; reprint, New York: Harper Perennial, 1991.

13. Press clippings from *Afro-American* (Baltimore), October 23 and November 6 1948; the *Iowa Bystander* (Des Moines), dated October 21 1948; and the *Ohio State News* (Columbus), October 23 1948. The clippings are in the Charles Scribner's Sons Archives, Author's File 3.

14. Hemenway, *Zora Neale Hurston*, p. 320.

15. Zora Neale Hurston to Carl and Fania Van Vechten, n.d., as quoted in ibid., pp. 321–2.

16. Zora Neale Hurston, *Their Eyes Were Watching God*, 1937; reprint, New York: Harper & Row, 1990, pp. 66–7.

17. Zora Neale Hurston to Burroughs Mitchell, October 2 1947, Charles Scribner's Sons Archives, Author's File 3.

18. Frank G. Slaughter, "Freud in Turpentine," *New York Times Book Review*, October 31 1948, p. 48, Herschel Brickell, "A Woman Saved," *The Saturday Review*, November 6 1948, p. 19.

13

The Politics of Fiction,
Anthropology and the Folk:
Zora Neale Hurston

The work of Zora Neale Hurston, in particular the novel *Their Eyes Were Watching God*, has been the object of more than a decade of critical attention. But, in addition to the critical consideration of Hurston's writings, her work has received the level of institutional support necessary for Hurston to enter the American literary mainstream. Two examples of this support would be the special Hurston seminar held at the Modern Language Association annual conference in 1975 and the award of two grants from the National Endowment for the Humanities to Robert Hemenway to write Hurston's biography. Hurston's work has also received institutional support from publishers: the rights to reprint *Their Eyes Were Watching God* in a paperback edition were leased to the University of Illinois Press by Harper & Row, but the 1978 Illinois edition has been so profitable that Harper & Row refused to renew leasing contracts and is reprinting *Their Eyes, Jonah's Gourd Vine, Mules and Men* and *Tell My Horse* itself with Henry Louis Gates as series editor. During the years between Hemenway's biography and the new Harper & Row/Gates monopoly of Hurston, there have been a variety of anthologies and collections of Hurston's essays and short stories, and in 1984, a second edition of Hurston's autobiography, *Dust Tracks on a Road*, was published.

As academics we are well aware that we work within institutions that police the boundaries of cultural acceptability and define what is and what is not "literature": our work as teachers and as critics creates, maintains and sometimes challenges boundaries of acceptability. Graduate students tell me that they teach *Their Eyes Were Watching God* at least once a semester; it is a text that is common to a wide variety of courses in African American Studies, American Studies, English or Women's Studies. It is frequently the case that undergraduates in the humanities may be taught the novel as many as four times, or at least once a year during their undergraduate careers. Traditions, of course, are temporal, and are constantly being fought over and renegotiated. Clearly, a womanist- and feminist-inspired desire to recover the neglected cultural presence of Zora Neale Hurston initiated an interest in her work, but it is also clear that this original motivation has become transformed. Hurston is not only a secured presence in the academy; she is a veritable industry, and an industry that is very profitable. The new Harper & Row edition of *Their Eyes* sold its total print run of 75,000 in less than a month.[1] The *New York Times* of February 4 1990 published an article on Hurston called "Renaissance for a Pioneer of Black Pride" in which it was announced that a play based on Hurston's life and entitled "Zora Neale Hurston: A Theatrical Biography" was opening in New York, and that another play, "Mule Bone," a collaboration with Langston Hughes, is scheduled to open this summer.[2] On February 14 1990, the Public Broadcasting System, in their prestigious American Playhouse series, broadcast "Zora is My Name" starring Ruby Dee in a dramatization of selections from *Mules and Men* and *Dust Tracks*. Although it could be said that Hurston has "arrived" as a contemporary, national, cultural presence, I await one further development: the announcement of a Hollywood movie.

I am as interested in the contemporary cultural process of the inclusion of Hurston into the academy as I am interested in her writing. I wonder about the relation between the cultural meanings of her work in the 1920s and 1930s and the contemporary fascination with Hurston. How is she being reread, now, to produce cultural meanings that this society wants or needs to hear? Is there, indeed, an affinity between the two discrete histories of her work? Certainly, I can see parallels between the situation of black intellectuals in the 1920s and 1930s, described now as a "Renaissance," and the concerns of black humanists in the academy in the 1980s. Literary histories could doubtless be written about a "renaissance" of black intellectual productivity within the walls of the academy in the post-civil rights era of the twentieth century.

Their Eyes Were Watching God now, of course, has a cultural existence outside of the realm of African American Studies and independent of scholars of the field, but how tenuous is this presence? Does the current fascination of the culture industry for the cultural production of black women parallel the white fascination for African American peoples as representatives of the exotic and primitive in the 1920s?[3] And will the current thirst for the cultural production of black women evaporate as easily? Will the economic crisis of the late 1980s and early 1990s be used, in a future literary history, to mark the demise of the black intellectual presence in the academy in the same way as the 1929 stock market crash has been used by literary historians to mark the death of the Harlem Renaissance? If there is a fragile presence of black peoples in universities, is our cultural presence secure or only temporarily profitable? With or without reference to our contemporary economic conditions, it is startlingly obvious that current college enrollment figures reveal a sharp fall in the numbers of black graduate students, figures which would seem to confirm the tenuous nature of our critical presence. But what I find most intriguing is the relation between the crisis of representation that shaped cultural responses to black urban migration after World War I and the contemporary crisis of representation in African American humanist intellectual work that determines our cultural and critical responses, or the lack of response, to the contemporary crisis of black urban America.[4]

However, let me make a theoretical intervention here. Edward Said has asserted that it is "now almost impossible . . . to remember a time when people were *not* talking about a crisis in representation," and he points to the enormous difficulties of uncertainty and undecidability that are a consequence of transformations "in our notions of formerly stable things such as authors, texts and objects."[5] In an attempt to be as specific as I can about the particular crisis of representation in black cultural production out of which, I am going to argue, Hurston's work emerges, I will try to define some terms.

The subaltern group that is the subject of Hurston's anthropological and fictional work is represented as the rural black folk. However, the process of defining and representing a subaltern group is always a contentious issue, and is at the heart of the crisis of representation in black intellectual thought in both historical moments.[6] The dominant way of reading the cultural production of what is called the Harlem Renaissance is that black intellectuals assertively established a folk heritage as the source of, and inspiration for, authentic African American art forms. In African American studies the Harlem Renaissance has become a convention particularly for literary critics, but it is, as is the case with all literary histories, an imagined or created historical perspective that privileges some cultural developments while rendering other cultural and political histories invisible. The dominance of this particular literary history in our work, as opposed to organizing a history around a Chicago Renaissance, for example, has uncritically reproduced at the center of its discourse the issue of an authentic folk heritage. The desire of the Harlem intellectuals to establish and re-present African American cultural authenticity to a predominantly white audience was a mark of a change from, and confrontation with, what were seen by them to be externally imposed cultural representations of black people produced within, and supported by, a racialized social order. However, what was defined as authentic was a debate that was not easily resolved and involved confrontation among black intellectuals themselves. Alain Locke, for example, who attempted to signal a change or a break in conventions of representation by calling his collection of the work of some Harlem intellectuals *The New Negro*, assumed that the work of African American intellectuals would be to raise the culture of the folk to the level of art.[7] Locke's position has been interpreted by contemporary critics as being very different from, if not antagonistic to, the dominant interpretation of the work of Hurston, who is thought to reconcile the division between "high and low culture by becoming Eaton-ville's esthetic representative to the Harlem Renaissance."[8]

In 1934, Hurston published an essay called "Spirituals and Neo-spirituals" in which she argues that there had "never been a presentation of genuine Negro spirituals to any audience anywhere." What was "being sung by the concert artists and glee clubs [were] the works of Negro composers or adaptors *based* on the spirituals."

> Glee clubs and concert singers put on their tuxedos, bow prettily to the audience, get the pitch and burst into magnificent song – but not *Negro* song. . . . let no one imagine that they are the songs of the people, as sung by them.[9]

Hurston was concerned to establish authenticity in the representation of popular forms of folk culture and to expose the disregard for the aesthetics of that culture through inappropriate forms of representation. She had no problem in using the term "the people" to register that she knew just who they were. But critics are incorrect to think that Hurston reconciled "high" and "low" forms of cultural production. Hurston's criticisms were not reserved for the elitist manner in which she thought the authentic culture of the people was reproduced. The people she wanted to represent she defined as a rural folk, and she measured them and their cultural forms against an urban, mass culture. She recognized that the people whose culture she rewrote were not the majority of the population, and that the cultural forms she was most interested in reproducing were not being maintained. She complained bitterly about how "the bulk of the population now spends its leisure in the motion picture theatres or with the phono-graph and its blues." To Hurston, "race records" were nothing more than a commercialization of traditional forms of music, and she wanted nothing more to do with them.[10]

Understanding these *two* aspects of Hurston's theory of folk culture is important. When Hurston complained about the ways in which intellectuals transformed folk culture by reproducing and reinterpreting it as high culture, she identified a class contradiction. Most African American intel-lectuals were generations removed from the "folk" they tried to represent. Their dilemma was little different from debates over proletarian fiction in the Soviet Union, in Europe, in the Caribbean, and in North America generally: debates that raged over the question of how and by whom should "the people," the masses of ordinary people, be portrayed.[11] Hurston identified herself both as an intellectual and as a representative figure from the folk culture she reproduced and made authentic in her work. However, asserting that she *was* both did not resolve the contradictions embedded in the social meanings of each category. When Hurston complained about "race records" and the commercialization of the blues, she failed to apply her own analysis of processes of cultural transformation. On the one hand, she could argue that forms of folk culture were constantly reworked and remade when she stated that "the folk tales" like "the spirituals are being made and forgotten every day."[12] But, on the other hand, Hurston did not take seriously the possibility that African American culture was being transformed as African American peoples migrated from rural to urban areas.

The creation of a discourse of "the folk" as a *rural* people in Hurston's work in the 1920s and 1930s displaces the migration of black people to cities. Her representation of African American culture as primarily rural and oral is Hurston's particular response to the dramatic transformations within black culture. It is these two processes that I am going to refer to as Hurston's discursive displacement of contemporary social crises in her writing. Hurston could not entirely escape the intellectual practice that she so despised, a practice that reinterpreted and redefined a folk consciousness in its own elitist terms. Hurston may not have dressed the spirituals in tuxedos but her attitude toward folk culture was not unmediated; she did have a clear framework of interpretation, a construct that enabled her particular representation of a black, rural consciousness.

Gayatri Spivak has pointed to an important dilemma in the issue of representing the subaltern. She sees "the radical intellectual in the West" as being caught either "in a deliberate choice of subalternity, granting to the oppressed . . . that very expressive subjectivity which s/he criticizes [in a post-structuralist theoretical world]" or, instead she faces the possibility of a total unrepresentability.[13] I don't know if the choice is always as bleak as Spivak claims, or is quite so simple and polarized. Langston Hughes, for example, in his use of the blues to structure poetry, represented a communal sensibility embedded in cultural forms and reproduced social meaning rather than individual subjectivity. In his blues poetry, the reader has access to a social consciousness through the reconstruction and representation of non-literary, contemporary cultural forms that embodied the conditions of social transformation. Hurston, by contrast, assumed that she could obtain access to, and authenticate, an individualized social consciousness through a utopian reconstruction of the historical moment of her childhood in an attempt to stabilize and displace the social contradictions and disruption of her contemporary moment.

The issue of representing the subaltern, then, involves not only the relation of the intellectual to the represented, but also the relation of the intellectual to history. In Hurston's work, the rural black folk become an aesthetic principle, a means by which to embody a rich oral culture. Hurston's representation of the folk is not only a discursive displacement of the historical and cultural transformation of migration, but also a creation of a folk who are outside of history. Hurston aggressively asserted that she was not of the "sobbing school of Negrohood" – in particular, to distinguish her work from that of Richard Wright – but she also places her version of authentic black cultural forms outside of the culture and history of contestation that informs his work. What the *New York Times* has recently called Hurston's "strong African-American sensibility" and is generally agreed to be her positive, holistic celebration of black life, also needs to be seen as a representation of "Negroness" as an unchanging, essential entity, an essence so distilled that it is an aesthetic position of blackness.

Hurston was a central figure in the cultural struggle among black intellectuals to define exactly who the people were who were going to become the representatives of the folk. Langston Hughes shaped his discursive category of the folk in direct response to the social conditions of transformation, including the newly forming urban working class and "socially dispossessed," whereas Hurston constructed a discourse of nostalgia for a rural community.[14] In her autobiographical writings, Hurston referenced the contradictory nature of the response of the black middle class and urban intellectuals to the presence of rural migrants to cities. In an extract written six months after completion of *Their Eyes Were Watching God*, Hurston describes this response:

> Say that a brown young woman, fresh from the classic halls of Barnard College and escorted by a black boy from Yale, enters the subway at 50th Street. They are well-dressed, well-mannered and good to look at . . .
>
> . . . the train pulls into 72nd Street. Two scabby-looking Negroes come scrambling into the coach. . . . but no matter how many vacant seats there are, no other place will do, except side by side with the Yale–Barnard couple. No, indeed! Being dirty and smelly, do they keep quiet otherwise? A thousand times, No! They woof, bookoo, broadcast. . . .
>
> Barnard and Yale sit there and dwindle and dwindle. They do not look around the coach to see what is in the faces of the white passengers. They know well what is there. . . . "That's just like a Negro." Not just like *some* Negroes, mind you, no, like all. Only difference is some Negroes are better dressed. Feeling all of this like rock-salt under the skin, Yale and Barnard shake their heads and moan, "My People, My People!" . . .
>
> Certain of My People have come to dread railway day coaches for this same reason. They dread such scenes more than they do the dirty upholstery and other inconveniences of a Jim Crow coach. They detest the forced grouping. . . . So when sensitive souls are forced to travel that way they sit there numb and when some free soul takes off his shoes and socks, they mutter, "My race but not My taste." When somebody else eats fried fish, bananas, and a mess of peanuts and throws all the leavings on the floor, they gasp, "My skinfolks but not my kinfolks." And sadly over all, they keep sighing, "My People, My People!"[15]

This is a confrontation of class that signifies the division that the writer as intellectual has to recognize and bridge in the process of representing the people. It is a confrontation that was not unique to Hurston as intellectual, but it was one that she chose to displace in her decision to re-create Eatonville as the center of her representation of the rural folk.

The Eatonville of *Their Eyes Were Watching God* occupies a similar imaginative space to the mountain village of Banana Bottom in Claude McKay's novel of the same name published four years earlier.[16] McKay's Jamaican novel, set in the early 1900s, re-creates the village where he grew up. Much of the argument of *Banana Bottom* emerges in the tension between attempts by missionaries to eradicate black cultural forms and the gentler forms of abuse present in white patronage of black culture. Against these forms of exploitation McKay reconstructs black culture as sustaining a whole way of life. But it is a way of life of the past, of his formative years, a place that the intellectual had to leave to become an intellectual and to which he does not return except in this utopian moment. Eatonville, likewise, is the place of Hurston's childhood, a place to which she returns as an anthropologist. As she states in her introduction to *Mules and Men*, she consciously returns to the familiar,[17] and she recognizes that the stories she is going to collect, the ones she heard as a child, are a cultural form that is disappearing.[18]

In returning to and re-creating the moment of her childhood, Hurston privileges the nostalgic and freezes it in time. Richard Wright, in his review of *Their Eyes Were Watching God*, accused Hurston of re-creating minstrelsy. Though this remark is dismissed out of hand by contemporary critics, what it does register is Wright's reaction to what appears to him to be an outmoded form of historical consciousness. Whereas Wright attempted to explode the discursive category of the Negro as being formed, historically, in the culture of minstrelsy, and as being the product of a society structured in dominance through concepts of race, Hurston wanted to preserve the concept of Negroness, to negotiate and rewrite its cultural meanings, and, finally, to reclaim an aesthetically purified version of blackness. The consequences for the creation of subaltern subject positions in each of their works are dramatically different. The antagonism between them reveals Wright to be a modernist and leaves Hurston embedded in the politics of Negro identity.

Eatonville, as an anthropological and fictional space, appears in Hurston's work before her first anthropological expedition in 1927.[19] Not all the stories and anecdotes in *Mules and Men* originated from her research, and many appeared in different versions in different texts.[20] Rather than being valued primarily as a mode of scholarly inquiry, anthropology was important to Hurston because it enabled her to view the familiar and the known from a position of scientific objectivity, if not distance. She could not see her culture for wearing it, she said: "It was only when I was off in college, away from my native surroundings, that I could see myself like somebody else and stand off and look at my garment. Then I had to have the spy-glass of Anthropology to look through at that."[21] Anthropology, then, is seen by Hurston as providing a professional point of view. Ethnography becomes a tool in the creation of her discourse of the rural folk that displaces the antagonistic relations of cultural transformation.[22]

George Marcus and Michael Fischer have described the ways in which anthropology "developed the ethnographic paradigm" in the 1920s and 1930s. "Ethnographies as a genre," they argue, "had similarities with traveler and explorer accounts, in which the main narrative motif was the romantic discovery by the writer of people and places unknown to the reader."[23] Hurston shares this romantic and, it must be said, colonial imagination. Her representation of Eatonville in *Mules and Men* and in *Their Eyes Were Watching God* is both an attempt to make the unknown known and a nostalgic attempt to preserve a disappearing form of folk culture.[24] Marcus and Fischer argue that there are three dimensions to the criticism that ethnography offered of Western civilization:

> ... they – primitive man – have retained a respect for nature, and we have lost it (the ecological Eden); they have sustained close, intimate, satisfying communal lives, and we have lost this way of life (the experience of community); and they have retained a sense of the sacred in everyday life, and we have lost this (spiritual vision).[25]

Whereas the other students of Franz Boas, Margaret Mead and Ruth Benedict, turned to societies outside of Europe and North America to point to what the West had lost but the cultural "other" still retained, Hurston's anthropological work concentrated upon the cultural "other" that existed within the racist order of North America.

In 1934, Ruth Benedict published *Patterns of Culture,* in which she asserted that black Americans were an example of what happens "when entire peoples in a couple of generations shake off their traditional culture and put on the customs of the alien group. The culture of the American negro in Northern cities," she continued, "has come to approximate in detail that of the whites in the same cities."[26] With this emphasis in the school of anthropological thought that most influenced Hurston, anthropology provided her not only with a "spy-glass" but also with a theoretical paradigm that directed her toward rural, not urban, black culture and folk forms of the past, not the present.

Hurston, like Benedict, was concerned with the relationships among the lives and cultures that she reconstructed and her own search for a construction of the self.[27] She lived the contradictions of the various constructions of her social identity and rewrote them in *Their Eyes Were Watching God.* Her anthropological "spy-glass," which she trained on the society that produced her, allowed her to return to that society in the guise of being a listener and a reporter. In her fictional return, Hurston represents the tensions inherent in her position as an intellectual – in particular as a writer – in antagonistic relation to her construction of the folk as community. It is in this sense that I think Hurston is as concerned with the production of a sense of self as she is with the representation of a folk consciousness through its cultural forms. Both, I would argue, are the motivating forces behind the use of anthropological paradigms in Hurston's work. But it is the relation and tension between the two, particularly the intellectual consciousness and the consciousness of the folk, that is present in the fictional world of *Their Eyes Were Watching God,* which is written between her two books of anthropology, *Mules and Men* and *Tell My Horse*. In this novel, we can see how Hurston brings into being a folk consciousness that is actually in a contradictory relation to her sense of herself as an intellectual.

Throughout the 1930s, Hurston is in search of a variety of formal possibilities for the representation of black rural folk culture. She produced three musicals – *From Sun to Sun, The Great Day* and *Singing Steel* – because she was convinced that folk culture should be dramatized. She returned to fiction as a form after a gap of six years when she wrote "The Gilded Six Bits" in 1933, and *Jonah's Gourd Vine*, which was published in 1934. Then Hurston seriously considered pursuing a Ph.D degree at Columbia in anthropology and folklore. After finalizing all the arrangements for the publication of *Mules and Men*, however, Hurston accompanied Alan Lomax on a trip to collect folk music for the Library of Congress in 1935. That fall she joined the Federal Theatre Project and was prominent in organizing its Harlem unit as well as producing a one-act play, "The Fiery Chariot." Between 1936 and 1938, Hurston spent a major part of her time in the Caribbean collecting material on voodoo practices. She spent six months in Jamaica, and *Their Eyes Were Watching God* was written while she was in Haiti.[28] In *Their Eyes* she reproduces Eatonville from a distance which is both geographical and metaphorical and politically inscribed with issues of gender and class. Hurston's work during this period, then, involves an intellectual's search for the appropriate forms in which to represent the folk and a decision to rewrite the geographical boundaries of representation by situating the southern, rural folk and patterns of migration in relation to the Caribbean rather than the northern states.

Henry Louis Gates, Jr, has explored in great detail matters of voice in *Their Eyes Were Watching God* in relation to a politics of identity by tracing Hurston's construction of a protagonist engaged in a search "to become a speaking black subject."[29] On the other hand, Mary Helen Washington and Robert Stepto have both raised intriguing questions about Janie's *lack* of voice in the text. Washington relates this silencing of a female protagonist to her reading of *Jonah's Gourd Vine* and concludes that "Hurston was indeed ambivalent about giving a powerful voice to a woman like Janie who is already in rebellion against male authority and against the roles prescribed for women in a male-dominated society."[30] However, both sides of this debate about the speaking or silent subject exist within the same paradigm of voice. I wish to introduce an alternative paradigm that suggests ways in which *Their Eyes Were Watching God* is a text concerned with the tensions arising from Hurston's position as writer in relation to the folk as community that she produces in her writing. In other words, I want to concentrate upon the contradictions that arise in the relation between the writer, as woman and intellectual, and her construction of subaltern subject positions rather than remain within critical paradigms that celebrate black identity.

The two chapters that frame the story of Janie's life and are central to arguments about the ways in which Hurston prepares the fictional space in which Janie can tell her own story, actually detail the antagonistic relation between Janie, as a woman alone, and the folk as community. The community sits "in judgment" as the figure of Janie, the protagonist, walks through the town to her house. This walk can be seen as analogous to crossing a stage and "running the gauntlet." Oral language, as it was embodied in the folktale in *Mules and Men*, was a sign of an authentic culture that enabled a people to survive and even triumph spiritually over their oppression. In the opening chapter of *Their Eyes Were Watching God*, however, oral language is represented as a "weapon," a means for the destruction and fragmentation of the self rather than a cultural form that preserves a holistic personal and social identity. Questions become "burning statements," and laughs are "killing tools."[31] Janie has broken the boundaries of social convention and becomes the accused. She doesn't act appropriately for her age, which is "way past forty" (p. 3). (Hurston was forty-five years old at the time the text was written, but on various occasions took between seven and nineteen years off her age.)[32] Also inappropriate are the class codes that Janie threatens in her behavior and in her dress: as a middle-class widow she should not have associated with the itinerant Tea Cake; and as a middle-class woman, her "faded shirt and muddy overalls" are a comforting sign to the folk as community who can ease their antagonism and resentment with the thought that maybe she will "fall to their level someday" (p. 11).

Hurston increases the tension between her protagonist and the community to which she returns through a series of binary oppositions between the intellect, or mind, and speech. The process of the analysis by the anthropological self in *Mules and Men* is reversed by the creator of fiction in *Their Eyes Were Watching God*. In the former, the oral tale is a sign of a whole healthy culture and community; in the latter, the individual functions of speaking are isolated and lack a center. Janie responds to her victimization through synecdoche. The community is indicted as a "Mouth Almighty," a powerful voice that lacks intellectual direction. Far from being spiritually whole, the folk who are gathered on the porch are reduced to their various body parts: in each, an "envious heart makes a treacherous ear" (p. 5).[33] This is the context that determines Janie's refusal to tell her story directly to the community, a refusal that distinguishes her story from the directly told and shared folktale. In the process of transmitting Janie's story, Hurston requires an instrument of mediation between her protagonist and the folk, and it is Janie's friend Pheobe who becomes this mediator. When Janie decides to tell her story through her friend – "Mah tongue is in mah friend's mouf" (p. 5), she says – Hurston creates a figure for the form of the novel, a fictional world that can mediate and perhaps resolve the tension that exists in the difference between the socially constructed identities of "woman" and "intellectual" and the act of representing the folk.[34]

Hurston's particular form of mediation appears to be an alternative version of the anthropological spy-glass that she needed to create a professional point of view between her consciousness of self and the subjects she was reproducing. Janie's definite refusal to tell her tale directly, as in a folktale, distinguishes not only her story from other stories that are communally shared, but also her position from that of the folk as community. Hurston's position as intellectual is reproduced as a relation of difference, as an antagonistic relationship between Janie and the folk. The lack in the folk figures, the absence of mind, or intellectual direction in the porch sitters, is symbolically present when Janie mounts her own porch.

In *Mules and Men*, the porch is the site for the expression of the folktale as an evocation of an authentic black culture. In *Their Eyes Were Watching God*, the porch is split and transformed. Whereas in *Mules and Men* the anthropological self is positioned on a figuratively unified porch, primarily as a listener and a recorder, in *Their Eyes Were Watching God* the anthropological role of listener is embedded in the folk as community and the role of recorder situated in the mediator – Pheobe/the text. In the novel, then, a listening *audience* is established for the narrative self, whereas in *Mules and Men* Hurston constructs a listening *anthropological subject*. It is Janie who can address and augment the lack in the folk as community and Janie who can unify the division between mind and mouth. Janie, of course, is placed in the subject position of intellectual and has the desire to "sit down and tell [the folk] things." Janie, as intellectual, has traveled outside of the community and defines herself as "a delegate to de big 'ssociation of life" (p. 6); her journey is the means by which knowledge can be brought into the community. As intellectual she creates subjects, grants individual consciousness and produces understanding – the cultural meanings without which the tale is useless to the community – "taint no use in me telling you somethin' unless Ah give you de understandin' to go 'long wid it," Janie tells Pheobe (p. 19). The conscious way in which subjectivity is shaped and directed is the act of mediation of the writer; it is this sense in which Pheobe becomes both Hurston's instrument of mediation and her text in an act of fictionalization.

The second part of the frame in the last chapter of *Their Eyes Were Watching God* opens with the resolution of the tension, division and antagonism that are the subject of the opening chapter. The pattern of division of the first part of the frame is repeated: Janie is verbally condemned by the folk as community because she killed Tea Cake. The folk "lack" the understanding of the reasoning behind Janie's actions, but this deficiency is compensated for only through Janie's defense of herself in a court of law. The folk on the muck finally end their hostility to Janie when Sop explains that Tea Cake went crazy and Janie acted to protect herself. Reconciliation, then, between the position of intellectual and the folk as community takes place through acts of narration. The discursive unity that is maintained in the framing of the text prefigures the possibility for reconciliation between the position of Janie, as both intellectual and woman, and the folk as community when Pheobe provides them with the understanding of Janie's life through what will be another act of narration. *Their Eyes Were Watching God*, as such an act of narration itself, offers a resolution to the tension between Hurston, as intellectual, as writer, and the people she represents. In a paragraph that reproduces the tension in relation of the intellectual to the folk, Hurston specifies the source of antagonism between Janie and the community as being a lack of knowledge.

> Now, Pheobe, don't feel too mean wid de rest of 'em 'cause dey's parched up from not knowin' things. Dem meatskins is *got* tuh rattle tuh make out they's alive. Let 'em consolate theyselves wid talk. 'Course, talkin' don't amount tuh uh hill uh beans when yuh can't do nothin' else. And listenin' tuh dat kind uh talk is jus' lak openin' yo' mouth and lettin' de moon shine down yo' throat. It's uh known fact, Pheobe, you got tuh *go* there tuh *know* there. Yo' papa and yo' mama and nobody else can't tell yuh and show yuh. Two things everybody's got tuh do fuh theyselves. They got tuh go tuh God, and they got tuh find out about livin' fuh theyselves. (p. 183)

The passage that I have quoted here is the final paragraph in Janie's story. It gains authority from claiming the tone of the preacher and the peda-gogue, and at the same time it evokes the dilemma of the intellectual. Hurston's journey away from the community that produced her and that she wants to reproduce has provided her with a vision of an alternative world. Although it is not actually present in the text, the novel ends with the possibility that that history could be brought into the community and suggests that Pheobe/the text is the means for accomplishing the transfor-mation necessary to reconcile difference. However, as a woman and as an intellectual, Hurston has to negotiate both gendered and classed construc-tions of social identity and subjectivities.

Critics often forget that Janie is a protagonist whose subject position is defined through class, that she can speak on a porch because she *owns* it. The contradictions between her appearance in overalls, a sign of material lack, and the possession of nine hundred dollars in the bank are important. Hurston's anthropological trips for *Mules and Men* were financed by a patron, Mrs Osgood Mason, to whom she dedicates the text. The folklore material that Hurston had collected she could not freely utilize as she wished: Mason had made it abundantly clear that she claimed proprietary ownership of all that ethnographic material. Hurston traveled to Jamaica and Haiti on her own Guggenheim grant, and, when she was writing *Their Eyes*, she must have pleasured in the sense that no-one else could claim ownership of her words and her work. However, the problem is that providing her protagonist with the financial independence that Hurston herself must have found necessary in order to occupy a position from which to write reinforces the division between Janie and her community. The text here echoes Janie's grandmother's demand for a place like the white woman's, a place on high. The fact that Janie does indeed mount and own her porch enables the story, but also permeates it with a bourgeois discourse that differentiates her from the folk as community.

But this intellectual and property owner is also a woman, and thus the problem of representation here is also a question of how a woman can write her story within a site that is male-dominated and patriarchally defined. In *Mules and Men*, Hurston addresses the social constitution of gender roles in particular tales and through brief narratives that describe the relations among the tale-tellers on the porch, but she does not inscribe a concern with gender within the terms of the professional role of the anthropologist itself.[35] However, the role of listener had its limitations. Hurston's conscious reversal of the role of anthropologist reveals the contradictions inherent in the processes through which an intellectual, an intellectual who is also a woman, can instruct a community about what is outside of its social consciousness. This is the problem that frames the novel. The final metaphor of the horizon as a "great fish-net" with "so much of life in its meshes" (p. 184) that Janie pulls in and drapes around herself is an appropriate image for a writer who can re-create and represent a social order in her narrative. But what this metaphor also confirms is the distance between the act of representation and the subjects produced through that act of representation. The assertion of autonomy implicit in this figuration of a discourse that exists only for the pleasure of the self displaces the folk as community utterly and irrevocably.

I have suggested ways in which the narrative strategies of *Mules and Men* and *Their Eyes Were Watching God* are different and yet similar in that they both evoke the romantic imagination so characteristic of ethnography in the 1930s. If, as Marcus and Fischer suggest, the main narrative motif of ethnography is the "romantic discovery by the writer of people and places unknown to the reader," then *Mules and Men* both discovers the rural folk and acts to make known and preserve a form of culture that embodies a folk consciousness. The folk as community remain the "other" and exist principally as an aesthetic device, a means for creating an essential concept of blackness. The framing of that novel is the process of working out, or mapping, a way of writing and discovering the subject position of the intellectual in relation to what she represents.

Hurston's journey to Jamaica and two trips to Haiti produced *Tell My Horse*, a text that Robert Hemenway has dismissed as Hurston's "poorest book." Hemenway argues that Hurston "was a novelist and folklorist, not a political analyst or traveloguist."[36] I would agree that Hurston's overtly political comments in *Tell My Horse* are usually reactionary, blindly patriotic and, consequently, superficial. The dominant tendency in Hurston scholarship has been to ignore or dismiss as exceptional some of her more distasteful political opinions, but, as Marcus and Fischer have explained, the ethnology and travelogue share a romantic vision (and I would add a colonial or imperial vision), making *Tell My Horse* not an

exception to Hurston's work at this moment in her life but an integral part
of it. In the second chapter of Part Two of *Mules and Men*, the section
entitled "Hoodoo," Hurston shifts away from a concern to record and
preserve a particular form of black culture, the folktale, and toward a
desire to create the boundaries of a cultural world in a relation of
difference to the dominant culture. The geographical boundaries of Hurston's black folk are rural, but their southernness is not defined through a
difference to northernness as much as it is related to cultural practices and
beliefs of the Caribbean. This shift is clear when Hurston, the anthropologist, moves from Florida to New Orleans and seeks to become a pupil of a
"hoodoo doctor."[37]

In her introduction to *Mules and Men*, Hurston explains that she chose
Florida as a site for the collection of folklore not only because it was
familiar, but because she saw Florida as "a place that draws people . . .
Negroes from every Southern state . . . and some from the North and West.
So I knew it was possible for me to get a cross section of the Negro South
in one state."[38] In the section of *Mules and Men* that is situated in Louisiana,
we can see a shift in Hurston's work to a stress on a continuity of cultural
beliefs and practices with beliefs and practices in the Caribbean. In *Their
Eyes Were Watching God* this system of reference is continued through the
way in which Hurston discursively displaces the urban migration of black
people in the continental United States. In her novel, as in *Mules and Men*,
migration is from the southern states further south to Eatonville, Florida.
Migration in a northerly direction is undertaken only by the Barbadians
who join Janie and Tea Cake on the "muck." After the completion of her
novel, Hurston continued her search for an appropriate vehicle for the
expression of black culture in *Tell My Horse* – a first-person account of her
travels in Jamaica and Haiti. Part Three of *Tell My Horse* completes the
journey, initiated in *Mules and Men*, in search of the survival of the ritual
and practices of Vodoun.[39]

The geographic boundaries that enclose *Their Eyes Were Watching God*
enlarge our understanding of the metaphoric boundaries of self and
community. The discourse of the folk, which I have argued is irrevocably
displaced in the figuration of a discourse of individualized autonomy
existing only for the pleasure of the self, is dispersed and fragmented in
a narrative of Hurston's personal initiation into African religious practices
in the diaspora. Hurston does not return again to a romantic vision of
the folk. Her next book, *Moses, Man of the Mountain*, is an extension
of her interest in the relations between and across black cultures because
it rewrites in fictional terms the worship of Moses and the worship of
Damballah that had first interested her in Haiti.[40] This figuration of
Moses/Damballah also transforms questions about the relation of the
intellectual to the folk as community into an exploration of the nature of
leaders and leadership. The intricate inquiry into the construction of
subject positions, as writer, as woman, and as intellectual, is also not

repeated. In *Dust Tracks on a Road,* an apparently autobiographical act, Hurston ignores her earlier attempts to represent the complexity of the relationship between public and private constructions of the self. She continues, however, to displace the discourse of a racist social order and maintains the exclusion of the black subject from history. This is the gesture that eventually wins her the recognition and admiration of the dominant culture in the form of the Ainsfield–Wolf Award for the contribution of *Dust Tracks on a Road* to the field of race relations.[41]

We need to return to the question why, at this particular moment in our society, *Their Eyes Were Watching God* has become such a privileged text. Why is there a shared assumption that we should read the novel as a positive, holistic, celebration of black life? Why is it considered necessary that the novel produce cultural meanings of authenticity, and how does cultural authenticity come to be situated so exclusively in the rural folk?

I would like to suggest that, as cultural critics, we could begin to acknowledge the complexity of our own discursive displacement of contemporary conflict and cultural transformation in the search for black cultural authenticity. The privileging of Hurston at a moment of intense urban crisis and conflict is, perhaps, a sign of that displacement: large parts of black urban America under siege; the number of black males in jail in the 1980s doubled; the news media have recently confirmed what has been obvious to many of us for some time – that one in four young black males are in prison, on probation, on parole or awaiting trial; and young black children face the prospect of little, inadequate or no health care. Has *Their Eyes Were Watching God* become the most frequently taught black novel because it acts as a mode of assurance that, really, the black folk are happy and healthy?

Richard Wright has recently been excluded from contemporary formations of the African American canon because he brought into fictional consciousness the subjectivity of a *Native Son* created in conditions of aggression and antagonism,[42] but, perhaps, it is time that we should question the extent of our dependence upon the romantic imagination of Zora Neale Hurston to produce cultural meanings of ourselves as native daughters.

1991

Acknowledgment

I would like to thank Richard Yarborough for his helpful suggestions and corrections made to an earlier version of this manuscript.

Notes

1. Personal communication with Henry Louis Gates, Jr, February 1990.
2. Rosemary L. Bray, "Renaissance for a Pioneer of Black Pride," *New York Times*, February 4 1990.
3. A more detailed consideration of this parallel would need to examine what Nelson George calls "selling race." The ability of the record industry to market and make a profit from "black talent performing black music" in the 1920s could be interestingly compared to the highly profitable publishing of the work of black women writers, the Book of the Month Club's distribution of Alice Walker's novel *The Color Purple*, and the subsequent film of the same name, and the success of Spike Lee's *She's Gotta Have It* and *School Daze*. See Nelson George, *The Death of Rhythm and Blues*, New York: Pantheon, 1988, pp. 8–9.
4. Hazel V. Carby, *Reconstructing Womanhood: The Emergence of the Afro-American Woman Novelist*, New York: Oxford University Press, 1987, pp. 163–6.
5. Edward W. Said, "Representing the Colonized: Anthropology's Interlocutors," *Critical Inquiry*, no. 15, Winter 1989, pp. 205–6.
6. See Gayatri Chakravorty Spivak, *In Other Worlds: Essays in Cultural Politics*, New York: Methuen, 1987, pp. 197–221. Spivak identifies and elaborates upon the concern of the work of subaltern studies with change as "confrontations rather than transition" and the marking of change through "function changes in sign systems." This rather awkward phrase, "function changes in sign systems," becomes in the process of Spivak's analysis the somewhat shorter phrase "discursive displacements."
7. See, for example, Robert E. Hemenway, *Zora Neale Hurston: A Literary Biography*, Urbana: University of Illinois Press, 1977, p. 50.
8. Ibid., p. 56.
9. Hurston, "Spirituals and Neo-spirituals," in *The Sanctified Church*, Berkeley, CA: Turtle Island, 1981, pp. 80–1.
10. Hemenway, *Zora Neale Hurston*, p. 92.
11. See Chapter 10 in the present volume.
12. Hurston, "Spirituals and Neo-spirituals," p. 79.
13. Spivak, *In Other Worlds*, p. 209.
14. See Ralph Ellison, "Recent Negro Fiction," *New Masses*, no. 40, August 5 1941, pp. 22–6.
15. Hurston, *Dust Tracks on a Road*, 1948; reprint, New York: Harper & Row, 1991, pp. 292–4.
16. Claude McKay, *Banana Bottom*, New York: Harper & Row, 1933.
17. Zora Neale Hurston, *Mules and Men: Negro Folktales and Voodoo Practices in the South*, 1935; reprint, New York: Harper & Row, 1990, pp. 17–19.
18. Ibid., p. 24.
19. See Hurston, "The Eatonville Anthology," *Messenger*, no. 8, Sept., Oct., Nov., 1926; pp. 261–2, 297, 319, 332.
20. See Arnold Rampersad's comments in his introduction to the new edition of *Mules and Men*, New York: Harper & Row, 1990, pp. xxii–xxiii.
21. Hurston, *Mules and Men*, p. 17.
22. See Hemenway, *Zora Neale Hurston*, p. 221, who calls this reconstruction of

Eatonville idealized but feels that Hurston chose to assert positive images "because she did not believe that white injustice had created a pathology in black behavior." I remain unconvinced by this argument because it simplifies to a level of binary oppositions between positive and negative images what are very complex processes of representation. It is interesting that Hemenway seems to realize this inadequacy in the next paragraph when he raises but cannot resolve the problem of "professional colonialism" in Hurston's anthropological stance.

23. George E. Marcus and Michael E. Fischer, *Anthropology as Cultural Critique: An Experimental Moment in the Human Sciences*, Chicago: University of Chicago Press, 1986, pp. 129, 24.

24. Hurston's desire to make black people and culture known is evident in letters she wrote to James Weldon Johnson. See Zora Neale Hurston to James Weldon Johnson, January 22 1934, in which she complains that the J.B. Lippincott Company is "not familiar with Negroes"; and May 8 1934, in which she says about the review of *Jonah's Gourd Vine* in the *New York Times* that she "never saw such a lack of information about us." Both letters are in the James Weldon Johnson Collection, Beinecke Library, Yale University.

25. Marcus and Fischer, *Anthropology as Cultural Critique*, p. 129.

26. Ruth Benedict, *Patterns of Culture*, Boston: Houghton Mifflin, 1934, p. 13.

27. See Margaret Mead's introduction to *Patterns of Culture*, written in 1958, which opens the 1959 edition, p. ix.

28. Hemenway, *Zora Neale Hurston*, pp. 184–5, 202–27, 230.

29. Henry Louis Gates, Jr, *The Signifying Monkey: A Theory of Afro-American Literary Criticism*, New York: Oxford University Press, 1988, pp. 170–216.

30. Mary Helen Washington, *Invented Lives: Narratives of Black Women 1860–1960*, New York: Doubleday, 1987, p. 245. Washington's rereading of *Their Eyes Were Watching God* is an admirable analysis of the ways in which this text has been romanticized, and initiates the important work of comparative analysis across texts. It was this essay that first encouraged and inspired me to follow her lead and think seriously of the relations between Hurston's texts. See also Robert Stepto, *From Behind the Veil: A Study of Afro-American Narrative*, Urbana: University of Illinois Press, 1979, pp. 164–7.

31. Zora Neale Hurston, *Their Eyes Were Watching God*, 1937; reprint, New York: Harper & Row, 1990, p. 2; hereafter page references given in the main text.

32. See Hemenway's introduction to the second edition of *Dust Tracks on a Road*, p. xi.

33. I am grateful to Richard Yarborough for pointing out to me that, of course, this aphorism is itself drawn from oral tradition. My emphasis is that in its application at this point in the novel, it stresses division.

34. I am implicitly arguing, therefore, that it is necessary to step outside questions of voice and issues of third-person (as opposed to first-person) narration in order to understand why Hurston needs an instrument of mediation between the teller of the tale and the tale itself.

35. This may have been because other women like Mead and Benedict were also using the role of anthropologist as a position from which to accumulate knowledge that was both authoritative and scientific. But this is just a guess. The relations among these three anthropologists have not been explored, as far as I know, but a comparative examination of the nature of their work would seem to be an interesting area for future study.

36. Hemenway, *Zora Neale Hurston*, pp. 248–9.
37. Hurston, *Mules and Men*, p. 239.
38. Ibid., p. 17.
39. It would be fruitful to explore the relationship between Hurston's interest in and use of the Caribbean in these years with the cultural production of intellectuals who turned to the Caribbean, in particular the island of Haiti, as a source for an alternative revolutionary black history. I am thinking here, among other works, of the production of the play *Touissant L'Ouverture* by C.L.R. James, which opened in London in March 1936 starring Paul Robeson, and the publication, in 1938, of *Black Jacobins*; Jacob Lawrence's series of paintings on Touissant L'Ouverture, 1937–38; Langston Hughes's *Troubled Island*, written for, but never produced by, the Federal Theatre; and the New York Negro Federal Theatre production of *Macbeth*, often referred to as the "voodoo" *Macbeth*, directed by Orson Welles in 1936. Other black units in the Federal Theatre performed *Black Empire* by Christine Ames and Clarke Painter, and *Haiti* by William Du Bois, a journalist for the *New York Times*.
40. Zora Neale Hurston, *Tell My Horse*, 1938; reprint, Harper & Row, 1990, pp. 139–40.
41. Hemenway, "Introduction" to Hurston, *Dust Tracks*, p. ix.
42. See Gates, *The Signifying Monkey*, pp. 118–20 and 181–4.

Dispatches from the Multicultural Wars

14

Schooling in Babylon

Emancipate yourselves from mental slavery
None but ourselves can free our minds.

Bob Marley

The educational response to the presence of black students in the British school system has been framed in terms of the "problems" for the system that these students pose. Since the sixties, educational theory has located these "problems" in the black child, his or her educational "failure" being explained through the application of common-sense racist assumptions: black students' language structures are inadequate and inhibit learning processes, or, as individuals and as a group, black students suffer from identity crises, negative self-images or culture shock. Having thus situated "failure" in the individual black student, educational theories trace the causes, or roots, of these "problems" to a cycle of pathology within the black communities: excessively patriarchal or matrifocal family structures, self-determined ghettoization, or generational crises precipitated by the repressive measures of black parents. This cycle of pathology arises in this scenario from the need to force their children to conform to social and cultural practices increasingly alien to sons and daughters born into, or maturing in, a society unquestioningly assumed to be more "enlightened" or "progressive" than that of the black parents' origin. From these examples or theoretical positions that mobilize a racist common sense, educational policies have been recommended or implemented that elaborate this common sense into an ideological system which justifies an exclusive focus on the black child in certain educational practices: practices which are remedial, compensatory or coercive.

This chapter will examine theories, policies and practices which have addressed the black child in school. An understanding of the relationship between the function of schooling as institution, and issues of race, is crucial to an understanding of the ways in which state intervention in schooling has become (and is becoming) more direct, overt and authoritarian. We will examine the race relations discourse emanating from local authorities, the Department of Education and Science (DES), Select Committee Reports,

Education Bills and the Manpower Services Commission. Black communities have been engaged in a struggle to redefine what constitutes education and have condemned the consequences of schooling in Britain for black students. Their actions, in defiance of dominant definitions of the practices and function of schooling, have profound implications for the whole of the British working class *vis-à-vis* its relation to the aims, objectives and achievements of the formal education system. The politics of white working-class subcultures have been the subject of much academic research.[1] Paul Willis in *Learning to Labour* refers to what he calls "patterns of racial culture"[2] and describes racism as present at the "formal" as well as the "informal" levels of school culture.

> Both "lads" and staff do share . . . resentment for the disconcerting intruder. For racism amongst the "lads" it provides a double support for hostile attitudes. The informal was, for once, backed up by at least the ghost of the formal.[3]

We will argue that the material interests of black students and the structure of social relationships in which these interests are embedded are distinct from those of white students. However, in being distinct (a struggle that is different to their white peers'), we cannot view the struggles of black students in schools as struggles of school students only. These forms of resistance must be understood within the wider context of the struggles of the whole of the black community: students practicing forms of resistance as members of the black fraction of the working class. As we shall illustrate, the requirements of white working-class parents of the formal schooling system have differed from the demands of black parents, and in fact the two have often appeared to be incompatible. The history of the transformation of the "popular" interests of the white working class into the formal mechanisms of the representation of "popular" interests through the Labour Party has been dealt with elsewhere.[4] Social-democratic initiatives in the field of education have always displayed profound contradictions, notably in the attempt to balance the perceived needs of the working class and the demands of capital. One attempt at a resolution of these conflicting interests is the construction of a "national interest." This resolution is apparent only, disguising conflict in its attempt to win consent. However, this consent has been won through the creation of a "national interest" that has been mobilized against and which excludes the black community.

Black struggles over educational processes and practices have occurred autonomously, outside of the formal mechanisms of representation. The expectations of what schooling in Britain would mean for the black community were shattered by the end of the sixties. The social-democratic rallying cry of "equality of opportunity" became demonstrably bankrupt. The research of Bernard Coard into the overrepresentation of black children in educationally sub-normal (ESN) schools presented what many black parents were already experiencing – formal schooling was not going to provide an alternative future for their children.

Numbers, Language and the Weather

We can characterize initial educational policy as embodying the philosophy of assimilation. Schools were viewed as the primary site for successful assimilation. Black parents were referred to only as potential, or actual, inhibitors of this process. In common-sense terms the system was seen as capable of absorbing black children; "race problems" would literally die away with the older generations. The Commonwealth Immigrants' Advisory Council reported that

> a national system of education must aim at producing citizens who can take their place in a society properly equipped to exercise rights and perform duties which are the same as other citizens' ... a national system cannot be expected to perpetuate the different values of immigrant groups.[5]

A year later, in 1965, the DES echoed this approach, defining the task of education as "the successful assimilation of immigrant children."[6] No adjustments in the system were seen to be necessary; all adjustments were to be made by the students. Attention was focused upon language and numbers as these were seen to be the major inhibitors to successful assimilation.

The first official reactions were in terms of numbers. In 1964 the Commonwealth Immigration Economist Intelligence Unit reported that there were 38,000 pupils in London schools of overseas origin compared to 8,000 in 1956. Four reports issued from the Home Office between 1963 and 1965: on Housing (Cmnd 2119, Cmnd 2796), on the Education of Commonwealth Immigrants (Cmnd 2766) and on Immigrant School Leavers (Cmnd 2458). The concern with numbers and their accuracy culminated in the Home Office White Paper of 1965 (Cmnd 2739) which instituted a quota system and formally acceded to increasing racist hostility against black people. Events in Nottingham and Notting Hill were interpreted as being the result of increasing numbers of immigrants and of their concentration in urban areas. The Commonwealth Immigration Act, which had met with Labour Party opposition in 1962, was approved for renewal by Labour in 1964. A consensus was reached that numbers were the "problem" and restriction the "solution."

The concentration of immigrants in significant numbers was seen by the DES to undermine the process of assimilation:

> ... as the proportion of immigrant children in a school or classes increases, the problems will become more difficult to solve and the chances of assimilation more remote.[7]

Numbers and white hostility were also equated in educational policy and it was the black children who were constructed as the threat, threatening to disrupt the education progress of white pupils.

... in areas of high immigration density, immigrant children can form large percentages in some schools. . . . This may cause racial tension, since parents are afraid that their children will be affected by the apparent lower standards of the immigrant children as the latter numbers increase.[8]

These policy documents express the widespread, common-sense notion that racism is imported into Britain with the black immigrant. This consensus was described in the seventies by Stuart Hall:

Neither side can nowadays bring themselves to refer to Britain's imperial and colonial past, even as a contributory factor to the present situation. The slate has been wiped clean. Racism is not endemic to the British social formation. . . . It is not part of the English culture, which now has to be indeed protected against pollution – it does not belong to the "English ideology". It's an external virus somehow injected into the body politic and it's a matter of *policy* whether we can deal with it or not – it's not a matter of *politics.*[9]

Assimilationist policy laid the ideological basis for practices designed to protect the indigenous population. Hostility, for example, was not conceived as being perpetrated upon black communities in the form of racist attacks and racist street corner politics, nor was it seen that it was the black community who needed protection. Rather hostility was seen to be the result of whites' *justifiable* fear of the very presence of blacks. In schools the situation for black students was an extension of the situation that their whole community faced. Their existence was a threat to their white counterparts. The Ministry of Education pamphlet N.43, 1963, outlined "administrative procedure" to deal with "this sudden influx into schools" whilst at the same time admitting that its advice to local authorities was not based upon research "since research evidence [was] not available." Bussing began in Southall in 1963. Though there was recognition that the institution of a quota system and dispersal were controversial, the DES continued to recommend in their Circular 7/65 that "the proportion of immigrant children in any one school should not be unduly high."

The ideological foundation was laid for policies and practices that would necessarily construct opposing material interests of the black and white working class. Powellism, as opposed to the individual pronouncements of Enoch Powell, which were formally rejected, became implicitly embodied in policies which seemed to promise that race problems would have a conclusive end (returning whence they came) and protect white interests in the process. The black community, on the other hand, organized around specific issues, such as bussing and testing in education, but from the common basis in the wider struggle of the right to stay. What has been referred to as a "structured antagonism" would characterize the relation between politics and race.[10]

Educational testing in the mid-sixties was taken to "prove" the educational inferiority of the black child. The National Foundation for Educational

Research (NFER) acknowledged that "the existence of colour prejudice and other social pressures may affect intelligence test scores as a result of differences in emotional and motivational climate."[11] Contemporary research, however, argued not for an examination of the "social pressures" in Britain, but on the contrary saw educational performance as a product of the conditions of the countries of origin, and concluded that if that performance was considered to be low the answer lay within the black community itself.

Vernon compared his study of West Indian boys made in 1961 with a study of English schoolboys made in 1965 and argued that "the factors which handicapped the children's environment" were previous "defective education," "family instability" and the "cultural level of the home." Children from "non-technical cultures," he stated, "are seriously handicapped in picture and performance tests as well." Vernon in 1966 concluded "that the whole pattern of a culture determines the educational and vocational potential and combines to reduce the effective intelligence."[12]

Consistent with a colonialist and imperialist reasoning, "the natives" were being condemned as "uncivilized" and, with a missionary zeal, the acquisition of the English language was seized upon as the key to successful assimilation. The only impediment was the language the child had already acquired. The intention was not just to teach a language but to rectify cultural and intellectual backwardness. To distinguish this process from processes of learning other languages, complicated systems of cataloguing were devised to "explain" the deficiencies of immigrant language structures. The findings of Alleyne were relied upon. The three categories he used were:

1. Total language deficiency; to describe the acquisition of a foreign language but no script.
2. Partial language deficiency; to describe the acquisition of a foreign language, some English and a script which may or may not be a western alphabet, and
3. Dialect impediments; where English may be fluent but dialect or "pidgin" English was spoken. West Indian Creole was seen to be the cause of problems of listening, interpreting and later reading and writing.[13]

A black child speaking a language from a black country was seen as backward not as actually or potentially bilingual. In fact the "greatest danger" Alleyne discerned "was that the child learns the language for a certain segment of the environment in which he [sic] will operate and another language for specific situations."[14] Assimilation through language was seen to be necessarily total; alternative languages were not to survive. The ability of black students to use language as a form of resistance can be seen in the teachers' fear of being excluded from communication between pupils; this has always been regarded as an unacceptable loss of authority. Black pupils using their own language is often referred to by teachers with the derisory comment "jabbering." In 1963 Jones outlined the conclusions of the Conference Commission on Communication by saying,

> The dialect or Creole English is an immature language which is clearly inadequate for expressing the complexities of present day life, for complete understanding of human motivation and behaviour.[15]

This statement outlines quite clearly the evolutionary notions behind these language theories and attitudes toward black cultures. Western societies were felt to be more advanced, not just technologically, but also intellectually, and language was the index of the stage of civilization reached. In terms of the total and partial language deficiency categories outlined above, speaking an Asian or African language didn't really count as having a language at all.

The two major strands, language and numbers, came together in a project sponsored by the Schools Council and conducted by Derrick, initiated in 1966. The aim was

> to establish the number of immigrant children born overseas *or here* who have not been brought up with English as their first language, and the number of West Indian children and of children of other immigrant groups; and to find out the arrangements, made by the local authorities to teach them.[16]

Language became the most obvious indication, in educational terms, of the black child's inferior intelligence, and confirmed the paucity, or complete lack, of a culture. In order to "work" as a theory, assimilationist concepts had to deny the existence of a viable culture in those to be assimilated. In the words of the NFER:

> It appears, therefore, that language is one major factor in this culturally induced backwardness of immigrant children and affects assessment of ability and actual school performance.[17]

Black children were perceived and treated as retarded. However, around the language issue gravitated other common-sense, racist notions to reaffirm the inferiority of blacks in general, and the pathology of their family structures.

> Many of the surveys listed indicate that of the three ethnic groups now settling in Britain . . . it is the West Indian group which appear to illustrate our difficulties most vividly. Linguistically, they seem to have an advantage over the other two groups, but it is their partial mastery of English, and their use of dialect which seems to be a major barrier to educational motivation and achievement. They also appear to be more susceptible to the climate, in terms of health, and pose difficulties for the host community because of the high incidence of broken families or children of varied parentage.[18]

Climate has gained a pivotal significance in the determination of other cultural and social characteristics. The economic relations of exploitation have been effectively disguised through the presentation of the Caribbean as a tropical paradise in which live a happy, smiling, though simple people – it becomes incomprehensible that they should ever wish to leave. At this point we can see clearly the transference of ideas from educational research into textbooks designed for use in teacher training. Moving from apparently "objective" educational surveys that attempt to naturalize social relations of exploitation, we find a more developed and sophisticated ideological use of "nature" as the determinant in the shaping of a social system, in handbooks that attempt to construct a sociological approach to teaching black children. In Ivor Morrish's *The Background of Immigrant Children*, we find the following paragraph:

> Life in the West Indies is, for the most part, a life spent in the open air in a warm, sunny and friendly climate; and the warmth of the atmosphere is translated also in terms of human relationships. In the Caribbean people live together in crowded kin-group communities, and they share one another's hopes, fears, joys, sorrows, troubles and all family occasions. When they come here they find a climate which is cold, wet and highly unpredictable; they have to live most of their lives indoors, and there is no common "yard" where all the street can congregate and engage in idle chatter. They begin to experience a pace of life which is greatly removed from the *dolce far niente* of the tropical Caribbean; its speed and unchanging, incessant routine are at first strange, and to some quite terrifying. If *we* suffer from "colour shock", they suffer from climate and culture shock.[19]

Racism becomes naturalized through the use of Sheila Patterson's concept of "colour shock," offering reassurance to the student teachers, for whom the book was intended, that their distaste for black skin is only natural. The reference to "crowded communities" acts as a naturalizing mechanism in relation to the explanation offered for the existence of ghettos later in Morrish's chapter. The weather as an unquestioned natural, biological force is used as the cause and justification for the existence of the concepts surrounding numbers and language that we have discussed. Blacks "naturally" crowd together, their language is "chatter" and, because it is "idle," it explains why they are culturally, intellectually and technologically "backward."

'Special Problems Need Special Treatment'

A recognition that assimilationist policies and practices had failed and could not hope to succeed emerges during the last half of the sixties. It is impossible to present a strictly chronological account of precisely when assimilation as a philosophy dies and integration in a pluralistic form

becomes the dominant ideology. Theories of assimilation have been associated with the period of optimism and economic expansion of the fifties
and early sixties, and their disappearance with the "profound social,
cultural and political polarization" evident in 1968.

> It is when the great consensus of the 50s and early 60s comes apart, when the
> "politics of the centre" dissolves and reveals the contradictions and social
> antagonisms which are gathering beneath.[20]

The formal education system had undergone an unprecedented period of
expansion and experimentation with "progressive" teaching methods. However, within the wider context of a perceived threat to the social order
from excessive permissiveness, schooling became linked to the "youth
crisis" and a loss of traditional standards. Liberal concepts of education for
"equality of opportunity" came under attack and stories of "blackboard
jungles" and the abdication of authority by teachers well popularized in
the press. It is within this atmosphere of a crisis in social relations that we
must situate the significance of the ideological shift from assimilation to
integration through cultural pluralism. This period also marks a more
general shift in race relations policy and is punctuated by a crisis of race.
Though there is often a disjuncture between official policy recommendations and the implementation of policy, official statements do reflect a
transition from indirect to more direct control over the schooling of black
children.

An illustration of this shift is the move from a predominant concern
with language to the construction of categories of the "complex disabilities"
of the black pupil. Language does not disappear as a problem but becomes
incorporated into a complex which also includes "culture shock," "cultural
conflict" and "generational conflict." The concern with cultural factors
contrasts with the previous denial of culture but many characterizations of
the structure of black communities remain, though granted greater significance as disabling factors to integration. At the axis of many of these
disabilities was placed the black family, constituted as a pathological family
structure. The black family, it is argued, is unable to provide the conditions
for, or acts as an inhibitor to, the successful educational progress of the
black child. Most frequently, in educational reports, the focus is placed
upon the black mother.

The report from the Select Committee on Race Relations and Immigration, 1968–69, hypothesized a generational conflict existing within the
black communities which would hinder integration. The Committee asked,

> Should the young Pakistani retain the clothes and manners of his [sic] parents
> or adopt those of his [sic] white contemporaries with whom he [sic] spends most
> of his [sic] time? The mother, in particular, usually at home and mixing little in
> British society, may object to her daughter in a mini-skirt.[21]

It has been around black women that pathological notions of the black family and the responsibility for the failure, or inability, to integrate have been secured. Common-sense constructions of the passive Indian or Pakistani wife and mother, speaking no English and never leaving the home, have been elaborated alongside constructions of the dominating Afro-Caribbean wife and mother, who is always out working and therefore never at home, into ideologies that justify increased state intervention into school and home. The report condemned the lack of contact between schools and black parents, which they saw as existing because

> many Asian parents, *particularly mothers*, speak less English than their children. *Many West Indian mothers* work during school-hours and cannot get to school meetings.[22]

Black children were labeled "disadvantaged" or "disabled" either because their mothers worked or because they didn't. The position of Asian women in the labor force has been ignored and common-sense conceptions of their passivity reinforced. Alternatively, it has been precisely the Afro-Caribbean woman's position in the labor force that has been used to imply the neglect of her children's interests. Hypothetical situations such as that over clothes, cited above, are used in an explanation of the failure of black and white youth to integrate. The report also refers to the "more rigid discipline" of Asian and Afro-Caribbean parents, which is described as being a contributory factor in a "conflict of culture and customs," a "barrier to would-be social integration in youth clubs and their neighbourhood." The portrayal of black parents as deficient, unable to equip their children to compete equally with white youth, has been used to justify increased state intervention to compensate for this supposed "failure" on the part of black parents.

In particular recommendations for action the Select Committee stressed the importance of intervention in the home. It suggested that social workers be appointed to "liaise with immigrant parents" and that special attention be paid to attempting "to overcome the language deficiencies of the parents of immigrant children – *especially Indian and Pakistani mothers.*"[23] This represents a significant shift from policies of assimilation which concentrated on the school–child relationship, toward an increasingly direct interventionist approach which links the social services, teachers and, most recently, the police in the schooling of black students. Direct intervention by the careers service was also recommended in the report to compensate for a perceived lack of parental guidance. "Much careers teaching" was seen by the Committee to be "uninformative about life on the factory floor," but, they argued,

> White boys and girls may learn from their fathers, relatives and friends. For the coloured immigrant the change from school to work may be more bewildering. He [*sic*] may therefore need particular advice and help.[24]

There was no discussion of how black parents managed to find their way onto the factory floor, into the transport services and into the National Health Service; intervention was perhaps more to ensure that the state established the mechanisms for the control of black youth.

This Select Committee report responded directly to the actuality and potentiality of black organization, resistance and rebellion. In its initial pages the "existence of sympathy to . . . 'black power' policies" is noted and concern is expressed that the "second generation may be less patient in surmounting difficulties that confront them than their parents have been."[25] Written against the background of the "youth crisis" of the sixties, the increased visibility of white male subcultures, gangs and social unrest on the streets, the anxiety of the Committee members about future "alienated" black youth can clearly be felt. Whilst they attempt a tone of optimism, there is also recognition, of prophetic proportions, that the optimism may be ill founded: "we have assumed there will be no widespread and sustained shortage of employment in this country."[26]

In relation to policing, the report is at pains to indicate a "much lower level of crime and juvenile delinquency among coloured people than white." Nevertheless, the report recognized the potential for "trouble" and the need for "monitoring" black youth.

In general terms the Committee laid the groundwork for policies to focus exclusively on the black student in school and during the transition to work. In comparison with the physically and mentally disabled, black youth were seen as disabled because they were black:

> . . . "equal opportunity" for coloured school-leavers does not flourish naturally in the crowded areas of our towns and cities. Many of them have special problems, whether because of their upbringing in another country or from discrimination, that handicap them in entering adult life. White school-leavers do not suffer the same handicaps.

In terms of policy, however, it was not the conditions of towns and cities that were under scrutiny but the black youth for whom separate, special provision should be made.

> Equality of opportunity does not always mean treating everyone in exactly the same way. . . . Special problems need special treatment.[27]

The Committee argued that this special treatment should be seen in the same light as that given to backward children and the special assistance provided for the physically handicapped in both education and employment. This correlation between being backward and being physically handicapped has remained and is enshrined in the extension of "special needs" and "special provision" in the Education Bill 1981.

In summary we argue that toward the end of the sixties an ideological shift to more direct forms of social control can be perceived in race relations policy. First, through increased monitoring (the Committee favoured the keeping of statistics on black youth); second, through direct intervention by the state into the home and school, under the guise of compensating for the inadequacies of black parents.

Alongside the establishment of mechanisms that would allow for more effective means of social control grew a sociology of race relations that was to concern itself with culture and ethnicity. Roy Jenkins had defined integration, in 1966, as "not the flattening process of assimilation but an equal opportunity accompanied by cultural diversity in an atmosphere of mutual tolerance." Around this doctrine, as Jenny Bourne has pointed out, was formed a

> school of thinking . . . which held that if racialism, seen as the cultural intolerance underlying and giving rise to racial discrimination, was educated away, equal opportunity would begin to flourish. This could be achieved not least through anti-discriminatory legislation which their guru Jenkins had promised. They approached race relations, then, in terms of cultural relations (like the earlier assimilationists) and not in terms of power relations, least of all state power.[28]

The development of the sociology of race relations has been criticized elsewhere, but it is important to note two dimensions that have implications for schooling in this shift from assimilation to cultural pluralism. The first is the central role given to education, and the second is the close relationship between the investigations of the sociology of race relations and policy making. As Deakin said in *Colour and Citizenship and British Society* (1970), a central text in the formation of a race relations discourse,

> Any proposals for the amelioration of relationships between minority and majority – and this book is intended principally as a constructive contribution towards policy making in this field – must be justified in purely practical terms.[29]

These two dimensions come together in the development of educational theories which used the findings of the sociology of race relations to formulate educational processes and practices. The pluralistic model acknowledged the existence of different cultures, different "ways of life," but ignored the way in which these cultures were produced and existed in social relations of power, of dominance and subordination. It was clear, from the first teacher training handbooks that argued for the adoption of cultural pluralism, which cultural factors were to be encouraged "to contribute to the enrichment of our society and its culture" and which were viewed as threatening to the British social fabric.

Ivor Morrish complained that "the isolation of immigrants in certain areas of our large cities will tend to encourage the retention of their own social systems rather than accommodation to those of their hosts." What this meant was that black family structures were not accepted in notions of cultural diversity. Morrish stressed that the "danger of the ghetto is the perpetuation of Caribbean familial concepts and values in the new society," that "the very forces which make for Sikh solidarity are at the same time the forces which prevent assimilation or integration," and that for Pakistanis Britain would offer "liberation from the narrowing limitations of an ancient, but parochial and stifling, hierarchical system."[30]

Cultures do not exist in egalitarian diversity and, therefore, cultural pluralism had to be "managed." One of the principal sites in which this managing has occurred is through the formal education system. Concepts of the white, nuclear family were to remain as indices of the "pathology" of black family structures. The responsibility for the transmission of black cultural forms was to be removed from the black family and undertaken by schools: interpreted, digested and made safe for consumption. Just as the sociology of race relations was to ignore the implications of increasingly militant black political consciousness, so educational theory advocated avoidance, at all costs, of "black power" politics.

> Most thinkers would perhaps agree that the concept of negritude, which involves "the awareness, defence, and development of African cultural values" . . . is a misguided one if applied to West Indian immigrants in our society. There is no common West Indian culture to which West Indian children in this country may turn; leaders such as Neville Maxwell . . . have, it is true, referred to "our original African culture" and its suppression by the acquisitive whites, but this is more in the nature of an *emotional appeal* than an anthropological statement. There are, and there have been, African "cultures", many of them; but no single, or original, African culture. Nor is the West Indian immigrant child likely to discover one, unless some new Ras Tafari movement should develop in our midst and create a pseudo-African culture.[31]

The concepts of a multicultural, multiracial or multiethnic society that grew from this pluralistic model assumed that equality could be achieved through cultural diversity and thus removed from the realm of politics. Race relations became totally absorbed with issues of black ethnicity at the expense of examining institutionalized racism. The educational philosophy of multiculturalism followed the sociologists of race relations in the reinterpretation of ethnic cultural forms for the classroom. In the words of the Select Committee on Race Relations and Immigration "much can also be done . . . to create better understanding of the national and cultural background of immigrants." It advocated

> specific teaching about the countries from which the immigrants in any particular town come. Here material direct from those countries can be displayed in the classroom by immigrant children. Children in primary schools in Hackney or Brixton, for example, could be taught West Indian songs, or children in Wolverhampton be shown Indian art, jewellery and costumes. This would help bring the immigrant children into the life of the school.[32]

Two aspects should be discerned in this approach. First, this implies that racial prejudice and racial discrimination would come to an end through an education in cultural diversity; racism was thus merely a matter of individual ignorance. Second, the articulation by black movements of the need for an awareness of black history and culture, formed in the struggles against imperialism and colonialism, and essential in the struggle against contemporary forms of racism, was turned by the state into a superficial gesture in an attempt to control the rising level of politicized black consciousness. The multicultural curriculum was from its inception part of state strategies of social control. Black culture and history were what the schools said they were. The state recognized the danger of the demand for Black Studies and determined to exercise control over what black students were taught. In 1973 the Select Committee on Race Relations and Immigration stated:

> The demand for Black Studies has arisen because the content of education in Britain is seen as Anglocentric and biased against black people. We can understand this. *But we doubt whether Black Studies in the narrow sense would make a contribution to wider education and better race relations and we are not attracted by the idea of black teachers teaching pupils in separate classes or establishments.* But the history, geography and cultures of the large minorities which now form a part of British society are worthy of study and appreciation, not least by indigenous children. We are certainly not suggesting that curricula be turned upside down.[33]

A critique of multicultural curricula has been made elsewhere and we will not repeat that analysis here.[34] It has not only been irrelevant to the black struggle in Britain but has also failed to address any of the crucial aspects of the relation between race and education. A recent Schools Council report[35] confirms that the multicultural curriculum, even in its limited approach to black cultures, has had very little impact on schools in Britain. The *Guardian*, in a review of the report, stated that most white schools "have carried on teaching as though multi-ethnic Britain never happened" and seemed surprised that white local education authorities "invariably replied that they thought a multi-ethnic society was not a matter which concerned them . . ."

> Three quarters of schools with few or no minority ethnic group pupils expressed similar views; most of those that did report including relevant teaching said that this was limited to R.E. [Religious Education][36]

On the contrary, this limited application of multiculturalism should not be surprising because, as we have argued, it had been conceived and applied as a method of social control over black children. The ways in which the curriculum content innovations were originally conceived, as an integral part of an overall strategy which was developing toward black youth, were neglected by teachers, their professional organizations and unions. The "progressive" boom in the industry of multiracial, multiethnic and multicultural teaching materials, journals, departments and organizations was doomed to be myopic, failing to address the issues around which blacks themselves were to organize.

From Containment to Policing

In 1971, Bernard Coard published the results of his research that exploded the myth of education for "equality of opportunity." He revealed the practices implicit in theories of the deficiencies and disabilities of black children.

> Thus the one way to ensure no changes in the social hierarchy and abundant unskilled labour is to adopt and adapt the educational system to meet the needs of the situation: to prepare our children for the society's future unskilled and ill-paid jobs. It is in this perspective that we can come to appreciate why so many of our black children are being dumped in E.S.N. [Educationally Sub-Normal] schools, secondary moderns, the lowest streams of the comprehensive schools, and "Bussed" and "Banded" about the school system.[37]

This book, published for the Caribbean Education and Community Workers' Association, made an intervention in educational debate and gave many black parents an understanding of what was happening to their children in British schools. Until then many black parents had been led to believe, by head teachers and local education authorities, that special education was "special" in the sense of giving their children additional educational advantages to succeed.

Many white, liberal teachers were shocked by the results of Coard's research and the early seventies saw a rapid increase in the production of research projects, reports, policy documents and teaching materials focusing upon the black child. Concern with language and numbers remained whilst approaches to a multicultural content in curricula expanded in number. It is beyond the scope of this essay to include an inventory of all policy documents and reports concerning the black child in school, but we will indicate the general trends and concerns and discuss any significant shifts or consolidations of policy and practice.

The National Association for Multiracial Education (NAME) was formed and issued its first journal *Multiracial Schools* in the autumn of 1971, indicating a commitment to concepts of cultural pluralism in its move from being the journal of the Association for the Education of Pupils from Overseas (ATEPO).

A Schools Council project on "Teaching English to West Indian Children" based at Birmingham University was tested during 1971–72 and published in the summer of 1972, with units designed to deal with the "problems" arising specifically from West Indian dialect. The Schools Council Working Paper on Religious Education recognized a "multifaith context" and two years later Working Paper no. 50 concentrated on curricular changes for a multiracial education.[38] The NFER undertook three major research projects: into the provisions made by local education authorities for immigrant pupils in England, in 1971; an investigation of "the opinions of teachers as to the need for development of materials" and an identification of "existing innovations," started in 1972; and, in response to a joint proposal of ATEPO, the National Union of Teachers and NFER, research into education for a multiracial society, to last from April 1973 to December 1976.[39]

The DES continued to be preoccupied with numbers, publishing the figures of New Commonwealth immigrant children in London and County Boroughs on January 1 1970, in January 1971, and became increasingly concerned with forms of assessment. In the same year the DES Education Survey no. 10[40] tried to assess "potential and progress in a second culture" but, because of Coard's work, also recognized that the practices of assessment were a contentious area in the acknowledgment of the "currently highly sensitive issue of West Indian children inappropriately placed in E.S.N. Schools."[41]

Completing the second phase of a three-phase research project for the DES, located at the NFER and entitled "Educational Arrangements in Schools with Immigrant Pupils," Townsend and Brittain complained of the inaction of education authorities and schools in the face of the "disturbing number of immigrant children underachieving."[42] Judith Hayes was also located at the NFER researching into the "educational assessment of immigrant pupils."

What would seem to be a move from a concern with "immigrants," as a distinct group, to a concentration on the wider aspects of a multiracial society was not, in fact, the significant change it appeared to be. We can see that a concern with language and assessment was shared by all the bodies participating in the above research. Though those preoccupied with developing multicultural curricular content expressed disquiet at culturally biased testing, the major concern was still the performance of the black child. Innovations in content were conceived as enabling the black child to improve his, or her, performance in ways that could be assessed. The social relations of power that sustained institutionalized racism and which are reproduced in the classroom were not seen as open to investigation. Content innovation concerned itself with "ethnic" cultural forms only, or with the removal of racist stereotyping from school textbooks. Multiculturalism has reacted to racism as if it were limited to a struggle over forms of representation – a struggle over images – in an attempt to disguise the social relations of domination and subordination in which it is situated and which it reproduces. In place of an analysis of schooling as a mechanism for increasing direct social control over black communities, those who advocated the adoption of "progressive methods" of teaching saw changes towards a multicultural curricular content as being the catalyst that would reverse the "underachievement" of black school children.

It is necessary, here, to indicate the background against which "progressive" support for the drive for the multicultural curriculum occurred. In 1960 the Albermarle Report on the Youth Service in England and Wales had associated a crime problem with a youth problem. In education the reaction to the "youth crisis" of the sixties was to increasingly associate delinquency with "educational failure" and, in turn, with the family and neighborhood culture of the working class.[43] Two Central Advisory Committee reports, Crowther and Newsom, emphasized the influence of home background on children's performance in school, and a third, the Plowden Report, recommended the diversion of extra resources to the deprived and disadvantaged.[44] The latter report endorsed "progressive" teaching methods and advocated the creation of educational priority areas. However, in the process, remedial or compensatory strategies still placed the "cause" of failure in the child and his or her family, in particular focusing upon inadequate mothering. We have already seen how the black mother was specifically addressed, as schools moved toward the kind of "client" relationship toward the working class of the other social services.[45] As schools moved in between children and the working-class family, "progressive" or child-centered methods were seen to be part of the strategy of compensation. Schools, it was suggested, should be part of their "community," and should aim at involving the working-class mother to teach her state-approved methods of mothering and thus break the "cycle of deprivation." However, in relation to the white working-class family this type of intervention by the state was viewed as an interruption in the process of social reproduction not as a disruption of this process. The white working-class family was seen as a unit capable of reproducing required labor power with some modification. As we have already argued, the black family was not, and has not been, considered a viable or desirable unit for social and cultural reproduction and, therefore, the state response has been one not of transformation but of negation. Changes in the immigration laws from immigrant to migrant status and the denial of black motherhood as constituting motherhood attest to this.

Thus, in arguing for the relevance of a multicultural curriculum to black children, "progressive" supporters were an integral part of an interventionist approach. Liberal and progressive teachers were reluctant to acknowledge their role in the wider aspects of social control, but, in the face of increasing classroom resistance by black students, the introduction of a multicultural syllabus was an attempt to pacify the recalcitrant. Curriculum development was an essential part of trying to streamline the school curriculum to meet the needs of industry[46] but multiculturalism did not question the nature of the relation between black students in the classroom and their future position as labor. "Progressive" teachers also failed to make the connections between their role, in what we have referred to as the management of the transmission of black culture, and the process the CCS Education Group describes as "the general manageability of labour," which "could only be strengthened through a heightened manageability of and through education."[47] Educational disadvantage was a waste of potential talent to industry, and educational disadvantage became more and more associated with black students.

In 1974, a White Paper, "Educational Disadvantage and the Educational Needs of Immigrants," was published by the DES in direct response to the Select Committee on Race Relations and Immigration's recommendations that ways be found to identify and prevent the growth of educational disadvantage. This report clearly illustrates ways in which state control over education and the curriculum was to be increased. Three units were to be established: an information center, the Centre for Educational Disadvantage; an administrative sector, the Educational Disadvantage Unit; but most importantly, the Assessment of Performance Unit as a branch of the DES. This latter unit was to:

> Promote the development of methods of assessing and monitoring the achievement of children at school and to seek to identify the incidence of underachievement.[48]

All black school children were identified as in need of increased centralized monitoring and assessment. This form of direct DES intervention contradicted the previous "power-sharing" role with local education authorities. It also confronted teacher professionalism, which had tried to establish autonomy of control over curricular innovation. The multicultural curriculum came to be used as the last bastion of control that teachers had over curriculum innovations.[49] But so defensive was the battle against encroachment on the territory of professionalism that the links between direct centralized control and schooling for industry were ignored by teachers, some of whom were busily being "multicultural" whilst really protecting the grounds for their own autonomy.

Teachers involved in multicultural teaching maintained that they were improving the self-concepts of black children, providing positive images and alleviating disadvantage. This role confirmed the importance of the autonomy of their position, their need to be professionals, and displays a liberal moral conscience of messianic proportions.

> Self-concept research is saying to the teacher: you are the backbone of the educational system, not the social scientist or the armies of advisers and petty officialdom. The teacher is a force in the classroom and in the field of self-concept he [sic] is a force for good, given he [sic] has the will to experiment and

succeed. Teachers can enhance self-concept through the provision of special curriculum materials ... through developing experimental curriculum projects designed to enhance self-worth in children and in general through becoming more person-oriented in the classroom.[50]

The parallels with missionaries following in the wake of the armies of colonialism are more than metaphorical. Like missionaries these teachers have not examined their own racism in their preoccupation with their own spiritual regeneration through "doing good" to black youth. Neither have they examined their own positions as agents of the state in a hierarchy of relationships in which they are in a position of control and ultimate authority in the classroom. It is in the lack of this form of analysis that "anti-racist" teaching has become a mere substitute for political action.

The Bullock Report[51] of 1975 reinforced earlier recommendations that the role of the teacher and social worker be interrelated through its encouragement to teachers to visit the parents of children in their home. The 1976 Great Debate on Education formalized the parameters for debate upon the relation school–industry and the crucial role for the new assessment procedures.

> In addition to establishing basic skills, the curriculum should enable children, as part of their essential general education, to understand the society of which they are a part, including the economics of everyday life and the role of industry and commerce in sustaining our standard of living.[52]

The application of the education–industry equation to schooling has been underestimated. Stuart Hall, in describing the "major restructuring of the state apparatus" during this period, argued that

> The D.E.S. has been set aside, and new state apparatuses capable of realizing the equation in more immediate and practical forms have moved into a central position in the field.[53]

The Great Debate, however, did re-emphasize the necessity for increased centralized control over the curriculum, through the DES and its new assessment units. The 1977 Green Paper, the product of this "debate," outlined the tasks that schools were expected to undertake in the reproduction of a future, disciplined workforce in its advocacy of the core curriculum.

> In addition to their responsibility for the academic curriculum, schools must prepare their pupils for the transition to adult and working life. Young people need to be equipped with a basic understanding of the functioning of our democratic political system, of the mixed economy and the industrial activities, especially manufacturing, which create our national wealth.[54]

What is actually involved in constituting "life-skills" will be discussed later, but it is important to note how ambivalent the notion of "skills" becomes. Basic skills had previously been defined as the acquisition of the 3 Rs but have now been extended to include an understanding of the "necessity" of capitalist modes of production and the importance of the reproduction of labor in a stratified form:

> Young people need to reach maturity with a basic understanding of the economy and the activities, especially manufacturing activities, which are necessary for the creation of Britain's national wealth. It is an important task of secondary schools to develop this understanding, and opportunities for its development should be offered to pupils of all abilities.[55]

Teachers' autonomy over the curriculum was to give way to "industry, the trades unions and commerce [who] should be involved in curriculum planning processes."[56] Also recognized was the need for the collection of statistical knowledge "essential for any effective policy" designed to meet "the special needs of ethnic minorities."[57]

The Green Paper, and the Great Debate which heralded it, were the last attempt at a "corporatist" solution to the schooling–industry relation in "crisis." This shift toward a more direct relation between schooling and industry has allowed for the disciplining into the wage relation of a large sector of unemployed youth. During the present economic recession the education system has had to adopt this role in the absence of employment which had previously been the site in which this disciplining would take place.

The Select Committee on Race Relations and Immigration, 1975–76, was concerned about black youth, who seemed to be escaping this process of disciplining. It noted the "reluctance of young West Indians" to use the services of the Manpower Services Commission (MSC) and the Careers Service because of what was termed "alienation." The Committee requested further information about this group "which would be of help to the agencies in ensuring that their market arrangements are such as to meet their special needs." The possibility of a group of youth who may escape the disciplining into the wage relation field obviously represents a threat to the state agencies of social control. And, we would argue, in relation to black youth it is increasingly becoming a priority that this disciplining occurs before they leave school and refuse to register as unemployed. Here, again, we see expressed the need for the increased monitoring of black youth. As well as statistical information the Select Committee suggested the need for "intensive counselling," a process that was intended to follow the strategy of entering in between black youth and the black family.

> Young West Indians, even though they have been born and educated in this country, may be handicapped to the extent that the advice and information

about employment opportunities available to them from their family, relatives and friends, which is one of the main sources of finding jobs, will often be less complete than that available to other young people.[58]

It is not a lack of knowledge but the form of knowledge held within the black communities about the state of the labor market which is really threatening to the smooth reproduction of the black labor force. Older brothers and sisters are increasingly likely to have more information about unemployment than about employment. It is precisely to disrupt the flow of this sort of information within the black communities that the state finds it necessary to intervene under the guise of intensive counseling in an attempt to counter strategies for survival and the ways and means of resisting.

Concurrent with the staging of the Great Debate and public discussion of the aims and objectives of schooling, new practices of training were being established in the schooling–industry relation. Intervention was felt to be necessary in the period of transition from school to work. The MSC through its Training Services Agency (TSA) expanded from training schemes in its own skill centers into massive representation in further education. The history of the formation of these agencies and courses and their relation to the phenomenon of growing youth unemployment has been thoroughly analyzed elsewhere.[59] We do not intend to re-present those arguments here but to concentrate only upon the implications and consequences of these training practices for black youth.

As Dan Finn has emphasized in "The Rise of Manpower Servicedom,"[60] the MSC

> in no way sees itself as engaged in a struggle against existing forms of class, sexual or racial privilege. Indeed, its activities to date simply reproduce and reinforce these fundamental distinctions emanating from the "world of work".

However, most research, so far, has concentrated upon the ways in which TSA (and later, Youth Opportunities Programme) training schemes transformed the role of further education, reproducing the class position of the youth enrolled. This research has ignored the gendered and racialized aspects of this training. Sheridan Welsh has exposed the ways in which research on the young unemployed has neglected the position of girls. She has pointed to "the invisibility of unemployed young women, who tend to be isolated in the home." The MSC, Welsh feels, has only "paid lip service to women as a source of potential and untapped labour . . . the focus has been on the potential dangers of a large male unemployed population."[61] Unemployment itself, argues Welsh, is generally regarded as a male "problem" "to the extent that the very term 'the unemployed' has masculine overtones."[62]

The aptitudes and capabilities that unemployed youth are seen to lack and the skills which are to be provided by Youth Opportunity Training Schemes are, in their very conception, sexually and racially specific. Very rarely do MSC or YOP reports specifically refer to black male youth or black or white young women. The discourse of their official documents abstracts a generalized category of unemployed youth. But this discourse already references common-sense divisions within the category, not only in terms of gender, as Welsh indicates, but also in terms of race. This form of training is not immune to the forms of common-sense racism which pervade society and which operate throughout the education system to structure its policies and practices. It would be naïve to conclude that because the official discourse is abstract that in practice the experience of YOP courses are the same for black and white, male and female youth. As we have seen above, "the unemployed" has predominantly masculine connotations but within this wider categorization racialized divisions will function with consequences for the practices of being trained for industry/ work. In terms of future careers Asian male youth are frequently categorized as holding unrealistically high aspirations. A training scheme consisting predominantly of this group will, as part of its function, attempt to make their aspirations "more realistic." The "life-skills" that Asian young women are seen to need are usually considered to be minimal as it is assumed that they will disappear into wifehood and motherhood at a very young age, literally vanishing into their homes, from which it is thought they will rarely emerge. In the Careers Service West Indian young women are thought to be most suitable for occupations as orderlies in the National Health Service and thus are encouraged to train for such jobs, the chosen few being channeled toward SEN nursing. Black youth are associated with low-paid, low-skilled jobs, jobs that their parents were encouraged to migrate to Britain to do. In common-sense terms, the relation has become "naturalized"; shit-work is all that the sons and daughters of those who fill those positions now can, will or want to do. A refusal to consent to this form of subordination is interpreted as a refusal to contemplate any type of labor.

The central contradiction remains. The MSC has predicated its course on the assumption that an entry into the labor market will follow for its students. However, this is less and less the case and YOP courses have to manage the potential and actual disaffection from the economic, political and social order that can arise from prolonged, structural unemployment. The "skills" that are necessary for these courses to inculcate, therefore, are not purely vocational. They also incorporate the instilling of what Dan Finn has called "work socialization."[63] This socialization process includes work disciplines: time-keeping, respect for workplace hierarchies and behavior modifications.

Attempts to alter behavior are thought to be particularly necessary for black youth, both male and female, but especially in the case of West Indian male youth. They are thought to lack discipline of any sort and have a history of a lack of regard for authority. They are, therefore, key targets for attempts at behavior modification. A study that was produced from Liverpool University reported that

> In Wolverhampton and Manchester, blacks had markedly better qualifications than their white peers. More than two-thirds had some qualifications on leaving school, compared with about one third of whites, and almost three times as many had some further education. Yet they had greater difficulty finding and keeping work.[64]

The reason offered to explain this dilemma is that black, particularly West Indian, youth have attitudes which are not attractive to potential or actual employers. We are offered yet more "proof" that West Indian youth "fail" to function in ways which could guarantee success. These attitudes become a prime cause of failing to achieve and, therefore, must be changed to make West Indian youth more acceptable to employers. YOP courses thus become involved in the changing of these attitudes and attempt to mold black youth into an acceptance of their position at the bottom of the very hierarchy that rejects them. It would appear that it is the behavior of black youth, the attitudes of defiance and resistance, that have come to be regarded as the least acceptable of the modes of behavior of any sector of youth. It is precisely this group that have transformed their position of wagelessness from being one of subordination and complete demoralization into the basis for new forms of politicization: a questioning of the basis of the social formation itself.

There is fear of the consequences of black youth unemployment for the social, political and economic order. Throughout MSC documents the "alienation," work-refusal and non-registration of black youth are described as potential and actual threats to the social fabric. The depth of this fear needs to be understood in the context of the entirety of black youth culture, which has been developed in the struggle against the demands of capital for certain forms of labor, being categorized as rebellious, anarchic and threatening. It is not an individual but a collective struggle and the fear is not fear of individual black youths whose mode of dress, style or way of talking are unacceptable to the status quo. Attempts to transform the behavior and attitudes of black youth are part of the rejection of their culture as a whole. Young adolescent West Indian women, for example, are frequently regarded by teachers as "unfeminine." Accused of being "too loud," of "flaunting" their sexuality as opposed to being demure but tempting, and of "talking back" when they are being repressed, they "fail" to reach Western standards of femininity. In practice, in relation to careers or job opportunities, West Indian girls are not regarded as suitable for work where an overt but malleable display of sexuality is required. These conditions apply to many office jobs where women are expected to display yet subordinate their sexuality, to flatter and amuse; to pamper a white, middle-aged male. Qualities thought desirable in racist ideologies of illicit sexuality and processed in the commodification of black female sexuality in international iconography are deemed unsuitable for the glass-domed reception area of a merchant bank in the City of London (the black women will usually be found in the post room). Pratibha Parmar has outlined instances of racialized gender differentiation in MSC programs.

> Schemes under the Youth Opportunities Programmes ... are another area in which Asian girls are seen as "problems". Unemployment for Black school leavers is three times higher for young Black women than men. The prevalence of sex role stereotyping existing in the wider context of society is reflected in YOP schemes through gender-appropriate training courses such as community service, sewing and typing for the young female trainees and building maintenance, carpentry and painting and decorating for the young male trainees. This gender-ascribed job training is compounded by specific cultural and racial features in the case of Asian girls. One YOP scheme in Yorkshire trained the predominantly Muslim female trainees by taking them out to the park for walks, and their work placement consisted of them watching male trainees dig up old people's gardens.[65]

The MSC sustains the mythological reason for its existence: it aims to correct the disparity between the aptitudes of young employees and the demands of employers. Politically it cannot afford to acknowledge the contradiction underlying the organization of provision for the young unemployed: namely that it is not the failings of youth that determine the distribution and availability of jobs. Consequently, neither the MSC nor the YOP schemes question the gender, racial or class ascriptions that structure their courses. It is the labor force itself, not the British economic structure, that is seen to be the "problem" and in need of transformation.

If, however, we posit the reverse of this formulation, we can argue that

> An understanding of the differentiation of groups within the labour market, and of the relationships between these groups, is possible only through an examination of the forces which operate in the labour market. An understanding of the labour markets which exist must precede an explanation of the circulation of individuals within these markets.[66]

Certain practices of MSC training programs can be seen to operate in line with theories that claim the existence of a dual labor market in Britain. Within this theoretical framework YOP training could be seen to be a mechanism for the maintenance of the majority of blacks in the secondary labor market.

> They are not chosen [trained?] for primary sector jobs because they are associated with secondary sector employee characteristics such as unreliability or low aspirations or because of anticipated hostility to them from other workers. By

relegating them to secondary sector employment, the labelling becomes self-fulfilling.[67]

The training programs themselves need to be investigated for the ways in which they reproduce and maintain a dual labor market and base their practices upon accepted social divisions of labor which are racist. Alternatively the application of the "reserve army of labor" thesis can be revealing when applied to the MSC. In this case it can be seen as a direct intervention by a state agency to discipline youth into the wage relation, outside of actual employment. This would mean that the programs were a part of an attempt to reproduce a transformed labor force, one that would be disciplined for future protracted periods of structural unemployment, and deskilled and available for use in possible future economic expansion.

Both these theoretical positions illuminate different aspects of MSC policies and practices and could be utilized in research that is needed into the reproduction of racially constituted gender roles through these training programs.

The 1981 Youthaid review of the Youth Opportunities Programme recommended that

> Black organisations should be encouraged to establish YOP projects so that young blacks whose pride and self-image has been damaged by the experience of discrimination can work with black people in positions of leadership and authority. Such projects would also help to attract "alienated" young blacks into the Programme.[68]

It would appear that the Youthaid review body have completely missed the point. Their suggestion sounds all too familiar, yet another "encouragement to black people to acquiesce in their own exploitation."[69] Whose interests do these YOP courses serve? Is it, in fact, in the black communities' interests to participate in them at all? The forms of resistance of black youth that these schemes have been attempting to manage and control are not about merely entering a hierarchy and leaving it untouched, but transforming that hierarchy and the sets of social relations that are oppressive.

Conclusion

In 1980 the Inner London Education Authority (ILEA) launched a £1.6 million program to provide disruptive units. Over fifty "sanctuaries" had been established within schools for disruptive children, and fifty off-site centers were being established to cater for approximately 2,000 pupils. In January 1981 a survey was demanded to establish the "ethnic origins of children in units for disruptive children" because of their use as a "'dumping ground' for blacks."[70] Concerted action by black parents in Haringey led the local education authority to abandon its program of establishing further disruptive units for the present.

Contemporary debate is still locked into a framework of assessing the educational "failure" of the black child. Underachievement is assumed and then tested to be proven. A general consensus appears to exist that testing will provide the "evidence" needed to be able to make "compensatory provision"; argument occurs only over how this testing is to be implemented. Black parents dissent and argue that their children now in school were born here and should no longer be treated as an alien sector of the school population. However, as we have seen, educational policy and practice actually constitute black children as an alien group that present "problems" that are external to "normal" schooling. A recent report from the Assessment of Performance Unit (APU) recommends the testing of children of "Afro-Caribbean" origin, 95 percent of whom the report says were born here.

> Though the unit's report gives no clue about which pupils would be included, it is understood that teachers would be expected to pick out such pupils by their appearance and on the basis of what they already know about their family. . . . West Indian children of Asian or Chinese extraction would be excluded and the unit has suggested that black African children can be distinguished by their names. Children of mixed marriages would be included if one of their parents was of West Indian origin.[71]

It was felt by the APU that such figures, however absurd the process of identification, would be useful to the Rampton Committee investigation into the "Education of Children from Ethnic Minority Groups."

The Rampton Committee was set up in 1979 in order to look at "the educational needs and attainments of children from ethnic minority groups taking account, as necessary, of factors outside the formal education system relevant to school performance, including influences in early childhood and prospects for school leavers."[72] In practice, however, its terms of reference in no way suggested that racism itself had to be analyzed in order to explain the "underachievement" of black pupils. In its submission to the Committee the Institute of Race Relations pointed out that:

> Your terms of reference are concerned with the "educational needs and attainments of children from all ethnic minority groups", particularly West Indian children. We feel, however, that an ethnic or cultural approach to the educational needs and attainments of racial minorities evades the fundamental reasons for their disabilities – which are the racialist attitudes and the racist practices in the larger society and in the educational system itself.[73]

The first interim report of the Committee was published in June 1981, under the title *West Indian Children in Our Schools*.[74] By then, however, the

Chairman had been replaced by a person thought more amenable to routine policy analysis, and the government had made it clear that social and political questions were not the main concern of the revamped Committee. These changes were a response to attempts by black members of the Committee to consider the place of racism as central to its considerations.

There is little likelihood, however, that governments are going to take seriously the view of blacks themselves that racism *is* the central issue. At one point in the Rampton report we find the following statement:

> Many West Indians insisted to us that the major reason for the underachievement of their children at school was racism (racial prejudice and discrimination), and its effects both in schools and in society generally. Many other people who gave evidence mentioned racism as a contributory factor.[75]

But such ideas are not discussed in the body of the report itself, and they seem to have had little impact on the formulation of policy alternatives. By implication the report seems to be saying that with increased special provision and more multiculturalism the problem of racism will disappear, at least from schools. In addition, by locating the source of racism in schools in the attitudes of teachers, Rampton failed to face up to the thorny problems of looking at the racism inherent in all state institutions.

Meanwhile – through an extension of the concept of "community" (noted earlier) used in conjunction with more direct control and the linking of educational services with social services – the police are in the classroom with black students. Under the Birmingham Inner City Partnership Programme (1979–82) the sum of £30,000, subsequently raised to £50,000, per annum for three years, was provided to be used exclusively with the jointly supported "Lozells Project." The original area of the project was modified to include the Holte School and the Wallace Lawler Centre. The objectives were seen as follows

1. to enable the police to develop closer links with the community;
2. to encourage local residents to participate with statutory agencies in the solving of community problems;
3. to reduce crime and vandalism in the Project area.[76]

What we wish to point to here is the close liaison between the police, the social services and the schools and to the association with the disciplining of black youth. It is interesting that modifications were made to include the Holte School, 80 percent of whose pupils are black, in the light of police intentions. The police, "with the support of teaching staff, will seek to assist within the schools in developing law-abiding young people."[77] The construction of the "fear" of crime by black youth is used as a justification to police them in schools. Policing them in the classroom also aids with identifying and monitoring black youth on the streets.

The Lozells Project is not an exceptional instance but an illustration of the direct control being exerted through the practice of "community relations." The reaction of the police to a hoax telephone call describing a "riot" at Archway School in London was to send six police cars and a helicopter! When the headmistress complained to the head of the juvenile bureau of the local police, she informed him that this police reaction had "totally destroyed much of the good community relations work *you and I* have been doing through the school in the last 18 months."[78]

Community relations, or what is often referred to as a "soft-centered" form of control, has replaced notions of integration.

> The state, the police, the media and race relations experts ascribe to young blacks certain objective qualities, e.g. alienated, vicious little criminals, muggers, disenchanted unemployed, unmarried mothers, truants, classroom wreckers etc. The youth workers, community workers, counsellors (teachers) and the rest start with these objective qualities as given, and intervene on the basis that through their operations they could render young blacks subjectively different, and make them people to whom those objective qualities could no longer be applied. When this is done in collaboration with control agents themselves, as in police–community liaison schemes, or instances in which professional blacks collaborate with schools in blaming black kids for their "failure", it is interpreted as progress towards "good community relations".[79]

Multiculturalists had visions of classrooms as microcosms of a race relations paradise. Proponents of community policing strategies are concerned to reap a harvest of information from the seed-beds of schools and youth clubs. Meanwhile, black youth recognize liberal dreamers and the police for what they are and act. They determine the terrain on which the next struggle will be fought – the street, the day. Intensive policing of all areas of black life – domestic, public, social and educational – testifies to the political strength and resilience of black culture. Black communities as a whole have withdrawn their consent to being governed in an increasingly authoritarian and racist way. Black youth have led the way in the redefinition of who's got the problem.

1982

Acknowledgments

I wish to thank Valerie Amos for hours of fruitful discussion in the shaping of the ideas for this essay and for being not only a friend but a sister. Andy Green also gave up much of his time debating with me the hotly contested issue of the role of multicultural and anti-racist teaching practices. I am sorry that I have not been able to do justice to his arguments but this essay had to concentrate on our brothers and sisters struggling in the classrooms and outside rather than on the struggle of teachers. That story should appear somewhere – I hope he will write it.

Notes

1. Phil Cohen, "Subcultural Conflict and Working-Class Community," in Stuart Hall, Dorothy Hobson, William Lowe and Paul Willis, eds, *Culture, Media, Language*, London: Hutchinson, 1980; S. Hall and T. Jefferson, eds, *Resistance Through Rituals*, London: Hutchinson, 1975; Angela McRobbie, "Working-Class Girls and the Culture of Femininity," in CCCS, *Women Take Issue*, London: Hutchinson, 1975; Angela McRobbie, "Settling Accounts with Subcultures," *Screen Education*, no. 34, Spring 1980; Paul Willis, *Learning to Labour*, Farnborough: Saxon House, 1977.
2. Willis, *Learning to Labour*, p. 47.
3. Ibid., p. 49.
4. CCCS Education Group, *Unpopular Education*, London: Hutchinson, 1981.
5. Commonwealth Immigrants' Advisory Council, *Second Report*, Cmnd 2266, London: HMSO, 1964.
6. DES, *The Education of Immigrants*, Circular 7/65, June 14 1965.
7. Ibid.
8. National Foundation for Educational Research, *Coloured Immigrant Children: A Survey of Research, Studies and Literature on Their Educational Problems and Potential in Britain*, London: NFER, 1966, p. 167.
9. Stuart Hall, "Racism and Reaction," in *Five Views of Multi-Racial Britain*, London: CRE, 1978, p. 24.
10. Ibid., p. 28.
11. NFER, *Coloured Immigrant Children*, p. 171.
12. Ibid., pp. 171–2.
13. Ibid., p. 173.
14. Ibid.
15. Ibid., p. 174.
16. Ibid., p. 169 (our emphasis).
17. Ibid., p. 173.
18. Ibid., p. 177.
19. Ivor Morrish, *The Background of Immigrant Children*, London: Unwin, 1971. See also Sheila Patterson, *Dark Strangers*, London: Penguin, 1965.
20. Hall, "Racism and Reaction," p. 29.
21. Select Committee on Race Relations and Immigration, 1968–69, *The Problems of Coloured School-Leavers*, London: HMSO, 1969, p. 16.
22. Ibid., p. 17 (our emphasis).
23. Our emphasis.
24. Ibid., p. 45.
25. Ibid., pp. 6–7.
26. Ibid., p. 10.
27. Ibid.

28. Jenny Bourne, "The Sociology of Race Relations in Britain," *Race and Class*, vol. XXI, no. 4, Spring 1980, p. 336. Jenny, at this point in her article, elaborates upon the work of Deakin *et al.* and a mode of thought that informed the research of the Institute of Race Relations during this period.

29. N. Deakin, *Colour and Citizenship and British Society*, London: IRR, 1970.

30. Morrish, *The Background*, pp. 87, 164 and 232.

31. Ibid., p. 90 (our emphasis).

32. Select Committee on Race Relations and Immigration, 1968–69, p. 41.

33. Select Committee on Race Relations and Immigration, *Education Report*, London: HMSO, 1973 (our emphasis).

34. See Chapter 15 of the present volume. Also Hazel V. Carby, *Multicultural Fictions*, occasional stenciled paper no. 58, Centre for Contemporary Cultural Studies, Birmingham University, 1980.

35. Alan Little and Richard Willey, *Multi-Ethnic Education: The Way Forward*, Schools Council Pamphlet no. 18, 1981.

36. Education Guardian, "The Mixture as Before," *Guardian*, March 10 1981.

37. Bernard Coard, *How the West Indian Child is Made Educationally Subnormal in the British School System*, London: New Beacon Books, 1971.

38. Schools Council Working Papers: no. 36, *Religious Education in Secondary Schools*, London: Evans/Methuen, 1971; no. 50, *Multiracial Education: Need and Innovation*, London: Evans/Methuen, 1973.

39. H.E.R. Townsend, *Immigrant Pupils in England: The LEA Response*, London: NFER, 1971; Schools Council Working Paper no. 50; Schools Council, *Education for a Multiracial Society*, 1976.

40. DES, "Potential and Progress in a Second Culture," *Education Survey 10*, London: HMSO, 1971.

41. NAME, *Multiracial Schools*, vol. 1, no. 1, 1971.

42. NAME, *Multiracial Schools*, vol. 3, no. 1, 1972.

43. CCCS Education Group, *Unpopular Education*.

44. Central Advisory Council for Education (CACE), *15 to 18*, Crowther Report, London: HMSO, 1959; CACE, *Half Our Future*, Newsom Report, London: HMSO, 1963; CACE, *Children and Their Primary Schools*, Plowden Report, London: HMSO, 1967.

45. CCCS Education Group, *Unpopular Education*.

46. Miriam David, *The State, the Family and Education*, London: Routledge & Kegan Paul, 1980, pp. 170–8.

47. CCCS Education Group, *Unpopular Education*.

48. DES, *Educational Disadvantage and the Educational Needs of Immigrants*, Cmnd 5720, London: HMSO, 1974.

49. Clara Mulhern, "Multicultural Education and the Fight against Racism in Schools," in *Teaching and Racism*, London: ALTARF, 1979.

50. Quoted in Maureen Stone, *The Education of the Black Child in Britain: The Myth of Multiracial Education*, London: Fontana, 1981.

51. DES Committee of Enquiry, *A Language for Life*, Bullock Report, London: HMSO, 1975.

52. DES, *Educating Our Children: Four Subjects for Debate*, London: DES, 1976.

53. Stuart Hall, "The Great Moving Right Show," *Marxism Today*, January 1979.

54. DES, *Education in Schools: A Consultative Document*, Green Paper, Cmnd 6869, London: HMSO, 1977, p. 41:18.

55. Ibid., p. 22:5.2.

56. Ibid., p. 35:7.5.

57. Ibid., p. 44:10.41.

58. Select Committee on Race Relations and Immigration, *The West Indian Community*, London: HMSO, 1976.

59. Merilyn Moos, *Government Youth Training Policy and Its Impact on Further Education*, General Series: SP no. 57, CCCS, University of Birmingham; Dann Finn and Simon Frith, "Education and the Labouring Market," in *The State and the Politics of Education*, Open University Educational Studies, E353, Block 1, Part 2, Unit 4, London: Open University Press, 1981; Dan Finn, "The Rise of Manpower Servicedom," in CCCS Education Group, *Unpopular Education*; Simon Frith, "Education, Training and the Labour Process," in Cole and Skelton, eds, *Blind Alley*, London: Hesketh, 1980; British Youth Council, *Youth Unemployment: Causes and Cures*, London: BYC, 1977.

60. See n. 59.

61. Sheridan Welsh, "Unemployment in the Transition from School to Marriage of Working-Class Girls in the East End of London," *Schooling and Culture: Gender and Education*, no. 8, 1980, p. 20.

62. Ibid.

63. Finn, "The Rise of Manpower Servicedom."

64. Diana Geddes, "Young Blacks' Attitudes: A Factor in Lack of Jobs," *The Times*, August 11 1980.

65. Pratibha Parmar, "Young Asian Women: A Critique of the Pathological Approach," *Multiracial Education*, vol. 9, no. 3, Summer 1981, p. 27.

66. M.D.A. Freeman and Sarah Spencer, "Immigration Control, Black Workers and the Economy," *British Journal of Law and Society*, vol. 6, no. 1, Summer 1979.

67. Ibid.

68. "Quality or Collapse," *Report of the Youthaid Review of the Youth Opportunities Programme*, London: Youthaid, 1981.

69. Gus John, *In the Service of Black Youth: A Study of the Political Culture of Youth and Community Work with Black People in English Cities*, London: NAYC, 1981.

70. *Guardian*, January 2 1981.

71. *The Times Educational Supplement*, January 16 1981.

72. Committee of Inquiry into the Education of Children from Ethnic Minority Groups, *Press Notice*, July 14 1981.

73. IRR, "Anti-Racist Not Multicultural Education," *Race and Class*, vol. XXII, no. 1, Summer 1980, pp. 81–2.

74. *West Indian Children in Our Schools*, Interim Report of the Committee of Inquiry into the Education of Children from Ethnic Minority Groups, Cmnd 8273, Chairman: Anthony Rampton, London: HMSO, 1981.

75. *West Indian Children in Our Schools*, p. 12.

76. West Midlands Police, "Lozells Project: Background and Objectives," unpublished document, 1980.

77. Ibid.

78. *Guardian*, March 19 1981.

79. John, *In the Service of Black Youth*, p. 155.

15

Multiculture

Anti-racist teachers are faced with a dilemma: how should they respond to the range of new policies that are affecting black students in British schools? On the one hand, "multiculturalism" offers one of the very few remaining areas in which resources are being made available for curricular innovation. As Clara Mulhern argues in a document produced in November 1979 by ALTARF (All London Teachers Against Racism and Fascism):

> In a climate of retrenchment and defensiveness in education, when many of the curricular innovations of the Sixties are under attack, practically the only present source of progressive perspectives on the curriculum is the concept of multiculturalism.[1]

But in the same month, the Organization of Women of Asian and African Descent pointed tellingly to a different aspect of policy.

> It is no coincidence that the cuts in education will not mean a reduction in the number of disruptive units. Some boroughs are even considering building more, despite their reduced budgets.[2]

The problem often seems to be that discussions about the nature of curricular changes that could adequately reflect a multiracial society tend to avoid – or at least to address only implicitly – issues of discipline and control which are central to education practice. The twofold strategy of educational policy at the moment is apparently to win consent in the classroom and, if and when that fails, to bring coercion into play; and increasingly it is black students who are subjected to coercive strategies. What therefore need examination are not just courses and curricula, but also the social relations of classrooms and schools in relation to the wider material and ideological structures within which both teachers and pupils are located. A distinction has to be drawn between attempts to confront racism by changing educational policy and an understanding of educational racism as one instance of institutionalized racism in the context of other forms of institutionalized racism within a racist society. Policy, in short, cannot be divorced from politics.[3]

In current educational debates, multiculturalism is generally accepted as a positive practice with which teachers committed to an anti-racist society should be engaged. But despite the useful teaching produced from this perspective and the importance of ALTARF in creating a space in which white anti-racist teachers can assess their work, there seems to be little questioning of what multiculturalism is. In this essay I shall therefore address the limitations of the approach – the exclusive way that the concept poses questions about race and its implications, as an educational theory, for educational practice.

Policy and Educational Theory

The terms in which the argument for a multicultural curriculum is usually posed are not new; they are drawn from earlier debates about the need to counteract working-class educational failure. Theories of "deficiency" and "deprivation" were mobilized in these to support policies of channeling increased resources to inner-city schools and creating Educational Priority Areas. A similar strategy of positive discrimination was embodied in the Race Relations Act, 1976, which obliged local authorities to take positive action to promote equal opportunities. In this context education is seen as central in forging a new, more egalitarian and more democratic society. The Inner London Education Authority's (ILEA's) 1977 report, A Multi-Ethnic Education, asserts that:

> Unequivocally the commitment is to all. Just as there must be no second-class citizens, so there must be no second class educational opportunities.[4]

The purpose of educational policies is thus to promote tolerance between social groups and so produce a society displaying an equilibrium among ethnic groupings and between classes. The school is made a site for containing the effects of racism.

The need for multicultural education has not been regarded only as an ideal, however. According to the 1977 Green Paper Education in Schools, it is a practical necessity for constructing the society of the future.

> Ours is now a multiracial and multicultural country and one in which traditional social patterns are breaking down . . . the comprehensive school reflects the need to educate our people for a different sort of society . . . the education appropriate to our Imperial past cannot meet the requirements of modern Britain.[5]

This reference back to "our Imperial past" does hint at the basis of interracial conflict in social relations of exploitation, but this is presented as a historical rather than a structural consideration. The "breaking down" of "traditional social patterns" is presented as a natural, evolutionary progress; the antagonism, conflict and contradictions inherent in the process are disguised. The specific contribution of schools to the development of a racially just society is to "tackle with sustained enthusiasm the problems of children from other cultures or speaking other languages and make a microcosm of a happy and co-operative world."[6]

A similar perspective informs the work of educational theorists like Robert Jeffcoate, whose book *Positive Image* draws on his involvement in the Schools Council report on multiracial education; he now works in the Racial Minorities Unit at the Open University. The multiracial classroom, he argues, should be "a place where pride in race is affirmed and where inter-racial friendship and understanding are celebrated."[7] By dismissing "tensions and animosities," the multiracial curriculum is supposed to create an environment in which "the kind of racial slurs ... traded in the playground [are] not traded in the classroom."[8] Jeffcoate assumes it can achieve these effects in isolation from "negative and divisive outside pressures." Such sentiments, common to both Jeffcoate and the Green Paper, are based on a shared assumption that schools somehow *reflect* society, that a classroom can be a microcosm of society. But schools are also seen as a catalyst – the creation of "happy and co-operative classrooms" *will* influence the wider society and help to bring about a "happy and co-operative world." In justifying (and celebrating) his optimism, Jeffcoate "pins his hopes" on the generation now at school rather than on any structural – political or economic – changes. He leaves unexplored the relationship between (a) his students' display of multiracial cooperation in his classroom, (b) their trading of "racial slurs" in the playground and (c) the "tensions and animosities" outside the school. He fails to conceptualize the students – and their teachers – as living in and subject to these "negative and divisive outside pressures."

It is this account of the school–society relationship in educational policy that needs to be called into question. Both the Green Paper and the ILEA report from which I have quoted are official documents produced within state institutions. One of their ideological effects is to conjure up a "national interest" based on an assumed consensus of social interests, problems and solutions. Through a range of discursive techniques,[9] this apparent unity is imposed upon and subsumes inherent contradictions and conflicting economic and political interests within and between racial, sexual or class groupings. This normative pluralism not only ignores the institutional differentiation of interests but actually makes it impossible even to raise the question of the *construction* of inequality. Increasingly rigid immigration laws designed to limit black entry into Britain, police harassment and inequalities in housing and employment are not just detrimental to the interests of the black community, but they actually construct certain racial groups as "less equal" than others. In these material conditions, black students *know* that they are second-class citizens – in school as much as anywhere else.

It is here that the theoretical insights of Cultural Studies are important. By insisting that "culture" denotes antagonistic relations of domination and subordination, this perspective undermines the pluralistic notion of compatibility inherent in *multi*culturalism, the idea of a homogeneous national culture (innocent of class or gender differences) into which other equally generalized Caribbean or Asian cultures can be integrated. The paradigm of multiculturalism actually excludes the concept of dominant and subordinate cultures – either indigenous or migrant – and fails to recognize that the existence of racism relates to the possession and exercise of politico-economic control and authority and also to forms of resistance to the power of dominant social groups. Based upon liberal, humanistic notions of the individual experience of other cultures, multiculturalism proposes the classroom as the locus in which the cultures of racial minorities in contemporary Britain should be shared. The greater understanding achieved at this level is then meant to flow outwards to create a more harmonious society. In this account, schools are expected to affect wider social relations but are paradoxically granted autonomy from the effects of that society. The social relations of schools and classrooms are reduced to the single question of the transmission of a curriculum. But, as Richard Johnson argues,[10] the material being worked on in a classroom – the texts – is separate from the cultures as lived in the school, the lived experiences brought to the school and lived in the social relations of the school by both teachers and students. Multiculturalism assumes that it is only the material taught that is problematic.

Robert Jeffcoate dismisses as "pathological" and "tendentious" any argument that sees racism as endemic in Britain or as a cultural norm which molds children's attitudes. He also complains that debates about race have "become confounded" with debates about immigration.[11] To argue that the two debates should not be confounded, though, actually ignores their structural and historical interrelationship. Imperialism used race as a mechanism for economic, political and socio-cultural forms of exploitation and dominance. At present a different form of exploitation is being experienced within the Mother Country of that colonial system. Although the specific nature of the relationship has changed, of course, race is still seen as "the issue." In the terms of common sense, white immigration is effectively disregarded: the policies of successive governments have been designed to prevent non-whites from entering Britain; there's no doubt about who "they" are in comments like "we don't want any more of them." "Immigrant" has become synonymous with "black." It is not therefore a question of the issues of race and immigration being confounded; rather, the immigration laws and the dominant forms of representation in this area of debate are profoundly racist.

The central proposition here is that "blacks are a problem." The Green

Paper refers to the "*problems* of children from other cultures"; the ILEA report addresses the *problem* of black students as low achievers, which has become associated with the corollary *problems* of black crime and unemployed black youth; Robert Jeffcoate sees the *problem* of black students' negative self-images as central. Thus black educational failure is taken to guarantee that the root problem is that of the ethnic minorities themselves.[12] Black people are constructed as a social problem; the concept of multiculturalism mobilizes a "race relations" discourse and a range of social (educational) policies to "deal with" the problem.

Texts

The aspect of policy that I am mainly concerned with in this article is the use of texts in the multicultural curriculum to promote "racial harmony" by creating an unproblematic understanding of the culture of "others." Robert Jeffcoate argues for a fairly common but oversimplified methodology: he implies that the complexities of racism can be reduced to a simple binary opposition of positive/negative and that negative images can be reversed, like a photograph, and displaced by prominent and positive representations. If they accept this logic, even teachers who would normally eschew the use of filmic, televisual or fictional literary texts to solve "real-life" problems can find themselves arguing that the use of texts which represent blacks positively somehow reflects the needs of ethnic minorities and would allow teachers to combat racism in the classroom. This notion of an imbalance in the curriculum which needs rectification ignores both the social, political and economic determinations on the school as an institution and also the class, gender and racial positions of subjects within that institution. In Richard Johnson's terms, the texts to be worked on and the "lived relations" present in the classroom are not held separate; they therefore become obscured and are reduced to equivalents.

If these two elements are not distinguished, it is impossible to take proper account of how both of them determine and constrain what teaching and learning can effectively be achieved. The reasons for a white student's refusal to read a "Paki book" or for students' resistance to watching a play by black girls cannot be deduced just from the "positive" texts. Nor can these "positive" texts be assumed (though they often are) to show "blacks as they really are," as against the misrepresentations in ethnocentric or racist texts – a notion which would appear ridiculous if applied so simplistically to white characters. Teachers should therefore not be as surprised as they sometimes have been when, say, Farrukh Dhondy's short stories provoke a hostile response; when white students harden their racist responses and black students adopt strategies to exclude whites in the classroom from the availability of certain meanings. This increased divisiveness, rather than the expected cooperation, cannot be understood or explained if the "culture of the classroom" is seen as separate from "outside" tensions and from the determinations upon the attitudes students and teachers bring to the texts and which are being lived in the classroom in spite of, not *because* of, the texts. The point is not that the texts have no effectivity or that they should not be analyzed in terms of their reconstruction of dominant ideologies (that's the pedagogic purpose); on the contrary, it is to draw attention to the unargued psychological assumption that *these* texts will have *these* effects on any individual student, and to question quite radically the notion that actual responses to a text are wholly determined by the way it "positions" its "reader." Because, as Paul Willemen argues in his "Notes on Subjectivity," the inscribed reader

> is itself already an imaginary unity, a mapping onto each other of different You's produced by the plurality of discourses that constitutes the text, the construction of that unity will differ according to the discourses (knowledge, prejudices, resistances, etc.) brought to bear by given readers on that place. It is in this sense that inscribed subject positions are never hermetically sealed into a text, but are always positions in ideologies. Texts can restrict readings (offer resistances), they cannot determine them.[13]

Multiculturalist approaches to the examination of black cultures in schools generally tend to be as reductionist as their use of texts. The main purpose often seems to be to do no more than prove that "blacks have a culture too." Thus the case is made for including established West Indian and Asian authors in an O level syllabus (see the *Times Educational Supplement,* October 13 1978) – "established" here indicating literary texts which can be assimilated into the pantheon of a high cultural tradition. Alternatively, the introduction of black culture is seen in terms of the *ad hoc* incorporation of forms considered "relevant" to pupils' "lifestyle" – reggae, the poetry of Linton Kwesi Johnson, young black people's own writing, Rastafarianism. Again, the tendency in such teaching is to reduce "black culture" to the artifacts produced within a limited number of "cultural" sites – the arts, religion, and so forth. These manifestations are thus divorced from the political and economic struggles of being black in Britain, whether in school or in the labor market; the ways in which a culture is produced from and about the social relations of these sites and struggles remain unexplored. To take one of the most common examples, much contemporary reggae music can be said to be about the forms of resistance of urban black youth, about their refusal to be perpetual victims. Many songs voice the need for this resistance; but they can lose any political relevance if they are treated as a purely "cultural" artifact that is "popular" as opposed to "high." It is also misleading to assume that these records unproblematically represent the students' own culture that can be brought into the classroom. As soon as questions about production and consumption are raised, it becomes obvious that urban black youth have no control over their marketing or distribution. Other interests are involved – multinational record companies seeking a mass audience for their product, for example, will consider the music's appeal to white consumers as well as a black audience. An expression of black consciousness can equally well be good to dance to at a white middle-class party.

Similarly, language itself should be seen as a site of struggle over meanings: this makes it possible to understand the relation between a white teacher's use of standard English and a black student's use of an alternative form as a mode of resistance. A teacher may be excluded from understanding through the student's use of patois or the student may be labeled as insolent by the teacher for rejecting the required set of meanings:

> "And no blue and green tights. I want all the girls to wear flesh coloured tights."
> "Whose flesh, miss?" Lorraine asked.[14]

The struggle over whose terms will be definitive is not restricted to texts, and these broader contexts also need to be explored. How are superior/inferior or correct/incorrect attitudes inscribed within language in and through the social relations between dominant and subordinated groups? Why do non-racist texts produce racist readings – refusals to accept the preferred reading encoded at the point of their production? Once we recognize that texts have to *work* to neutralize contradictions and produce imaginary resolutions, we then need to examine not only the way texts are produced but also the differential nature of the responses they evoke. Instead of assuming that all texts are incorporated into a dominant ideology, we should ask what contradictions are present and how they are being handled. Why, for example, is romance mobilized in the BBC series *Empire Road* to resolve (at an imaginary level) racial conflict? Rather than asking how accurately it represents black life, *Empire Road* could be questioned in the light of a comment by the show's leading actress, Corinne Skinner-Carter.

> Writers don't like writing for women – even Michael [Abbensetts] . . . I've always accused him of being a chauvinistic pig. The women in *Empire Road* are passive. I'm only there because Norman must have a wife – because if he wants a cup of coffee he can't make it for himself.[15]

Invisible Woman

From the pedagogic point of view, the really important question is the specific ways in which texts are used, where and by whom. In the context of multicultural education, black or anti-racist books, films and television programs are used mainly by white teachers for the purposes of under-standing black cultures; the black voice is noticeably absent from the debate about the multicultural curriculum. I can illuminate these points by looking at a specific question – the "invisibility" of black women. Courses in Black Studies or Black History are usually male-centered and relate to white patriarchal society; in the same way, Women's Studies courses focus almost exclusively upon aspects of white women's lives. In sociological and cultural research, it is the forms of subcultural resistances by black male youth that are analyzed. Sexism is implicit in the stories of Farrukh Dhondy and, despite a contradictory sequence showing the Grunwick dispute, the woman's voice is not heard in the film *Blacks Britannica.* Black women are seldom recognized as a particular socio-cultural entity, nor as important enough to merit serious academic consideration.

How could a white woman teacher rectify this omission? There now exist texts in which black women write about the influence of white societies and confront the past and present in personal and historical terms; they address the need to reverse the present order through an increasing awareness of self and understanding of the political and economic press-ures that underlie present conditions. The writings of Ama Ata Aidoo, Toni Cade Bambara, Buchi Emecheta, Rosa Guy, Joyce Ladner, Toni Morrison, Alice Walker and Amrit Wilson are part of the struggle to challenge dominant white conceptions of black women and to voice the need for economic, political and personal power to change the fantasies that limit and construct the black woman.[16] They are part of a growing body of work which can be used by women teachers to explore not just the process of growing up female in a patriarchal society, but also the ways in which growing up female and black means coping with racial oppression at an early age and developing self-reliance and resilience. The specter of white beauty can here be seen as hauntingly destructive:

> I destroyed white baby dolls. But the dismembering of dolls was not the true horror. The truly horrifying thing was the transference of the same impulse to little white girls. The indifference with which I could have axed them was shaken only by my desire to do so. To discover what eluded me: the secret of the magic they weaved on others. What made people look at them and say, "Awwwww," but not for me. . . . The best hiding place was love. Thus the conversion from pristine sadism to fabricated hatred, to fraudulent love. It was a small step to Shirley Temple. I learned much later to worship her . . . knowing, even as I had learned, that the change was adjustment without improvement.[17]

The point of this extended example is to illustrate the potential and also the problems of introducing such texts. They should certainly help white teachers to understand the culture of black women. But this does not mean that they can be granted a privileged status. They do not simply express the experience of black women; like the other texts I have mentioned, they represent that experience in particular ways that have to be worked on by readers. Returning to Richard Johnson's two moments of a culturally informed pedagogy, the continuing absence of such texts from schools and from Women's Studies courses means that useful teaching about how black women are constructed as a category cannot even begin. Including these texts in a teaching program is only half the problem, though, because Johnson's second moment, the cultures brought to bear by students, still obtains. For example, a white woman teacher, maybe for feminist reasons, may care about the position of black women and want to learn about them, understand them and teach them. Nevertheless, it would be important that she should recognize the implications of white womanhood for black womanhood, clarify what are the social relations with those she teaches, and understand the nature of their responses to her teaching. Inevitably in this process, the anger evoked by texts representing the oppression of black women could not be separated from anger directed at the white teacher, herself implicated as a direct source of oppression. This conflict-ridden duality in the pedagogic role will remain unperceived if teachers interested in black culture are too comfortable or complacent in their own anti-racism.

It is also these hierarchical relationships that are misrecognized in the unifying concepts of "national interest," "community" and "multicultural-ism." The "black" of *Blacks Britannica* and its use in this essay to designate "non-white" should be seen in the context of a political consciousness which threatens these integrative concepts and their implications of an equality that is all too obviously a myth:

> I mean, it's something that was sort of generated from school. They were saying, "You're gonna want a car, you're gonna want a house, and you gotta do this and you gotta do that, and you wanna earn a wage about a certain amount." It's all drummed into you, you know, time after time. "You're gonna need this, and you're gonna want that, and so on – you're gonna need a holiday at least once a year, and all them things; and you gotta study, you know." And what they didn't tell you was that "you're black, and we're going to stop you doing all this, we're going to do our best to stop you getting all this".[18]

1980

Notes

1. Clara Mulhern, "Multicultural Education and the Fight Against Racism in Schools," *Teaching and Racism,* London: ALTARF, 1979.
2. "Education Cuts, from Sin-Bins to Social Security," *Fowaad, Newsletter of the Organization of Women of Asian and African Descent,* London: OWAAD, 1979.
3. For a fuller account of some of these arguments, see my stenciled occasional

paper no. 58, *Multicultural Fictions*, Centre for Contemporary Cultural Studies, Birmingham University, 1980.

4. Inner London Education Authority, *A Multi-Ethnic Education: Joint Report of Schools Sub-committee and Further and Higher Education Sub-committee*, London: Waterlow, 1977.

5. Department of Education and Science and Welsh Office, *Education in Schools*, Cmnd 6869, London: HMSO, 1977, paras 1.10–1.11.

6. Ibid., Foreword.

7. Robert Jeffcoate, *Positive Image: Towards a Multiracial Curriculum*, London: Writers' and Readers' Cooperative, 1979, p. 122.

8. Ibid., p. 63.

9. Among the most common of these is the play on "we" and "our"; for a detailed exploration of this process see James Donald, "Green Paper: Noise of Crisis," *Screen Education*, no. 30, Spring 1979.

10. Richard Johnson, "Cultural Studies and Educational Practice," *Screen Education*, no. 34, Spring 1980, pp. 5–16.

11. Jeffcoate, *Positive Image*, p. 26.

12. Other theories of deprivation also have the failing or problem child at their center through causative factors: the urban environment, poor living conditions, a family structure regarded as inadequate, and so on. The school's role is one of compensation; compensating for all the inadequacies focused in the student. For example, linguistic deprivation theories of the working-class child are applied to the black child, whose language becomes regarded as not adequate for the learning processes. Increased resources are then considered needed for remedial provision. Essentially the argument is for a more intense application of schooling rather than a structurally different form of an education system.

13. Paul Willemen, "Notes on Subjectivity," *Screen*, vol. 19, no. 1, Spring 1978, pp. 62–3.

14. Farrukh Dhondy, *Come to Mecca*, London: Fontana Lions, 1978, p. 67.

15. In *Radio Times*, August 18–24 1979.

16. See Ama Ata Aidoo, *No Sweetness Here*, London: Longman, 1970, and *Our Sister Killjoy*, London: Longman, 1978; Toni Cade Bambara, *Gorrilla, My Love*, New York: Random House, 1972; *The Seabirds Are Still Alive*, New York: Random House, 1977, and Bambara, ed., *The Black Woman*, New York: Mentor, 1970; Buchi Emecheta, *In the Ditch*, London: Allison & Busby, 1979; *Second Class Citizen*, London: Fontana, 1977; *The Bride Price*, London: Fontana, 1976; *The Slave Girl*, London: Fontana, 1979, and *The Joys of Motherhood*, London: Allison & Busby, 1979; Rosa Guy, *The Friends*, Harmondsworth: Puffin, 1977, and *Ruby*, New York: Bantam, 1979; Joyce Ladner, *Tomorrow's Tomorrow: The Black Woman*, New York: Doubleday Anchor, 1971; Toni Morrison, *The Bluest Eye*, New York: Pocket Books, 1972; *Sula*, New York: Bantam, 1975, and *Song of Solomon*, New York: Signet, 1978; Alice Walker, *In Love and Trouble*, New York: Harvest/HBJ, 1973; *The Third Life of Grange Copeland*, New York: Harvest/HBJ, 1977, and *Meridian*, New York: Pocket Books, 1977; Amrit Wilson, *Finding a Voice*, London: Virago, 1978.

17. Morrison, *The Bluest Eye*, p. 22.

18. Draft transcription of *Blacks Britannica* quoted in Arthur Paris, "*Blacks Britannica*: Race, Cinema and the Public Sphere," *Socialist Review*, no. 48, November–December 1979, pp. 4–5.

16

The Racism behind the Rioting

A sense of history has been lacking in analyses of the rebellions in Britain in 1981. Britain has a long history of the rebellion and repression of its black population, and that history can be found in a special issue of *Race and Class*.[1]

"Britain is a profoundly racist society": the opening sentence of the editorial disperses any lingering romanticism about traditions of British liberalism or the fair play of the British sense of justice. The recurring theme is of the increasing authoritarianism of the state, supported not by the friendly "bobby" but by the racist "blues." The rebellion of black youth is a response to this institutionalized racism, supported and perpetuated by the police.

"Blacks" is not the modern equivalent for Negro. It is how "Afro-Caribbeans and Asians, particularly the young, choose to describe themselves" as it expresses their common experience of racism. The first article, by Ambalavaner Sivanandan, outlines the history of the organizations Asians and West Indians formed against the racism they encountered when they arrived in Britain as immigrant labor. Sivanandan carefully traces both individual and collective forms of resistance and grounds them in the traditions that both groups brought with them. The connections made between colonialism, imperialism and racism were crucial in founding coordinated campaigns from the Pan-African Federation to the Indian Workers' Association.

Sivanandan documents the formations of organizations around every aspect of institutionalized racism – housing, schooling, immigration control legislation and the workplace. Internationally, he examines the influence of the politics and political organizations of "home" countries as well as the effects of black nationalism and the Black Power struggles in the USA. In the mid-seventies, Sivanandan argues, youth emerged as "the vanguard of the black struggle." The establishment of black women's groups in the seventies culminated in the formation of the Organization of Women of Asian and African Descent (OWAAD), a national-linked organization of autonomous groups in black communities.

This growth of black community organization is interwoven with the history of increasing state racism, the growth of fascist groups and the inability of the white left and trade unions to develop anti-racist strategies. Sivanandan describes Britain today as becoming a "pass-law" society: the new Nationality Bill creates classes of citizenship, and black citizens need a passport to get the shrinking services of the welfare state. Black youth, Sivanandan concludes, are "not the unemployed, but the never employed. . . . Theirs is a different hunger – a hunger to retain the freedom, the lifestyle, the dignity which they have carved out from the stone of their lives." The police represent "an army of occupation."

In another article, Tony Bunyan places the immediate cause of the "riots" "at the door of years of aggressive policing policies." Bunyan provides a comprehensive history of the coercive agencies of the British state, especially the police.

He describes the two major policing strategies in mainland Britain today: reactive or "fire-brigade" tactics of special units like the Special Patrol Group (SPG); and the preventative strategy called "community policing," with an emphasis on information-gathering and intelligence systems. Given the running down of industry and high unemployment, Bunyan concludes that Britain is entering a "period of greater repression – and resistance."

Lee Bridges analyzes the results of structural unemployment and assesses policies and programs of "containment directed at the least unionized, increasingly dis-employed white and black residents of the inner-cities." He also examines community policing projects and experiments that have been advocated as positive alternatives to the use of special units like the SPG and finds that they are complementary. Community policing is a model for forms of local police states. Louis Kushnick, meanwhile, explores the responses in the US to the ghetto uprisings of the sixties as "an important body of data that can illuminate the range of choices open to the British state."

Kushnick sees common patterns of harassment and invasion in both societies. A detailed account of the notorious "Sus" laws explains the procedures used to arrest blacks either for "acting suspiciously" or "on suspicion" of being an illegal immigrant.

Kushnick's conclusions are bleak: "ideological disarray" among liberals in the USA where "race" is an unfashionable subject, and Los Angeles mayor Tom Bradley's solution for "losers": a "24-hour-a-day controlled environment for uncooped members of the underclass." Is William Whitelaw's use of army camps as prisons for Britain's rebellious youth precisely this type of controlled environment?

Perhaps the most complex article is the last: Paul Gilroy argues that Marxist theory "has been at best 'race blind' and at worst eurocentric." He states that there can be no "general theory of 'race' or 'race relations'"; specific forms of racism have to be analyzed in specific social formations under particular historical conditions. The British left, he claims, has been unaffected by the black dialogue with Marxism to be found in the work of Marcus Garvey, George Padmore, C.L.R. James and Richard Wright, preferring to subsume black struggles under those of the working class.

Gilroy argues that "race is the modality in which class is lived." Since culture is a terrain of class conflicts, cultures of resistance are "one aspect of the struggle against capitalist domination which blacks experience as racial oppression. This is a class struggle *in* and *through* race." Gilroy feels it imperative that the "boundaries of the concept 'class struggle'" be redrawn to include "the relentless processes by which classes are constituted – organized and disorganized – in politics, as well as the struggles between them, once formed." He uses a concept of community to reveal the "ties between the struggles of blacks outside the workplace and those who remain within the wage relation," and explores the class character of black cultural struggles in Britain.

It is a pity to have to bewail the absences in such a well-organized, informative and thought-provoking collection of essays, but black women's voices are not heard, although many of the contributors obviously are aware of the existence of a black feminist presence emerging from autonomous black women's organizations. Understanding the position of black women is crucial to an understanding of the workings of racist ideologies that describe the black family as pathological; it is central to any attempt to link workplace and community; and it is integral to any understanding of resistance to institutionalized racism.

1982

Note

1. *Race and Class*, vol. XXII, 1981, Special Issue: "Britain '81: Rebellion and Repression."

17

The Blackness of Theory

Henry Louis Gates's *The Signifying Monkey* is bound to be controversial for what is at stake is the "blackness" of theory.[1] What Gates proposes is a theory of criticism which is inscribed within the black vernacular tradition but also shapes the African American literary tradition. In this project *The Signifying Monkey* has its historical and theoretical origins in a reaction against the Eurocentric dominance of literary theory in the United States and in particular the dominance of the "Yale School" of criticism of a decade ago.

As an essay, "The Signifying Monkey" had its first public presentation in 1980 when Gates, then an untenured assistant professor, lectured to the formidable ranks of the Yale English Department, before whom many had been cowed. The atmosphere was electric because, far from being intimidated, Gates proved to these stuffy and somewhat pompous arbiters of literary critical power not only that there was an entity that could be called black literature but that black scholars could use and manipulate theory. Those of us in the audience who were black offered support and solidarity through our historically recent and all too visible presence in these particular halls of academe. It almost seemed as if the moment could be compared to the escaped slave proving his or her humanity to the abolitionists by demonstrating the skills of literacy. The Civil Rights movement propelled our entry into universities in significant numbers, and Gates's contention that the vernacular and the theoretical can be combined appears to link the lives of critics with those on whom the doors of integration and upward mobility have been securely slammed shut. The vernacular is embodied in the privileged concept of Signifyin(g). Using Roger D. Abrahams's definitions, Signifyin(g) is a black figurative mode of language use including "the ability to talk with great innuendo"; "to carp, cajole, needle, and lie"; "the propensity to talk around a subject, never quite coming to the point"; and it is also "the language of trickery, that set of words achieving Hamlet's 'direction through indirection.'" Signifyin(g) is often associated with the everyday practice of the "dozens," and "coming down" on somebody with words.

Gates's use of the concept depends upon the construction of a link between the frequently esoteric use of a critical discourse and an everyday language practice of the people who live adjacent to but do not enter Yale except to clean and service it.

The political project to imagine a black literary theory and tradition has to define that tradition and set of theoretical premises against both a dominant cultural formation and other subordinate ethnic formations. The impulse toward establishing critical and cultural autonomy rests on the assumption that an aggressive assertion of the existence of a unique tradition is both desirable and necessary. The logic of such an assumption is that in order to confront, effectively, the exclusions of a literary canon, alternative canons should be created. Of course, the function of canons is precisely to exclude, and in African American literary criticism black feminists have been creating alternatives to the dominance of great black male thinkers. The concern to establish a canon or tradition is a conventional literary project, there is nothing inherently black or feminist about it, but the question of whether it is indeed necessary or desirable to create traditions rather than to develop a critique of the process of canon formation remains unasked.

"Signifyin(g)," Gates explains in the Preface, "is not the only theory appropriate to the texts of our tradition. But it is one that I would like to think arises from the black tradition itself." From a close reading of Ralph Ellison's collection of essays *Shadow and Act*, and Ishmael Reed's novel *Mumbo Jumbo*, Gates constructs a theory of criticism which he directs toward an "ideal reader" and theorist of the black vernacular, Houston Baker. The emphasis then is on readings of culture and of texts which are internal to the category of "blackness" rather than what Gates calls in his Introduction "literary theories appropriated from without."

In the first half of the book Gates makes a very complex and sophisticated argument that the principles of a black tradition of formal language use and its intepretation have their origins in the Yoruba myths of Esu-Elegbara and Fon myths of Legba. A detailed exposition of this mythological structure reveals an indigenous black hermeneutical principle. This principle, Gates argues convincingly, can be found in the New World transposition of tales of the Signifying Monkey, tales in which a monkey always outwits his physical superior, the Lion, by his extraordinary power to manipulate language, and is also present in the rhetoric and semantics of the practice of Signifyin(g). The Signifying Monkey and its "Pan-African cousin," Esu-Elegbara, Gates situates as functionally equivalent figures of rhetoric and interpretation. The mastery of Signifyin(g), a complex system of rhetoric which is "fundamentally black," creates "*homo rhetoricus Africanus*," Gates asserts, and this power to manipulate language is what he proposes as enabling black people to move freely across the boundaries between the white and the black discursive universes.

It is possible to be at once dazzled by the insights into the linguistic

complexities of Signifyin(g) and its relation to Yoruba and Fon hermeneu-
tics and at the same time to remain skeptical of the project of establishing
an essentially black theory and practice of criticism. Gates himself appro-
priates from without and is very eclectic in his use of structural, post-
structural and even Marxist literary and linguistic theory. The exposition
of uniquely black literary strategies is accomplished as much through the
work of Geoffrey Hartmann, Harold Bloom, Jacques Lacan and Tzvetan
Todorov, readings of Jacques Derrida by Gayatri Spivak and Jonathan
Culler, and the insights of Mikhail Bakhtin as it is through the formidable array of critics of African American culture, who include Houston
Baker, Amiri Imamu Baraka, Kimberly Benston, Sterling Brown, Ralph
Ellison, Claudia Mitchell-Kernan, Ishmael Reed, Geneva Smitherman,
John Edgar Wideman and Al Young. Gates's insights about the relation
between Signifyin(g) as a linguistic form and jazz as a musical form, both
of which depend upon complex processes of repetition, revision and
reformulation, are not applied to the ways in which African American
cultural forms have revised, reinterpreted and rewritten dominant cultural
paradigms. Emphasis on the intertextual relations between the narratives
and works of fiction that Gates selects frequently discounts the historical
conditions that shaped the production of a text. His assertion that there
is a simple division between black content and a white-influenced form is
inadequate to explain how struggles between social groups with unequal
access to power are reproduced on the terrain of culture. Indeed, *The
Signifying Monkey* cannot resolve its contradictory political positions
between Gates's appeal to a Black Nationalist rhetoric with its essentialist
understanding of "blackness" and his simultaneous claim that "race" is a
trope. The most significant weakness of Gates's analysis is that the concept
of race is not understood as a historically constructed and politically
contested category.

Part two of *The Signifying Monkey* is concerned with reading the tradition
and establishing the trope of the "Talking Book" as the central trope that
unites a tradition of black texts. Gates produces perceptive and subtle close
readings of texts as diverse as four narratives from the late eighteenth and
early nineteenth century, Zora Neale Hurston's *Their Eyes Were Watching
God*, Ishmael Reed's *Mumbo Jumbo* and Alice Walker's *The Color Purple*. But
he also inflects his definition of blackness and a black tradition through a
North American nationalist lens. The early narratives establish Gates's
subject as being black literature in English; he does not establish paradigms
for us that could be traced through narratives in Spanish or Portuguese;
neither does he suggest ways in which the theories and practices of
Signifyin(g), and thus his theory of blackness itself, could be applied to
diasporic writing and writers.

Gates creates an imagined unity of texts and writers which, like all
traditions, more effectively establishes imagined continuities than disconti-
nuities. While no critical book that outlines the parameters of a tradition

could, or should, attempt to discuss all texts that would respond to its paradigms, what is always an interesting question is what texts are excluded from that community. Gates peremptorily rejects Richard Wright from inclusion in his community of writers and critics and even from his definition of "blackness." Wright's centrality to black modernism is ignored. In terse phrases of condemnation, Wright is accused of creating "a class of ideal individual black selves" that included only himself, and of achieving his humanity "only at the expense of his fellow blacks." He is expunged as "an exception," characterized as "a noble black savage," and expelled in favor of Zora Neale Hurston's wholesome portrayal of the rural folk as an ethically and morally preferable source of twentieth-century African American writing.

The other intriguing absence is embedded in the field of criticism that Gates constructs and with which he is principally engaged. His admirable intention to see women writers as equally significant to his construction of a tradition as men is not paralleled by a theoretical engagement with black feminist criticism or black feminist critics. This is not because Gates is antipathetic to feminist criticism – his dialogue with the work of Barbara Johnson is important and enlightening. But he is silent about the substantial body of black feminist criticism on the work of Hurston, Reed and Walker, and the very significant theoretical interventions by Deborah McDowell, Hortense Spillers, Barbara Smith, Valerie Smith and Mary Helen Washington among others that have constituted a critical field during the last decade. Is it possible that, like Richard Wright, black feminist critics and black feminist criticism must remain on the margins of the formation of blackness?

Ultimately, we have to ask the question: is Gates Signifyin(g) on us all? His book is a complex and frequently dense repetition, revision and reformulation of both Eurocentric and African American theoretical paradigms. *The Signifying Monkey* is still deeply marked by the desire to prove its legitimacy and authenticity to a skeptical audience. The need for a "black" critical theory emanates from the fact that African American Studies in general, and African American literary criticism in particular, has had a significant influence on debates about curriculum. Most English departments in universities in the United States feel that they should employ a Professor of Black Literature. This does not mean that black literature is no longer ghettoized; what it signifies is that many more universities offer effectively ghettoized black literature courses than ten years ago. A black face also "proves" the sincerity of a commitment to minority recruitment, and most English departments feel that they should have "one," making the annual recruitment of recent black Ph.Ds look like a department store rush for the January sales. The conditions for the study of African American literature, then, are not necessarily better but they are different. *The Signifying Monkey* is symptomatic of the mutually contradictory tendencies in the intellectual struggle to control the dominant paradigms that will determine the politics of African American literary critical practice.

1989

Note

1. Henry Louis Gates, Jr, *The Signifying Monkey: A Theory of Afro-American Literary Criticism*, New York: Oxford University Press, 1988.

18

The Canon:
Civil War and Reconstruction

Like Toni Morrison, I too can hear the dull thud of a war machine contained within the contemporary debate about "the canon." I think of the American Civil War, of Reconstruction, of European and American imperialism, of post-colonial societies, and of the previously colonized drawn to live and work in the metropolitan heartlands of colonial power: in London, Los Angeles, New York and Paris. Each of these battlegrounds has involved intense struggles to define "Americanness," or "Britishness," to distinguish a Euro-North American cultural and political heritage from its "other," whether that be "blackness," "Orientalism" or "the Amerindian." Clearly, an Aryan, Greco-Roman, European history, purged of semitic and continental African influence, was created in conjunction with imperial ideologies of manifest destiny. Upon the *tabula rasa* of the New World a European future was to be imprinted from a purified European past. Thus, the genocide of the Lucayan and Tainan Arawaks and the Carib peoples was rendered, and remains, invisible and the enslavement of African peoples became the Christian salvation of their savage souls. But whether the means be cultural and political erasure or the contemporary institution of visible signs of minority status, like Margaret Thatcher's four grades of British citizenship, the struggle of definition in relation to or against Euro-Americanness shapes our past, our present and our futures. As W.E.B. Du Bois said in 1903, "The problem of the twentieth century is the problem of the color-line, – the relation of the darker to the lighter races . . . in Asia and Africa, in America and the islands of the sea."[1]

But I am not certain that we stand in the most effective place in relation to the contemporary (the fashionable description would be postmodern) debate about the canon. In attacking the canon are we, in fact, concentrating all our efforts upon one weapon aimed in our direction while losing a sense of what the whole battle is about? I think that, in many ways, the academic debate about teaching canonical versus non-canonical texts, in which so many of us are embroiled, disguises what we are really fighting about, indeed disguises what our real differences are.

We are all familiar with the contemporary "discovery" of the black woman writer by the publishing industry and by the academy. In February 1988, women, as producers of culture, were the focus of a debate about the canon. A columnist in the *Wall Street Journal* asserted, however erroneously, that books by Alice Walker were taught more frequently than Shakespeare in departments of English. This was an assertion that had originally been made in a January 1988 issue of the *Chronicle of Higher Education.* The article continued by claiming that the texts of women writers, and in particular black women writers, were the arsenal in the war against the canon. The implication of the article was, predictably, that the consequences for the transmission of high culture are devastating; black women writers were used as the cultural sign of the threat to the traditional curriculum.

However, I would argue that debates about the canon are misleading in many ways. Arguments appear to be about the inclusion or exclusion of particular texts and/or authors or about including or excluding types of books and authors ("women" and "minorities" are usually the operative categories). It also appears as if debates about the canon are disagreements about issues of representation only. Here, I am using the word "represen-tation" in two ways. First, it appears that if an agreed-upon percentage of texts by women and various minorities were included in academic syllabi debate would be resolved. But what is also implied in the argument for including these texts is that they represent, in the sense of reflect, the experience or point of view of previously excluded sectors of society. So, authors become representative figures for defined groups of people and their work is taken to be representative of that group's or community's response to the cultural formation in which they live.

Contrary to what the debate appears to be about, talking about the canon means that we avoid the deeper problem. Focusing on books and authors means that we are not directly addressing the ways in which our society is structured in dominance. We live in a racialized hierarchy which is also organized through class and gender divisions. Reducing these complex modes of inequality to questions of representation on a syllabus is a far too simple method of appearing to resolve these social contradictions, and yet this is how the battle has been waged at Columbia and Stanford, to take two examples of campuses engaged in debating the importance of canonical works of Western culture. What is absurd about these hotly contested and highly emotive battles is that proponents for radical change in canonical syllabi are forced to act as if inclusion of the texts they favor would somehow make accessible the experience of women or minorities as generic types. The same people who would argue in very sophisticated critical terms that literary texts do not directly reflect or represent reality but reconstruct and re-present particular historical realities find themselves demanding that the identity of a social group be represented by a single novel. Acting as if an excluded or marginalized or dominant group is represented in a particular text, in my view, is a mistake.

On the other hand, if you work in a somewhat liberal, or enlightened university like mine, a university where a significant number of people in departments of American and English Literature have become convinced that the canon does need revision, how is change implemented? Key words like "flexibility" and "diversity" advertise what I call a "supermarket" theory of education. Minority and women scholars and Minority and Women's Studies are included, but on what terms? We have achieved the democracy of the supermarket where the structural assumption of choice reigns through the multiple brands and flavors of ice cream we offer. Shakespeare courses thrive in the catalogue next to Caribbean fiction; before lunch you can attend the "Third World and Imperialism" course and for dessert can sample a course described as "some indispensable texts that every educated person should know," presumably without suffering indigestion. Of course, the ideology of equality in the supermarket makes invisible certain important inequalities: those who cannot afford fresh fruit and vegetables appear to choose not to eat them; the limited purchases demanded by food stamp allowances dictate diet; and the relations of exploitation and dependency between the metropolitan nations and the so-called "Third World" are hidden in the large display of bananas imported from Central America courtesy of a corporate entity more powerful than many small nations, the United Fruit Company.

I teach courses on African American and Caribbean Literature and am very critical of the boundaries within which courses like it exist. There are structural inequalities that implicitly define what is regarded as canonical, in terms of what every student should know, in the requirements for majors. Courses on culturally marginalized literatures are not part of those requirements. While a course on Caribbean Literature can be counted as an English or American Studies course, it has an exotic relation to what is regarded as the central area of study. The students occupy the position of tourist, a position which reproduces dominant American attitudes that regard the Caribbean as a romantic vacation paradise and a position that renders culturally and politically invisible the presence of thousands of migrant workers from Jamaica who, every autumn, live and work in the area that surrounds our school. The ideological common sense among both students and faculty about the actual content of the course is that Caribbean fiction is intensely political. But, of course, that is OK because culturally marginalized literature is a suitable subject for the sort of politicized discussion deemed inappropriate for culturally centralized literature. It is the latter that is thought to embody universal moral values which demand an aesthetic and politically neutralized response. The conclusion I draw from the fact of the existence of the Caribbean Literature course and courses like it is, therefore, that the mere presence of marginalized cultures in the curriculum changes very little.

As I have argued elsewhere,[2] teaching about marginalized culture in the context of metropolitan universities presents both students and teachers with some fundamental political dilemmas. Our teaching needs to make connections with, as well as provide a critique of, dominant ideologies and meanings of culture which structure the curricula of departments of English and American Studies. Teaching marginalized cultures must involve a constant and consistent critique of the forms of knowledge production that maintain the European and American cultural hegemony in which our students are embedded; either that or we will remain politically marginal. If we are not in a state of constant political confrontation with the imperialist discourse that structures metropolitan education systems, then we merely confirm our exoticism. Approaches to culture offered by programs in Comparative Literature offer no satisfactory alternative to English or American Studies, for historically they too are overwhelmingly Eurocentric. If we are to develop any sort of challenge to the ways in which educational institutions organize and structure forms of knowledge about marginalized peoples, then we have to be able to offer a coherent alternative political vision: a way of thinking critically across relations of cultural production in the, so-called, "Third," "Second," and "First" Worlds.

As Toni Morrison has argued,[3] one way to rethink the relationship between the social, political and cultural construction of blackness and marginality, on the one hand, and assumptions of a normative whiteness within the dominant culture, on the other, is to examine the ways in which that dominant culture has been shaped and transformed by the presence of the marginalized. This means a public recognition that the process of marginalization itself is central to the formation of the dominant culture. The first and very important stage is, as Morrison emphasizes, to recognize the cultural and political category of whiteness. It seems obvious to say it but in practice the racialization of our social order is only recognized in relation to racialized "others." For example, in the world of Women's Studies the politically correct thing to do is to make sure that your collection of essays, or your conference, includes the obligatory black perspective. That contribution has to carry the whole weight of racialization. Each time I am invited to speak somewhere, or invited to contribute to a collection of feminist essays under these conditions, I state that "whiteness" is the unrecognized and unspoken racial category and that we must end this silence; the response is usually astonishment.

Likewise, to return to my example of my Caribbean Literature course, I think that the presence of marginalized cultures within the university should transform the way in which the dominant political and cultural order is viewed. What Caribbean fiction does is not only assert an African and/or Asian presence in the New World but it transforms European definitions of the meaning of Western civilization. In an essay called "Discovering Literature in Trinidad: The 1930s," published in 1969, C.L.R. James talks about his formation as a black Caribbean intellectual. He states that "the origins of [his] work and thought are to be found in Western European

literature, Western European history and Western European thought." He
continues:

> I have had a lot to say that is valid about the underdeveloped countries. That is
> important. But what I want to make clear is that I learnt this quality in the
> literature, history and philosophy of Western Europe. I didn't *have* to be a
> member of an underdeveloped country, though I know a lot of people who are,
> and yet don't know anything about those countries. I didn't *have* to be an
> exploited African. It is in the history and philosophy and literature of Western
> Europe that I have gained my understanding not only of Western Europe's
> civilization, but of the importance of the underdeveloped countries. . . . I didn't
> learn literature from the mango-tree, or bathing on the shore and getting the
> sun of colonial countries; I set out to master the literature and philosophy and
> ideas of Western civilisation. That is where I have come from and I would not
> pretend to be anything else. And I am able to speak of the underdeveloped
> countries infinitely better than I would otherwise have been able to.[4]

As the essay continues, James situates the colonized within the heart of
colonial culture, where the black intellectual reads through and transforms
the meanings of the dominance of Western culture.

We should not be satisfied, then, with our mere inclusion in the
academy. My Caribbean course, for example, should be part of the process
of redefining the Englishness that is implied in the structural organization
of English departments. That English literature means, in practice, the
literature of England should be challenged as a racist definition which is
part of an English imperialist discourse and which excludes most of the
English-speaking peoples of the world and most of the literature written in
English. At the same time we should be engaged in rereading the literature
of England, written since the sixteenth century, as being centrally concerned with the formation of a national subjectivity and ideology that
constructed and simultaneously excluded a racialized other.

The formation of modern America is likewise a racialized struggle over
the definition of Americanness. If we are to unpack the dimensions of this
struggle to understand the terms and consequences of competing meanings of Americanness, then the categories of race, gender and class need
to be our conceptual and analytic tools. Preserving a gendered analysis for
texts by women or about women and an analysis of racial domination
for texts by or directly about black people will not by itself transform our
understanding of dominant cultural forms.

What is at issue here is how we look at and think about culture. Both
the historical creation of a canon and arguments in defense of the
preservation of the canon, as we know it now, depend upon the idea of a
pure and authentic culture that can be embodied in a careful selection of
texts. However, in African American Studies we too have been searching
for a pure and authentic culture.

First we have established the basis of an African American literary tradition in the narratives of ex-slaves through a critical practice which, in the work of Henry Louis Gates, Jr, elaborates a "black intertextual or Signifying relationship" in order to produce a "formal literary history of the African American tradition." Narrative strategies repeated through two centuries of black writing are argued to be the link that binds the slave narrative to texts as disparate as Booker T. Washington's *Up from Slavery*, *The Autobiography of Malcolm X*, Ralph Ellison's *Invisible Man*, Richard Wright's *Black Boy*, Zora Neale Hurston's *Their Eyes Were Watching God*, and Ishmael Reed's *Flight to Canada*. As readers and writers we become receivers of a textual experience that creates the unity of an African American literary tradition. This unity is established by an African American literary discourse that seamlessly links a particular form of cultural production that reconstructs one specific historical condition (slavery) as the basis of the entire narrative tradition. Second, our ideas of an African American literary tradition are dominated by an ideology of the black "folk" – a "folk" emerging from and still influenced by the slave condition. The critical project that situates the ex-slaves writing their "selfhood" or their "humanity" into being as the source of African American literature also reconstructs black culture as rooted in a "folk" culture. The ex-slave consciousness becomes an original "folk" consciousness.

We have also developed a critical vocabulary that we argue is appropriate to the task of analyzing representatives of African American subjectivities and sensibilities because its source is the vernacular of the African American "folk." Indeed, the critical language itself, it is argued, not only reproduces and preserves this vernacular but becomes a form of an African American vernacular. This process claims the autonomy of our heritage in relation to particular cultural forms and in relation to the critical project. What has been established is the "purity of our childhood," to use Martin Bernal's[5] phrase. At the same time we have defined the boundaries of an authentic culture in a language which can define authenticity *because* it is itself authentic. We have, in other words, established a canon and in the process we have dissolved historical difference. I would argue that our project in African American Studies is like the construction of the dominant canon to the extent that it displays a desire to create unity out of disunity and to resolve, if not make invisible, the social contradictions or differences between texts. And, after all, the function of traditions is to create the illusion of unity.

I would suggest that instead of searching for cultural purity we acknowledge cultural complexity. I would hope that the history of black culture will not be an antiquarian collecting and cataloguing of nostalgic artifacts, a romantic longing for a "folk" past at the expense of the urban present. The history of culture should be the history of the social relations between the industries producing cheap commodities for mass entertainment and recreation, the symbolic forms and practices, both traditional and newly invented, of black communities, and the attempts by the dominant white and colonizing cultures to police and reform the culture of the colonized or marginalized. This does not mean that we abandon ideas of cultural difference. Black cultures have not only been different from but antagonistic to cultures of domination. But, I would argue, this is not because there are pure, autonomous cultures that belong to particular groups or classes of people, the working class, or women, or black people. Rather, I think difference should be located, first, in relation to material conditions of life and, second, in relation to the boundaries drawn between what is designated Culture and non-Culture in the exercise of cultural power. As Stuart Hall has described this process:

The cultural process – cultural power . . . depends, in the first instance, on this drawing of the line, always in each period in a different place, as to what is to be incorporated into the "great tradition" and what is not. Educational and cultural institutions, along with the many positive things they do, also help to discipline and police this boundary. . . . from period to period, the contents of each category changes.

We should not freeze black cultures into a timeless descriptive framework but should situate analyses of culture within the relations of power which divide it into preferred and marginal categories.

The boundaries of culture in the exercise of cultural power can be moral as well as aesthetic ones, and Toni Morrison[6] has elaborated the ways in which particular cultural forms can ascend and descend the cultural escalator. Though we can delineate the racialized structuring of society in the terms of which there is an African American culture that has been racialized and defined as black – a culture with its center of gravity among black people, a set of practices, institutions and symbolic forms used, created and shaped by black people – neither its rhetoric nor its boundaries are strictly of "race." African American culture is not completely autonomous. It is intertwined with a commercial culture that is not the self-creation of black people and it is always subject to the influence and power of the dominant culture. Culture does not belong to particular people, and cultural analysis should not be about the ownership of cultural forms. For culture is the terrain of struggle *between* groups, "a continuous and necessarily uneven and unequal struggle," and there is no whole, authentic, autonomous black culture which lies outside of these relations of cultural power and domination.

It is the possibility that we can develop cultural analyses that are directed toward the complexity not the purity of culture that can free us from the limitations of canonic debates. This is the hope of work like Martin Bernal's *Black Athena* that Toni Morrison praises. *Black Athena* not only challenges the boundaries of dominant forms of historiography but challenges those of us who work to undermine relations of cultural power and domination to search not for purity but for complexity.

1989

Notes

1. W.E.B. Du Bois, *The Souls of Black Folk*, 1903; reprint, New York: New American Library, 1982, p. 54.
2. See Chapter 10, p. 135 above.
3. Toni Morrison, "Unspeakable Things Unspoken: The Afro-American Presence in American Literature," *Michigan Quarterly Review*, vol. 28, no. 1, Winter 1989, pp. 1–34.
4. C.L.R. James, "Discovering Literature in Trinidad: The 1930s," in *Spheres of Existence*, London: Allison & Busby, 1980, pp. 237–8.
5. Martin Bernal, *Black Athena: The Afroasiatic Roots of Classical Civilization*, London: Free Association Books, 1987.
6. Morrison, "Unspeakable Things Unspoken."

19

The Multicultural Wars, Part One

As a black intellectual, I am both intrigued and horrified by the contradictory nature of the black presence in North American universities. We are, as students, as teachers, and as cultural producers, simultaneously visibly present in and starkly absent from university life. Although it costs approximately $20,000 a year to attend Yale and approximately $50,000 a year to reside in a New York jail, black males are being incarcerated at unprecedented rates. The press and the culture industry, having "discovered" the black woman writer for the first time in the 1970s, are now finding it increasingly profitable to market narratives of the lives of successful black men. Articles about black males who have "made it" are no longer to be found only in the entertainment or sports sections of national newspapers: musicians and basketball stars have been joined by black male film directors and academics in the pages of our Sunday magazines.

In particular, the very existence of black male professors seems to fascinate the *New York Times*. On April 1 1990, the *Times* ran a cover story in its magazine entitled "Henry Louis Gates Jr.: Black Studies' New Star." Stanley Fish, Chair of the English Department at Duke University, patronizingly described Professor Gates's professional success as "entrepreneurial P.T. Barnumism." Adam Begley, the author of the *Times*'s story on Gates, concluded that with "a phone in his Mercedes-Benz, a literary agent in New York, and an impressive network of contacts in the academy, publishing and the arts, [Professor Gates] seems more like a mogul than a scholar."[1] The *Times* article is, at best, ambivalent toward its black subject, and frequently adopts such an incisive tone of ridicule that one wonders if the newspaper's editorial staff consciously decided to create an April 1 cartoon of Black Studies as a ship of fools. A much more serious, considered and sober article about Cornel West appeared in the same magazine, describing him as "Princeton's Public Intellectual."[2]

In stark contrast to the attention paid to individual black professors, the glaring absence of any equivalent publicity accorded the fact of the paltry presence of non-white regular faculty in universities receives little attention: 3.8 percent are Asian; 4.1 percent are black; 0.4 percent are Native

American; and 1.3 percent are Latino.[3] Derrick Bell, a professor at the Harvard Law School, argued that

> a widespread assumption exists that there is an irreconcilable conflict between achieving diversity in law school faculties and maintaining academic excellence. . . . It serves as a primary reason why most college and university faculties across the nation remain all-white and mostly-male almost four decades after the law barred them from continuing their long-practiced policies of excluding minorities and women because of their race and sex without regard to their academic qualifications.

These "contentions," Bell maintains,

> are simultaneously racially insulting and arrogantly wrong: They are insulting because they insinuate that the old rules of racial segregation rightly correlated color with intellectual inferiority. They are arrogant in that they assume that all of those with upper-class-based qualifications are by definition exemplary scholars and teachers.[4]

Bell continued by stressing that "minorities who achieve are deemed 'exceptions'" while those "who fail are deemed painful proof that we must adhere to hiring standards that subsidize the well-placed members of our society while penalizing those, white as well as black, from disadvantaged backgrounds." The fact that more than 90 percent of all faculty members across the nation are white is a scandal but is not, apparently, a cause for journalistic outrage or newspaper headlines.

The percentage of black students in college populations has steadily decreased throughout the last decade, as has the number of BAs awarded to black students, even though the absolute number of bachelor's degrees awarded has been increasing nationally. In graduate schools the proportion of American graduate students who are black is also decreasing, and the proportion of doctorates awarded to black people is also in significant decline. The number of tenured black professors has increased slightly but the number of untenured black appointees is decreasing.[5] Clearly, if the black student population continues to decline at the undergraduate and graduate levels, the current black intellectual presence in academia, small as it is, will not be reproduced.

During the past two years debate about the introduction of the inclusion of peoples from a variety of ethnic, national and class backgrounds as appropriate subjects for educational study and research has become focused in a public way around the institution of what is now commonly referred to as the "multicultural curriculum." Multiculturalism appears to be a controversial issue at all levels of the national educational system; debate about multiculturalism is not confined to universities. Despite the apparent uniformity of issues that are being fought over, in what I like to refer to as the "multicultural wars of position," there are, in fact, significantly different interests in play and at stake, as these battles take place regionally and in the public and private spheres of education. However, it is important to recognize that even though this debate is differently inflected at different levels, all aspects constitute a debate about contemporary meanings of race in North America. Indeed, I would argue that *multiculturalism* is one of the current code words for *race*, a code that is just as effective in creating a common-sense awareness that race is, indeed, the subject that is being evoked as is the word "drugs" or the phrase "inner-city violence."

Since the fall of 1990, we have witnessed a barrage of journalistic attacks on both the concept of multiculturalism and attempts to institute multicultural curricula. These reports have either implicitly or explicitly acknowledged that multiculturalism is a discourse about race, and have frequently asserted that there are close and disturbing links between multiculturalism, affirmative action and threats to freedom of speech guaranteed by the First Amendment. In common-sense terms, affirmative action is no longer referred to by the media as a necessary corrective social policy, but, instead, as a social problem that itself needs correction. The press's perceptions of the threats to freedom of speech and expression have shaped a moral panic about allegedly terroristic attempts to institute "politically correct" thought and behavior. Indeed, this danger is thought to be so real that it has elicited condemnation from President Bush himself. It is as if the historical contradictions between the original Constitution, which sanctioned slavery, and the Fourteenth and Fifteenth Amendments have returned to haunt us yet again, only to be dispelled by a form of executive exorcism.

The fundamental contradictions of a society structured by racial inequality since its founding moment have been shaped in the 1990s by an administration in Washington that is not only unsympathetic toward any demands for civil rights, but blatantly antagonistic to such demands. If we also consider the moral panics about affirmative action, anti-sexist and anti-racist codes of behavior, and multiculturalism in the pages of numerous journals like *Time*, *Newsweek*, the *Atlantic Monthly*, the *New Republic*, the *Chronicle of Higher Education*, the *Boston Globe* and the *New York Times*, it would appear that liberal, as well as conservative, opposition to increasing cultural and ethnic diversity in higher education is becoming entrenched.[6]

For those of us who recognize the need for transformations in our educational systems, and in the ways in which we organize fields of knowledge, it is frequently dismaying to consider what is sometimes thought to constitute change in educational policy and practice. Departments and programs in many private universities, for example, will proudly point to an "integrated" curriculum while being unable to point to an integrated student body – except in photographs in their student handbooks: photographs that contrive to demonstrate "diversity" by self-consciously including the pitiful handful of black, Latino, Asian, Chicano and perhaps even fewer Native American students on campus. As Nicolaus Mills argued in his survey of 1990 college publications, the contemporary college-view book presents an idealized world in which the dominant code word is "diversity."

> "Diversity is the hallmark of the Harvard/Radcliffe experience," the first sentence in the Harvard University register declares. "Diversity is the virtual core of University life," the University of Michigan bulletin announces. "Diversity is rooted deeply in the liberal arts tradition and is key to our educational philosophy," Connecticut College insists. "Duke's 5,800 undergraduates come from regions which are truly diverse," the Duke University bulletin declares. "Stanford values a class that is both ethnically and economically diverse," the Stanford University bulletin notes. Brown University says, "When asked to describe the undergraduate life at The College – and particularly their first strongest impression of Brown as freshmen – students consistently bring up the same topic: the diversity of the student body."

In this context, Mills concluded, diversity means that "a college is doing its best to abolish the idea that it caters to middle-class whites."[7]

The varying cultural and political presences of black women in universities provide particularly good examples of the contradictions that are embedded in the various curricular practices that occur under the aegis of "diversity." On many campuses, coalitions of marginalized and non-marginalized women, students and professors have formed alliances to ensure inclusion of the histories of black women and other previously excluded categories of women in the university curriculum. But the result has been a patchwork of success and spectacular failures. Clearly, the syllabi of some courses, particularly within Women's Studies and African American Studies programs, have been transformed, and the demand for the establishment of programs in Ethnic Studies is both vocal and assertive. However, changes too frequently amounted only to the inclusion of one or two new books in an already established syllabus, rather than a reconsideration of the basic conceptual structures of a course.

Within Women's Studies and some literature departments, black women writers have been used and, I would argue, abused as cultural and political icons. Regardless of the fact that the writings of black women are extraordinarily diverse, complex and multifaceted, feminist theory has frequently used and abused this material to produce an essential black female subject for its own consumption, one that represents a single dimension: either the long-suffering or the triumphantly noble aspect of a black community throughout history. Because this black female subject has to carry the burden of representing what is otherwise significantly absent in the curriculum, issues of complexity disappear under the pressure of the demand to give meaning to blackness.

Certainly, we can see how the black female subject has become very profitable for the culture industry. The HarperCollins reprint of all the previously published books of Zora Neale Hurston, for example, has been an extraordinarily profitable publishing enterprise based primarily on sales within an academic market.[8] We need to ask why black or other non-white women are needed as cultural and political icons by the white middle class at this particular moment. What cultural and political need is being expressed, and what role is the black female subject being reduced to play? I would argue that it is necessary to recognize the contradictions between elevating the black female subject as a major text within multiculturalism, and the failure of multiculturalism to lead students to understand the possibility of an integrated society or promote the integration of student and faculty bodies on a national scale. Instead of recognizing this contradiction, the black female subject is frequently the means by which many middle-class white students and faculty cleanse their souls and rid themselves of the guilt of living in a society that is still rigidly segregated. Black cultural texts have become fictional substitutes for the lack of any sustained social or political relationships with black people in a society that retains many of its historical practices of apartheid in housing and schooling.

The cultural, political and social complexity of black people is consistently denied in those strands of feminist and multicultural theory that emphasize "difference" and use it to mark social, cultural and political differences as if they were unbridgeable human divisions.[9] But this theoretical emphasis on the recognition of difference, or otherness, requires us to ask, different from and for whom? Black texts have been used in the classroom to focus on the complexity of response in the (white) reader/student's construction of self in relation to a (black) perceived "other"; the text has been reduced to a tool to motivate that response. The theoretical paradigm of difference is obsessed with the construction of identities rather than relations of power and domination,[10] and, in practice, concentrates on the effect of this difference on a (white) norm. Proponents of multiculturalism and feminist theorists have to interrogate some of their basic and unspoken assumptions: to what extent are fantasized black female and male subjects invented, primarily, to make the white middle class feel better about itself; and, at what point do theories of "difference," as they inform academic practices, become totally compatible with – rather than a threat to – the rigid frameworks of segregation and ghettoization at work throughout our society?

We need to recognize that we live in a society in which systems of domination and subordination are structured through processes of racialization that continuously interact with all other forces of socialization. Theoretically, we should be arguing that everyone in this social order has been constructed in our political imagination as a racialized subject. In this sense, it is important to think about the invention of the category of whiteness as well as of blackness and, consequently, to make visible what is rendered invisible when viewed as the normative state of existence: specifically the white point in space from which we tend to identify difference. If, instead, we situated *all* North American peoples as racialized subjects of our political imagination, we would see that processes of racialization influenced all our work. But processes of racialization, when they are mentioned at all in multicultural debate, are discussed as if they were the sole concern of those particular groups perceived to be racialized subjects. Because the politics of difference work with concepts of individual identity rather than structures of inequality and exploitation, processes of racialization are marginalized and only given symbolic and political meaning when the subjects are black.

My argument for the centrality of the concept of race is not the same as the assertion – from within the politics of difference – that everyone has an ethnicity. I am not arguing for pluralistic research paradigms, nor for a politics of pluralism, the result of much work on ethnicity. But I am arguing for educational politics that would reveal the structures of power relations that are at work in the racialization of our social order.

As a final exercise in thinking about the ways that the female subject has been addressed and, to a great extent, invented within the curricular practices designed to increase "diversity," I would like to question the marginalization of the concept of race in the phrase "women of color." This phrase carries a series of complex meanings. It has its origin in the need of subordinated, marginalized and exploited groups of women to find common ground with each other and in the assertion of their desire to establish a system of alliances as "women of color." But what happens when this phrase is then taken up and inserted into the language of difference and diversity? Does "women of color" have other meanings inflected by theories of difference and diversity? I know we are all supposed to be familiar with who is being evoked by this term, but do we honestly think that some people lack color? Do white women and men have no color? What does it mean, socially, politically and culturally not to have color? Are those without color not implicated in a society structured in dominance by race? Are those without color outside of the hierarchy of social relations and not racialized? Are only the "colored" to be the subjects of a specialized discourse of difference? And, most importantly, do existing power relations remain intact and unchallenged by this discourse?

We need to ask ourselves some serious questions about our culture and our politics. Is the emphasis on cultural diversity making invisible the politics of race in this increasingly segregated nation, and is the language of cultural diversity a convenient substitute for the political action needed to desegregate? In considering a response, we would be wise to remember Malcolm X's words: "There is nothing that the white man will do to bring about true, sincere citizenship or civil rights recognition for black people in this country. . . . They will always talk it but they won't practice it."[11] While the attention of faculty and administrators has been directed toward increasing the representation of different social groups in the curriculum or the college handbook, few alliances have been forged with substantial forces across this society that will significantly halt and reverse the declining numbers of black, working-class, and poor people among university student bodies or faculty.

From one perspective, academic language in the 1980s appeared to be at odds with the growing conservatism of the Reagan years. It seemed, at times, as if life in the academy was dominated by questions about the monolithic (and mono-ethnic) nature of courses in Western civilization, about texts that constituted all white and male literary and historical "canons," and about issues of "diversity" and "difference." Students on campuses all over the country formed movements that condemned apartheid in South Africa and vigorously worked to persuade university administrations to divest their economic holdings in that country. However, we have to confront the fact that the white middle and upper classes in this country, from which these students predominantly come, have, simultaneously, sustained and supported apartheid-like structures that support segregation in housing and education in the United States. Comparisons with South African apartheid are a part of the language of black American daily life: the Bronx becomes "New York Johannesburg"; Chicago is called "Joberg by the Lake"; and the *Minneapolis Star Tribune* is known by black politicians as the "Johannesburg Times."[12]

In Connecticut, the state where I live and work, the constitution provides for free public elementary and secondary schools, and specifically states that "No person shall be subjected to Segregation or Discrimination because of Religion, Race, Color, Ancestry or National Origin."[13] According to a recent report, 450,000 children attend school in Connecticut and 1 out of every 4 is non-white. But 8 out of 10 "minority" students "are concentrated in 10 percent of the school districts. By the year 2000, minority enrollments in Hartford, Bridgeport, and New Haven public schools will be approaching 100 percent."[14]

Such systems of segregation ensure that the black working class and the urban poor will not encroach on the privileged territory of the white middle and upper classes, or into the institutions that are the gatekeepers and providers of legitimate access to power – universities included. The integration that has occurred has been primarily due to class assimilation, and affirmative action has become an important mechanism for advancing a very limited number of black people into the middle class. Good examples are the admissions practices at Harvard University, discussed in a recent report on affirmative action:

> Harvard has sought to avoid the problem [of attrition] by ensuring that most of its black students come from middle-class families and predominantly white schools. As an admissions officer explained, "It is right for Harvard and better for the students, because there is better adjustment and less desperate alienation."[15]

Because entry into the professions is a major port of entry into the middle class, universities have been important and contested sites in which to accomplish the transformation of the previously outcast into an acceptable body for integration.

The social and political consciousness of the undergraduate population currently enrolled in universities has been formed entirely during the Reagan and Bush years, and the disparity between the groups that have benefited from, and those that have been radically disadvantaged by, the social policies of conservatism is stark. Public systems of education in particular regions have had to respond rather differently than overwhelmingly white private or public universities to questions of diversity and difference. In some schools and colleges in the New York City educational system, for example, the so-called minority groups are overwhelmingly in the majority and issues of difference and diversity are not theoretical playthings at odds with the context in which teaching occurs. New York public schools, which seem to have the most radically diverse and transformed curriculum in the country, find that this curriculum is now under vigorous attack by the New York Regents. At the same time, it is precisely the state and city educational systems with a majority population of black and Latino/a students that are disastrously underfunded. The withdrawal of federal funds and drastic cuts in state and city financing promise to decimate what is left of the promise of the city's schools and colleges.

Meanwhile, the National Association of Scholars, its friends and allies, and the media campaign against curricular reform have had significant effects in turning the general climate in the universities with money against educational reform and affirmative action. Not the least of these effects is the example of the $20 million donation to Yale University for the promotion of scholarship in Western civilization, a donation that was only one of four equivalent donations from the same family within one year. There is no equivalent donation that has ever been made to institute courses in non-Western civilizations that I have been able to find, but I can imagine the difference to the New Haven public school system that an injection of $80 million might make.[16] In the public sphere, the most recent presidential educational initiative seeks to replace federal funding of the public schools with corporate funding. One has to ask: will this mean corporate control of the curriculum as well?

In the post-civil-rights era, one has to wonder at the massive resources that are being mobilized in opposition to programs or courses that focus on non-white or ethnically diverse topics and issues. One wonders too about the strength of the opposition to affirmative action when social mobility has been gained by so few black people, and black entry into the so-called mainstream has been on the grounds of middle-class acceptability and not the end of segregation. Perhaps it is not too cynical to speculate that the South African government has learned a significant lesson by watching the example of the United States in the last two decades: some of the most important aspects of an apartheid system can be retained without having to maintain rigid apartheid legislation. It is in this social, political and economic context that I feel it essential to question the disparity between the vigor of debates about the inclusion of black subjects in a syllabus, and the almost total silence about and utter disregard for the material conditions of most black people.

From the vantage point of the academy, it is obvious that the publishing explosion of black women's fiction has been a major influence in multicultural curriculum development, and I have tried to point to the ways in which the texts of black women sit uneasily in a discourse that seems to act as a substitute for the political activity of desegregation. But it is also evident that in white suburban libraries, bookstores and supermarkets, an ever-increasing number of narratives of black lives are easily available. The retention of segregated neighborhoods and public schools and the apartheid-like structure of black inner city versus white suburban life mean that those who read these texts lack the opportunity to grow up in any equitable way with each other. Indeed, those same readers are part of the white suburban constituency who refuse to support the building of affordable housing in their affluent suburbs, aggressively oppose the bussing of children from the inner city into their neighborhood schools, and who would fight to the death to prevent their children from being bussed into the urban blight that is the norm for black children. For white suburbia, as well as for white middle-class students in universities, these texts are becoming a way of gaining knowledge of the "other": a knowledge that appears to satisfy and replace the desire to challenge existing frameworks of segregation. Have we, as a society, successfully eliminated the desire for achieving integration through political agitation for civil rights and opted instead for knowing each other through cultural texts?

1992

Notes

1. Adam Begley, "Henry Louis Gates Jr.: Black Studies' New Star," *New York Times Magazine*, April 1 1990, pp. 24–7.
2. Robert S. Boynton, "Princeton's Public Intellectual," *New York Times Magazine*, September 15 1991, pp. 39, 43, 45, 49.
3. These figures are from the American Council on Education, Office of Minority Concerns, "Seventh Annual Status Report on Minorities in Higher Education," Table 13, as quoted in "Recruitment and Retention of Minority Group Members on the Faculty at Yale," the report of a committee chaired by Judith Rodin, Yale University, 1.

   In the National Research Council's report *A Common Destiny*, the outlook for black faculty is gloomy: "Figures for 1977–1983 show a drop of 6.2 percent in the number of full-time black faculty at public four-year institutions and of 11.3 percent at private institutions. Black under-representation is greatest at elite universities and at two-year colleges. There is little prospect for growth in black representation in light of the declines in both the percentage of blacks going on to college and the percentage pursuing graduate and professional degrees." *A Common Destiny: Blacks and American Society*, ed. Gerald David Jaynes and Robin M. Williams, National Research Council (Washington, DC: National Academy Press, 1989), p. 375.

4. Derrick Bell, "Why We Need More Black Professors in Law School," *Boston Sunday Globe*, April 29 1991, p. A1.

5. See "Recruitment and Retention of Minority Group Members on the Faculty at Yale," p. 1.

6. There have been a number of articles in the national and local press that have been extremely critical of what is called "the hegemony of the politically correct," and which have described attempts to transform the canon as "liberal fascism" or terrorism. See, for example, "The Rising Hegemony of the Politically Correct," *New York Times*, October 28 1990, sect. 4, p. 4; "Opening Academia Without Closing It Down," *New York Times*, December 9 1990, sect. 4, p. 5; "Proponents of 'Multicultural' Humanities Research Call for a Critical Look at Its Achievements," *Chronicle of Higher Education*, November 28 1990, pp. A5–A10). An issue of *Newsweek* even went so far as to inscribe the words "Thought Police" on stone on its cover ("Watch What You Say: Thought Police," *Newsweek*, December 24 1990, pp. 48–55). In contrast the *Boston Globe Magazine* (October 13 1991) ran a much more sympathetic article on multiculturalism as a phenomenon of the "melting pot," entitled "The New World." However, it concluded with a negative article on multicultural education by Kenneth Jackson, "Too Many Have Let Enthusiasm Outrun Reason" (pp. 27–32).

7. Nicolaus Mills, "The Endless Autumn," *Nation*, April 16 1990, pp. 529–31.

8. Presumably influenced by the possibility of sharing some of the massive profits realized by the publishing industry through marketing the black female subject, film distribution companies have recently begun to vigorously market films about black women to university professors for course use. See Chapter 4 in the present volume.

9. I would like to thank Paul Gilroy for the many conversations we have had sharing our ideas on this issue. His influence upon my thinking has been profound.

10. See Elizabeth Weed, "Introduction: Terms of Reference," in Elizabeth Weed, ed., *Coming to Terms: Feminism, Theory, Politics*, London: Routledge, 1989, p. xvii.

11. Video interview with Malcolm X from *A Fan* (1989), an installation by David Hammonds at the New Museum, as quoted in Maurice Berger, "Are Art Museums Racist?", *Art in America*, September 1990, pp. 69–77.

12. John Matisonn, reporting for National Public Radio's "All Things Considered," Weekend Edition, Saturday (February 2 1991), transcript, p. 21.

13. Constitution of the State of Connecticut, 1965, as quoted on the PBS special "Schools in Black and White," produced and written by Vivian Eison and Andrea Haas Hubbell, September 4 1991.

14. Ibid.

15. Andrew Hacker, "Affirmative Action: The New Look," *New York Review*, October 12 1989, p. 64.

16. Giving this extraordinary amount of money, $80 million, to an already well-endowed institution, needs to be measured against initiatives to support inner-city schools by using black churches as sites for supplemental educational classes and activities. The Association for the Advancement of Science has spent $800,000 over a period of four years for educational programs in 800 churches in seventeen cities. The largest donation by a private foundation for church-based educational programs appears to be $2.3 million spread among nine cities from the Carnegie Corporation. See the *New York Times*, August 7 1991, p. A1.

20

The Multicultural Wars, Part Two

I would like to begin this essay on *Brown* v. *Board of Education*, originally presented to the conference "Brown at Forty," by returning, briefly, to a set of concerns and specific questions with which I concluded an essay entitled "The Multicultural Wars," published in the fall of 1992 in the journal *Radical History Review* [reproduced here as Chapter 19 – HVC].[1] There I argued that contemporary debates about cultural integration most commonly rage under the banner of "multiculturalism" in our schools and colleges but that the content of these debates seemed to me to be a totally inadequate political response to the conditions of social, political and economic devastation present in the daily lives of those who are poor and designated members of so-called "minority" populations in the United States.

An enormous amount of our individual and collective political energy in the academy, I am convinced, has been directed toward increasing the diversity of cultural representation through curricular reform. Agitation for increased cultural representation has, of course, a long history in black cultural politics, but the specific link to curricular reform in educational institutions is a legacy of the *Brown* paradigm – having fought to integrate our educational institutions, should we not now also struggle to integrate the curriculum? However, in many educational institutions across the country it appears that most advocates of multiculturalism are ignoring the fact that forty years after *Brown* v. *Board of Education* we still live with widespread educational and residential apartheid. Multiculturalists, it seems to me, limit their political imagination and vision to dreams of culturally integrated syllabi instead of agitating for the institutionalizing of a political vision of a just and equitable social formation; indeed, the former seems to be a comforting substitute for the latter. So, forty years after what is considered to be the victory of the *Brown* decision, it is important that we question the apparent reluctance of these proponents of multiculturalism to confront not only the continuing maintenance but increasing strength of an apartheid system in residence and education in this society. In addition, it is imperative that we develop a political critique of the discourse of multiculturalism and condemn its lack of a complex political vision for aggressive political action: action which would not only desegregate this society but would seek to create a just and equitable alternative social order.

I reassert this question, in the context of a discussion of *Brown* v. *Board of Education*, because I feel that our contemporary discursive legacy from *Brown*, multiculturalism, has at its heart a complete disregard for cultural, political and economic justice.[2]

Many of the daily practices of multiculturalism have spawned an obsessive engagement on the part of its practitioners with issues of identity politics, a form of politics which has focused upon questions of the personal, the subjective and the emotive. The emphasis on increasing personal, or subjective, awareness of difference is thought to take place in conjunction with a selection of cultural texts, but this process, frequently imagined to be an engagement in cultural politics, takes place at the expense of an engagement with the politics of culture and cultural production. In other words, what is deeply disturbing is that, as multiculturalism is currently practiced, the attention paid to cultural forms does not necessarily extend to a systematic interrogation of the nature of cultural formations. I would argue that it is not only necessary but urgent that we shift from this intense concentration on cultural forms, on textual representation and the subjectivity of identity politics, to an analysis of the relation between the production of cultural forms and the state of cultural formations, the material conditions which shape our collective as well as our individual existence.[3]

What we need to ask ourselves is if the vision of cultural integration implicit in the paradigm of "Brown at Forty" is, in fact, an adequate conceptual and political framework within which to understand the complexity of our contemporary systems of apartheid. I would argue that it is a very inadequate frame of reference and would evoke Antonio Gramsci's warning about becoming complacent about the nature of the battle in which *Brown* was only an opening sortie: "It was right," Gramsci asserts,

> to struggle against the old school, but reforming it was not so simple as it seemed. The problem was not one of model curricula but of men [and women], and not just of men [and women] who are actually teachers themselves but of the entire social complex which they express.[4]

Any analysis of identity politics, of the subjective and emotive expressions of the social order, must be part of an active and rigorous critique of, and engagement with, the "social complex" in order to embody a vision of social, political and economic transformation.

Throughout the nineteenth and twentieth centuries, issues of representation have consistently been present within the spectrum of black politics and political organizations. However, in the academic field of African American Studies, which has been in existence for more than twenty-five years,[5] there seems to be an assumption that the cultural politics of textual representation, as first articulated by black modernists, has an integral if not a seamless relationship to issues of political representation and the achievement of equal rights of citizenship. Thus, much of our energy as black intellectuals, cultural producers or critics has been aggressively directed toward increasing the force of our cultural presence, with pen and paper, in front of or behind cameras, or with paint or clay, as part of a wider political struggle. However, now these cultural forms, particularly mass cultural forms, easily penetrate the boundaries that the black working class or the black poor are forbidden to cross: rap music, or Spike Lee's, Stephen Carter's and Cornel West's cultural texts become metaphorical substitutes for the presence of young black male bodies in the white middle-class suburb. I want to stress that it is not a problem of authorship or of artistic practices that I am trying to name. The fact that our cultural forms have a social mobility and accessibility that is denied to the majority of black people is a structural issue with which the field of African American Studies should be centrally concerned. What I want to contest, here, is an assumption of cultural integration that has dominated African American humanist thinking: an assumption that if cultural forms embody our undeniable humanity, they will help advance our demands for justice and equality in the society at large.

In African American Studies we can loudly applaud our own "difference" and assert our distinct cultural presence in ways that resemble the valorization of difference within the discourse of multiculturalism, but we do so at great risk, if not at our peril.[6] As Paul Gilroy has argued, theories of cultural difference are becoming as absolute in their demarcation of the racial boundaries of humanity as the biological theories that supported scientific racism.[7] Indeed, the most notable feature of contemporary racist formations is that they no longer have to depend upon theories of biological heredity for their existence but, on the contrary, emphasize "the insurmountability of cultural differences" instead. Rather than "postulate the superiority of certain groups or peoples in relation to others," what is articulated is " 'only' the harmfulness of abolishing frontiers, the incompatibility of life-styles and traditions." As Etienne Balibar has characterized this shift, this new racism is "a racism without races . . . a differentialist racism," in which culture functions like nature. What has changed, he continues, is that contemporary racist discourse "naturalizes not racial belonging but racist conduct."[8]

Our contemporary fascination and obsession with cultural difference and cultural belonging is, thus, entirely compatible with a hegemonic ideology of apartheid that structures our contemporary social formation. An emphasis on cultural difference and cultural belongingness supports, for example, one of the most pernicious practices of university administrations and departmental politics, a practice which is frequently justified by appealing to the discourse of cultural integration. On a daily basis

university administrators and departmental chairs conflate the need to
increase the presence of minority faculty with particular fields of knowlege.
For example, African American faculty are drafted to teach African American Studies, Latino and Latina, Chicano and Chicana, and Asian American
professors are considered only in the context of a variety of ethnic studies
programs. We, therefore, exist in the academy as professionalized ethnic
or racialized presences. It was not the vision of *Brown* but maybe it is its
legacy that our professionalized ethnicity, or professionalized blackness,
has become a required academic commodity – a commodity that is in
demand and can be utilized as a type of academic currency.

If *Brown* was about the practice of inserting bodies into integrated
educational environments, are the current academic practices of reducing
bodies to spheres of knowledge a crucial element of the insidious and
pervasive practices of physical and mental ghettoization? And is the physical
and mental ghettoization experienced by so many so-called "minority"
faculty the more comfortable, though still unacceptable, academic equivalent of the brutal residential and educational apartheid of the wider
society? If you exist as a racialized or ethnicized intellectual, it is difficult
to speak or to be heard outside of the boundaries of the body/field of
knowledge equation: of casting a critical eye upon the narrow reach of
mainstream disciplines, for example, or of daring to confront the structures
of masculinity and patriarchal practices that shape and penetrate the
academic world. But, unfortunately, the reduction of bodies to spheres of
knowledge also has the effect of constructing those fields of knowledge as
political turfs, as fields of influence over which ethnicized and racialized
intellectuals feel that they have an exclusive claim or within which they
consider, usually quite correctly, that they have their only chance to gain
an academic job.

The metaphor of war that I intentionally evoked through my title of the
1992 essay, "The Multicultural Wars," was not used lightly. On the contrary,
I would describe the state of "minority" intellectual presences in the
academy, as students and as faculty, as embattled. *Brown* was only one of
many charges that we are going to have to make against the forces of racist
reaction and retrenchment, and maybe we should revise our strategies of
war to take account of what we did not achieve through the *Brown* decision.
Antonio Gramsci's analysis of the difference between wars of position and
wars of maneuver I have found to be very useful in thinking about the
complexities of our struggle for justice and equality.

> In wars among the more industrially and socially advanced States, the war of
> manoeuvre must be considered as reduced to more of a tactical than a strategic
> function. . . .
>   The same reduction must take place in the art and science of politics, at least
> in the case of the most advanced States, where "civil society" has become a very
> complex structure and one which is resistant to the catastrophic "incursions" of

the immediate economic element (crises, depressions, etc.). The superstructures of civil society are like the trench systems of modern warfare.[9]

The same thing happens in the art of politics as happens in military art: war of movement increasingly becomes war of position and it can be said that a state will win a war in so far as it prepares for it minutely and technically in peacetime. The massive structures of the modern democracies, both as state organizations, and as complexes of associations in civil society, constitute for the art of politics as it were the "trenches" and the permanent fortifications of the front in the war of position: they render merely "partial" the element of manoeuvre. . . .[10]

The cultural politics of multiculturalism, far from being a war of movement, a wing in a larger war for radical transformation of which *Brown* was a part, has, in fact, become merely a discursive strategy in a war of position. Whereas proponents of multiculturalism like to see themselves as part of an attack on the racist formation, they have actually become stuck in the first line of the trenches of textual representation and seem incapable of climbing the next hurdle and challenging the injustice and inequity of our contemporary racialized social order. Indeed, I would go even further and suggest that our legacy of cultural integrationism works in harmony with, not in opposition to, the anti-civil rights hegemony first secured during the Reagan and Bush years and now being elaborated through an anti-affirmative action backlash and the Republican "Contract With America." The liberal consensus on the attainment of justice and equality, as it was embodied in the demands of the expanded civil rights agenda of the sixties and seventies and which we believed was the legacy of *Brown*, has clearly been revoked and instead we are offered a vision of cultural integration, multiculturalism, as a pacifier, an antidote to the anger and outrage that we bitterly repress.

Forty years after *Brown* v. *Board of Education*, the interests of the white and a significant portion of the black bourgeoisie are aligned in a battle over one of our most important public resources – the public school system. In a maneuver that increasingly resembles the historical mobilization of states' rights to retain the disenfranchisement of masses of black southern residents, the white suburban middle class, rallying to the cry of "the right to local control," is virtually privatizing sectors of the public educational system in its own class interests. Now that corporations, rather than the middle class, control capital accumulation, the bourgeoisie seek to retain control over the production of what Immanuel Wallerstein has called "human capital."

Human capital is what these new-style bourgeois have in abundance, whereas our proletarian does not. And where do they acquire the human capital? . . . in the education systems, whose primary and self-proclaimed function is to train people to become members of the new middle-classes, that is to be the professionals, the technicians, the administrators of the private and public enterprises which are the functional economic building-pieces of our system.

In a situation in which the children of the bourgeoisie can no longer be assured of inheriting capital, the middle class is in a battle to retain its control over quality education as a legacy for its children.[11] Many members of the black middle class are aligned with the white bourgeoisie in this struggle and have adopted similar political strategies either by supporting the establishment of black private schools or through attempting to gain privileged access into magnet schools as a legacy for their children. The result is an apparent social consensus to the significant drain of economic, physical and material resources away from the poor.

The paradigm of *Brown* from a legal perspective is completely inadequate to counter this drain of resources. Indeed, the current role of the courts is to support the bourgeoisie as our educational system has entered the front line of this political struggle. We need, therefore, to drastically revise our perspective on the role of the law in the achievement of change. We need to interrogate the history of the role of the courts in the achievement of legal definitions of cultural integration while, at the same time, we develop a critique of the contemporary role of the law in the defeat of social justice and equality. As Jonathan Kozol has argued, the legal redress offered by *Brown* has been invalidated by the Supreme Court rulings in *San Antonio Independent School District* v. *Rodriguez* and *Milliken* v. *Bradley*, decisions which have effectively denied the legitimacy of claims for educational equality and justice.[12]

Surely, in the face of the despair and suffering of poor black, Native American, Latino(a) and Chicano(a) children we must try to develop an alternative to the *Brown* paradigm which asks us to place our hopes for radical social transformation in the courts of this land. The question is: who will take up the cause for social justice and equality that the courts refuse to defend? Our public school system must be defended as a public resource that no group has the right to use or abuse in its own narrow class interests. Through which channels do we articulate what we want to demand of a public education system in a democracy?

"Democracy, by definition," Gramsci stressed, "cannot mean merely that an unskilled worker can become skilled. It must mean that every 'citizen' can 'govern' and that society places him [or her], even if only abstractly, in a general condition to achieve this."[13] Or, to make the point through the phrase that C.L.R. James used as the title of one of his essays, "every cook can govern."[14] Our present language of cultural integrationism, multiculturalism, must be replaced by an active politics of social, political and economic transformation, a politics that is not satisfied with understanding and bewailing the inequities of the social order but develops a commitment to ending present injustices and inequalities and redistributing wealth through a socialist vision of the future in the present. To conclude in the words of Etienne Balibar, the "destruction of the racist complex presupposes not only the revolt of its victims, but the transformation of the racists themselves and, consequently, the internal decomposition of the community created by racism."[15] This is our actual legacy from *Brown*, a legacy that should force us to undertake the work that *Brown* left undone, to confront and dismantle the forces that not only protect but nurture the racist community.

1994

Notes

1. Although this paper was written for the "Brown at Forty" conference, I am taking this opportunity to address some of the issues raised in response to this earlier essay. In particular, I am intending to implicate an audience working in the field of African American Studies. As Thelma Foote stated in response to "The Multicultural Wars":

   . . . although Carby provides an incisive critique of multiculturalism's failings, she limits her analysis to the consequences those failures hold for the political awakening of white middle-class students, while ignoring the fact that curricular reforms have important consequences for the politicization of black students also.

   See Thelma Wills Foote, "The Black Intellectual, Recent Curricular Reforms, and the Discourse of Collective Identity," *Radical History Review*, no. 56, Spring 1993, p. 52.

2. The term "cultural justice" has been coined by Andrew Ross in the following context. "I see cultural studies as the quest for cultural justice, which is my preferred term for political correctness." Andrew Ross, "*Cultural Studies Times* Interviews," *The Cultural Studies Times*, vol. 1, no. 2, Fall 1994, p. A11.

3. See Eric Lott, *Love and Theft: Blackface Minstrelsy and the American Working Class*, New York: Oxford University Press, 1993, pp. 10–11, for a similar argument which is elaborated in his critique of strands of Cultural Studies in North America.

4. Antonio Gramsci, *Selections from the Prison Notebooks*, New York: International Publishers, 1971, p. 36.

5. The African and Afro-American Studies Program at Yale University was established in 1969. It was preceded by a conference in the spring of 1968, one of the first in the nation, to examine the nature of Afro-American Studies. The program formally changed its name to African and African American Studies in 1994. Thank you to Lorrie Trotter in the Office of Public Information, Yale University.

6. See Etienne Balibar,

   . . . it is not a question of setting a collective identity against individual identities. *All identity is individual*, but there is no individual identity that is not historical or, in other words, constructed within a field of social values, norms of behaviour and collective symbols. . . . The real question is how the dominant reference points of individual identity change over time and with the changing institutional environment.

   Etienne Balibar and Immanuel Wallerstein, *Race, Nation, Class: Ambiguous Identities*, London: Verso, 1991, p. 94.

7. I absolutely agree with Paul Gilroy when he states, "where black art and aesthetics are debated in conference after conference it is becoming harder to dislodge the belief that ethnic differences constitute an absolute break in history and humanity." See, Paul Gilroy, "Cruciality and the Frog's Perspective: An Agenda of Difficulties for the Black Arts Movement in Britain," *Third Text*, no. 5, Winter 1988/89, p. 37.

8. See Balibar and Wallerstein, *Race, Nation, Class*, pp. 21–2.

9. Antonio Gramsci, *Selections from the Prison Notebooks*, London: Lawrence & Wishart, pp. 234–5.

10. David Forgacs, ed., *An Antonio Gramsci Reader: Selected Writings 1916–1935*, New York: Shocken Books, 1988, pp. 226–7.

11. Balibar and Wallerstein, *Race, Nation, Class*, p. 150.

12. Jonathan Kozol, "Romance of the Ghetto School," *The Nation*, May 23 1994, p. 703.

13. Forgacs, ed., *An Antonio Gramsci Reader*, p. 318.

14. C.L.R. James, "Every Cook Can Govern," in *The Future in the Present: Selected Writings*, London: Allison & Busby, 1977, pp. 160–75.

15. Balibar and Wallerstein, *Race, Nation, Class*, p. 18.

21

Imagining Black Men:
The Politics of Cultural Identity

There is perhaps more intense controversy over the meaning of the life of Malcolm X than over the significance of any other black leader who has ever lived. Spike Lee's announcement that he intended to develop James Baldwin's screenplay of Malcolm X's life sparked widespread and acrimonious debate that has emphasized how Malcolm's death was a minor interruption to the ever-increasing political importance of his life. Twenty-five years ago Marvin Worth acquired the rights to *The Autobiography of Malcolm X*, cowritten with Alex Haley, from Betty Shabazz, Malcolm's widow. James Baldwin was commissioned to write the script. Baldwin expressed severe doubts and fears about Hollywood in his memoirs and felt that his agreement to write a screenplay was unlikely to bring him anything but grief. Baldwin faced a battle to determine whose vision would control the film and eventually he was defeated. Over the years two novelists, David Bradley and Calder Willingham, and two dramatists, Charles Fuller and David Mamet, have also worked on the production of a screenplay, and two directors, Norman Jewison and Sidney Lumet, have abandoned the project.

Spike Lee maintains that only a black director can film the life of Malcolm X. Yet Lee is also very aware that if Hollywood had wanted to make the film at any point in the last quarter-century it would have done so. As he argued in a recent episode of the PBS arts programme *Edge*, the only reason Warner Brothers is making this film now is that "they see all these kids with these Malcolm X hats on, they see all these rappers with Malcolm X included in their lyrics, they can smell a dollar better than anybody."

If the publishing industry discovered a profitable market for the fiction of black women in the eighties, the last decade of the century appears to be the time to sell the lives of black men. Certainly the remarkable success of Arnold Rampersad's important two-volume literary biography *The Life of Langston Hughes*[1] must have been a factor in the significant increase in the number of biographical and autobiographical books recently published.

But it is sobering to reflect on the irony of this moment. At a time when young black men are generally considered to be the socioeconomic segment of society most "at risk" and when black males are being jailed at unprecedented rates (the figures doubled in the eighties), the availability of narratives of successful black men has increased dramatically. No longer are articles about black males who have "made it" confined to the entertainment or sports pages of our newspapers: musicians and basketball stars have been joined by film directors and even academics in the pages of the Sunday magazines. Yet the absence of serious, sustained public debate about the inadequacy of governmental responses to the living conditions of urban black populations means that these success stories become Horatio Alger tales – reinforcing middle-class beliefs in individual rather than collective responsibility for social conditions.

From the recent crop of biographies and autobiographies about black men I have chosen four to illustrate a range of the different contemporary narrative constructions of male racial identities being produced. Bruce Perry in *Malcolm: The Life of a Man Who Changed Black America*[2] measures the intellectual life of Malcolm X by the dubious tenets of pop psychology. His premise is that the entire adult career of Malcolm X needs to be understood through the lens of the events of his childhood. Under the guise of providing a sympathetic portrait of a man who "helped to transform America," Perry tries to account for Malcolm X's political development, allegiances and interventions entirely through the framework of understanding a child who grew up "emotionally disfigured and maimed." For example, Perry speculates about the relation, on the one hand, between Malcolm X's desire to study international law and his inability to afford to go to school and, on the other hand, his decision to join the Nation of Islam. Citing an observation of Eric Hoffer, Perry concludes facilely that "people who feel thwarted frequently join a mass movement in the hope that its achievements will compensate for their failures."

In a series of shallow comparisons between Malcolm X and Martin Luther King, Jr, Perry describes Malcolm as a charismatic leader who did not offer any incisive and meaningful analysis of political oppression but was popular simply because he articulated the anger of his followers:

> King's penchant for lofty phrases did not diminish his moving, eloquent appeals for racial brotherhood, which were so unlike Malcolm's machine-gun-like, unbrotherly outbursts. Whereas Malcolm gave his followers leave to express their hatred of their hateful oppressors, King gave his followers the courage to confront them. Eventually, King's . . . approach would prove more effective politically.

Both King and Malcolm are reduced in the next paragraph to men who became leaders because they could, finally, eclipse their "tyrannical fathers" only by "rebelling against more powerful tyrants." Eventually, Perry situates

Malcolm himself as a "tyrant" behind the scenes who was incapable of providing effective leadership.

> Martin Luther King, Jr., gathered about him a group of articulate, independent-minded co-workers who could make him see his mistakes. While King and his aides transformed their disagreements into a consensus that produced creative political solutions to pressing political problems, Malcolm permitted . . . disagreements to tear his stillborn movement apart.

Aspects of Malcolm X's life that could be illuminated by references to history are displaced by narrow and uncritical interpretations of his childhood. For example, Perry maintains that "instead of expressing his negative feelings about his Christian parents, he vented his wrath upon Christianity itself." Perry continually explains and interprets Malcolm X's political beliefs in terms of his youthful repression of emotions, his rebellion against parental authority, and his self-hatred. What should be analyzed as the development of a series of complex and varied political critiques arising from Malcolm's response to particular social conditions at specific times warrants only the most superficial references to the conditions of the nursery. Perry's book could not be a more devastating attempt to undermine the political significance of the life of Malcolm X had it been written by the CIA as an exercise in disinformation. Perry concludes that Malcolm X was a "political chameleon," but in the context of reading his biography this tells us as much as if what we had read were merely an extensive record of his potty training.

Stephen Carter's *Reflections of an Affirmative Action Baby*[3] is a testimony to the ways in which the grounds of racial identity, established during childhood, can be reworked to incorporate new dimensions of political meaning. For Carter, a Professor of Law at Yale, the label "affirmative action baby" exists both as an individual affiliation and as an appropriate description for his generation. His narrative is reminiscent of the structure of the slave narrative – manhood is denied or its terms mitigated through the imposition of a racial identity that limits entry into full and equitable recognition as a citizen. But this structure has been significantly revised. William McFeely, Professor of American History at the University of Georgia, argues in his *Frederick Douglass*[4] that Douglass brought his full cultural and political presence "into being" through his speeches, political writings and autobiographies. In other words, Douglass asserted his powers as an intellectual in order to be regarded as a man. But Stephen Carter maintains that the very terms of the process of preferential treatment that has enabled him to function as a intellectual have denied him his intellectual equality, and thus his common humanity.

Whereas McFeely illustrates how Douglass located slavery in his *Narrative of the Life of Frederick Douglass, an American Slave* as a condition into which he was born but not trapped, Carter states categorically that "to be black and an intellectual in America is to live in a box":

> Affirmative action has been with me always. I do not mean to suggest that I have always been the beneficiary of special programs and preferences. I mean, rather, that no matter what my accomplishments, I have had trouble escaping an assumption that often seems to underlie the worst forms of affirmative action: that black people cannot compete intellectually with white people.

For Carter, affirmative action has meant losing the chance to prove himself on his own merit. It is as though he owned both the boots and the straps but someone came, uninvited, and pulled them up for him. A crucial moment in this narrative of the denial of intellectual equality is a chapter entitled "The Best Black." Carter explains how in order to be awarded a National Achievement Scholarship for "outstanding Negro students" when a graduating senior he had to forfeit the chance to be awarded a National Merit Scholarship for which he had qualifying scores: "People who get National Achievement Scholarships," he was informed, "are never good enough to get National Merit Scholarships." When he told his teacher that he wanted to attend Stanford, the teacher replied that Carter would get in not because he was smart but because he was "black and smart." Carter wanted, he insists, to be regarded simply as the *best*, not as the "best black," but that recognition has eluded him; his first chapter opens with the statement "I got into Law School because I am black."

Slave narratives were important ideological and political weapons for the anti-slavery movement. In these narratives it was crucial that the history of the ex-slave as slave be carefully documented and emphasized. The protagonist's construction of his or her cultural identity as slave and ex-slave was the privileged site of abolitionist activism. On the evening of August 16 1841, in Nantucket, Frederick Douglass made his first public address to members of the American Anti-Slavery Society, and the story he told was the tale of a runaway slave. William Lloyd Garrison immediately recognized the value of this demonstration of the slave's humanity and the importance of Douglass himself to anti-slavery propaganda. But if, for example, Douglass had chosen a different political identity and had stood up and attacked racism in the "free" northern states and had told of how, despite his training as a caulker in Baltimore, he was excluded because of his color from being a skilled laborer in the boatyards of New Bedford, it is doubtful whether his value to the abolitionist cause would have been so quickly recognized.

Stephen Carter's adoption of a primary identity as an affirmative action baby has definite political effects that not only shape the way he writes of his social experiences as a black person but influence the way these experiences are to be read and understood. Circumstances that are usually regarded as promoting the chances of academic success, like the fact that he grew up as the son of a Cornell University professor in an atmosphere where intellectual work was valued, encouraged and could be financially supported, are displaced to preserve the narrative dichotomy of progress through merit alone versus progress through affirmative action. A particular racialized identity is being shaped when the phrase "affirmative action has been with me always" is selected over, for example, "books have been with me always," a phrase that refers to a rather different and more class-specific cultural identity. Indeed, Carter argues that affirmative action policies only benefit those already socially advantaged enough to profit from them. While this claim supports Carter's narrative creation of himself as an affirmative action baby, it contradicts the results of social scientific research. William L. Taylor, writing in the *Yale Law Journal* in 1986, summarized the results of such research:

> Although one criticism of affirmative action remedies has been that they tend to benefit minorities who are already advantaged or middle class, the results . . . suggest otherwise. The focus of much of the effort has been not just on white-collar jobs, but also . . . on areas in which the extension of new opportunities has provided upward mobility for less advantaged minority workers. Nor does the criticism appear valid for the professions. Studies show that of the increased enrollment of minority students in medical schools during the 1970s, significant numbers were from families of low income and job status, indicating that the rising enrollment of minorities in professional schools stemming from affirmative action policies reflects increased mobility, not simply changing occupational preferences among middle-class minority families.

Carter's vision of a meritocracy in which he has been uniquely handicapped is also somewhat disingenuous. Merit is consistently qualified by other categories operating in admissions procedures for universities and colleges. The preference shown in many schools to children of alumni and to athletes, for example, reveals that merit is but one of many criteria. But to have considered affirmative action in conjunction with a series of preferential policies for college admissions would have weakened Carter's offensive against his political target.

Reflections of an Affirmative Action Baby is at times an eloquent and persuasive plea for the recognition of the diversity not only of black social experiences but of black political agendas. Carter is outraged by attacks by some black intellectuals on other black intellectuals who dissent from a civil rights agenda, and he explores why he thinks that the label "black conservative," one from which he assertively distances himself, functions only as a pejorative. He is also angered by the lack of confidence that the conservative movement, in particular the Republican party, has in its black members. But at times the book reads like a diatribe against open debate even as it aims to "spark a dialogue." To argue for complexity and diversity of opinion must mean to be prepared for vigorous opposition and criticism. It will, I am convinced, mean facing the challenge of political turbulence. But Carter seems to yearn for a narrow definition of dissent. In the final chapter, on the relation of the black intellectual to questions of racial solidarity, earlier arguments about the multifarious nature of black voices have disappeared, replaced by an undifferentiated "we" that is embroiled not in complex debate but in constant "squabbling" and "internecine warfare."

If Carter closes by reducing his concerns to his own imagining of a black community, William McFeely expands the landscape that his subject inhabits. McFeely imagines Douglass not as an ex-slave who becomes a black intellectual and leader but as an important American intellectual and leader. He deliberately and consciously presents Douglass as functioning in relation to the national entity, and this is reinforced by the narrative structure of the biography.

To establish Douglass's role as a national intellectual, McFeely is careful not to limit Douglass's presence as intellectual to any single community of interests. The biography is thus organized by place. We move from Tuckahoe, Maryland, where Douglass was born Frederick Augustus Washington Bailey in 1818 and where he lived with his grandmother, through the various sites of his captivity to Baltimore, where he escaped from slavery. In New Bedford he made his first home with Anna Murray and became a father, and in Nantucket he entered into the abolitionist movement. In this fashion each chapter is named after and situated within a different place, which gives the book a sense of perpetual movement and Douglass's life a quality of incessant wandering until the book closes at Cedar Hill, the house that overlooked the city of Washington and in which Douglass died on February 20 1895. This organization makes the reader respond to Douglass's political activity, to his speaking, and writing, from a number of locations and communities, which emphasizes the national and even international character of his existence as an intellectual: Douglass was appointed minister to Haiti in 1889. For McFeely, Douglass as an American intellectual both articulates and characterizes the tensions and contradictions of his moment. Douglass embodies, for the author, the schisms of the nation.

For Charles Hamilton, Professor of Government at Columbia, the American dilemma can be described as the distance between society's ideals – the American creed – and how much American institutions fail to embody or practice those ideals. At different moments, Hamilton argues, Americans have decided to rationalize, ignore, deny or act to eliminate the "gap." Moments of intense political activity to make American institutions live up to American ideals, Hamilton argues, are times of "creedal passion" politics. Attempts to rationalize contradictions between ideals and practice lead to feelings of "moral helplessness," ignoring it leads to "creedal passivity," and denial is an attempt to redefine reality as if it were consistent with professed values and ideals. *Adam Clayton Powell, Jr.: The Political Biography of an American Dilemma*[5] is an accomplished and informative account of the congressman from Harlem who was elected in 1944, the year that the Swedish scholar Gunnar Myrdal published *An American Dilemma*, his account of the discrepancy between American values and the way black people were treated.

Hamilton portrays Adam Clayton Powell, Jr, as "a mirror, as a reflection of what others saw and understood to be the state of the American Dilemma Myrdal and others so aptly described." He argues that as a leader Powell was dedicated to the issue of how America treated black people in particular and the downtrodden in general.

> These were the people who elected him; these were the people to whom he turned when he needed political protection, as was often the case. His official policy positions were never absent of attention to this issue. This is so whether the particular concern was civil rights and racial segregation, as it was earlier in his career, or broader socioeconomic issues in the 1960s. How one responded to Adam Powell reflected how one responded to the American Dilemma. His personal eccentricities made the response more difficult, but in a sense this made it more meaningful. . . . Powell always required that everyone – friend or foe – question whether his being black was the *real* reason he was attacked so often or indicted for income tax problems or refused his seat in Congress toward the end of his career. More often than not, his supporters had to take an "in-spite-of-Adam" stance in order to defend what he "stood for." In other words, they had to engage the American Dilemma that Powell exposed, notwithstanding the source of the exposure.

Hamilton's insights about the connection between how one responded to Powell and how one responded to the American dilemma can equally characterize the possible reception of his political biography. The book is published at a time when the Reagan–Bush hegemony has been secured upon the establishment of a consensus of opinion that would deny the existence of a discrepancy between social conditions and the ideals embodied in the Constitution. But Hamilton, like Powell, forces us to engage the contradictory and tenuous nature of this apparent consensus.

Adam Clayton Powell, Jr, was a flamboyant and controversial figure who as a politician had, in today's slang, an "in your face" attitude toward the establishment. His life provides endless source material for currently popular forms of interpretive psychobiography. But Hamilton, in this magnificent book, has scrupulously resisted any attempt to reduce Powell's life either to that of an exceptional (best black) individual or to a representative type or voice. Although Hamilton's account of Powell is so detailed that we can imagine Powell as a passionate, contrary individual who embodied at once the most morally principled and the most ambiguous politics, Hamilton consistently challenges us to read Powell in relation to his times. Adam Clayton Powell, Jr, is presented as both a product of his historical moment and a means for reading the political history of this nation between the 1930s and 1960s, which he helped to shape and give voice to and which ultimately rejected him.

On November 30 1991, a front-page article in the *New York Times* asserted that "not since the tumultuous 1960s has there been such an intense focus on blackness," challenging readers to face yet another crisis in the "ever-changing black experience in America." The article focuses on what Lena

Williams, the journalist, calls the black "quest" for identity in the 1990s, and her central argument is this: "The 'race question' in America has deeply troubled blacks since the days of slavery, when a 'single drop of black blood' classified a person as Negro. Today, increasing efforts to define blackness and what many blacks view as internal pressure to 'choose sides' dramatize the persistence of the conflict, and the confusion over racial identity." Williams stresses that it is black people who are "deeply troubled" by the "race question," but the process of racial classification itself involves no social agents: it is as though Williams imagines that the "single drop of black blood" rather than a set of social, political and economic practices actually did the classifying. Within the context of the article the issue of "racial identity" is a matter of "conflict" and "confusion" only for people defined as black by the magical makeup of their bodies.

Williams's article is indicative of how processes of racialization are commonly discussed as if they were not only generated by but the sole concern of the racialized subjects themselves. Black people in general are increasingly viewed as responsible for their social condition and for its amelioration. Such thinking accords with the shift in the general political climate of the Reagan–Bush years – one marked by the massive cutbacks in federal funding from urban areas and the withdrawal of federal support for civil rights legislation and affirmative action policies. The language of the article is also a good example of a general refusal to recognize significant "confusion" and "conflict" within the dominant social order over the meanings of racial identity and a persistent white fascination with meanings of blackness.

Much of the apparent current concern with racial identity in the media is generated in direct response to the interest of a white, not a black, audience. Many branches of the media, for example, are reluctant to produce programming directed primarily to black audiences, the long-standing exception being the recording industry, which introduced "race records" that were distributed to black consumers as early as the 1920s. The publishing industry in particular is notorious for its reluctance to recognize the existence of a black reading public as a significant sector of its consumer market. In other words, if narratives, visual or written, by or about black people are to sell in profitable quantities, the culture industry in general markets its products primarily to white consumers. If indeed the unacknowledged white readers of the *New York Times* are the primary consumers of a story about a crisis of racial identity, then perhaps we should reject assumptions that only black people are experiencing recurring identity crises and instead ask how much these so-called "crises" about the meanings of blackness determine the boundaries of what can be legitimately established as white, or non-black.

We are living in a time when, because of these cultural texts, it should no longer be possible for anyone to imagine that there is only one way to be black. It is difficult, though not impossible, to believe in the existence of what is now referred to as "the essential black subject," a figure that in the past has functioned as the voice of the "Negro" or embodied a representative black experience. The disappearance of this figure who thinks and acts in a predictable way for the dominant culture marks the beginning of a series of political adjustments that our society must make in order to grasp the turbulent consequences of recognizing the multifarious social experiences of people designated as black. As a society we have to ask if we are finally ready to confront the fact that the processes of racialization, so fundamental to the formation and development of the United States, have invented, not just sustained, categories of racial identity. What do we do with the realization that race is a product of our social, political and cultural imaginations? And how do we release the very real power that these imaginary categories have over all aspects of all our lives?

The institutionalized racism of our society without question has had and continues to have violent and horrifying effects, particularly on young black lives. But it is absolutely necessary to confront the consequences of the ways we live the racial identities that are the products of our political imagination. Those consequences are agonizingly evident in the material deprivation of our urban landscapes of racism and devastation.

1992

Notes

1. Arnold Rampersad, *The Life of Langston Hughes*, 2 vols, New York: Oxford University Press, 1986–88.
2. Bruce Perry, *Malcolm: The Life of a Man Who Changed Black America*, Barrytown, NY: Station Hill Press, 1991.
3. Stephen L. Carter, *Reflections of an Affirmative Action Baby*, New York: Basic Books, 1991.
4. William McFeely, *Frederick Douglass*, New York: W.W. Norton & Company, 1991.
5. Charles V. Hamilton, *Adam Clayton Powell Jr.: The Political Biography of an American Dilemma*, New York: Atheneum Publishing, 1991.

Acknowledgments

"The Sexual Politics of Women's Blues," first published as "It Jus Be's Dat Way Sometime: The Sexual Politics of Women's Blues," *Radical America*, vol. 20, February 1987, pp. 9–22.

"Policing the Black Woman's Body in an Urban Context," *Critical Inquiry*, vol. 18, no. 4, Summer 1992, pp. 738–55, © 1992 by the University of Chicago. All rights reserved.

"Black Women's Blues, Motown and Rock and Roll," first published as "Powerful Voices," *Women's Review of Books*, vol. 4, no. 12, 1987, pp. 1–4.

"They Put a Spell on You," first published as "In Body and Spirit: Representing Black Women Musicians," *Black Music Research Journal*, vol. 11, no. 2, Fall 1991, pp. 177–92.

"White Woman Listen! Black Feminism and the Boundaries of Sisterhood," in Centre for Contemporary Cultural Studies, *The Empire Strikes Back: Race and Racism in Seventies Britain*, London: Hutchinson, 1982, pp. 212–35.

"Race and the Academy: Feminism and the Politics of Difference," in Isabel Caldeira, ed, *O Canone Nos Estudos Anglo-Americanos*, Coimbra, Portugal: Livararia Minerva, 1994, pp. 247–53.

"National Nightmares: The Liberal Bourgeoisie and Racial Anxiety," in Herbert W. Harris, Howard C. Blue and Ezra E. Griffith, eds, *Racial and Ethnic Identity: Psychological Development and Creative Expression*, New York: Routledge, 1995, pp. 173–91 (revised version of "Encoding White Resentment: *Grand Canyon* – A Narrative for Our Times," in Cameron McCarthy and Warren Crichlow, eds, *Race, Identity, and Representation in Education*, New York: Routledge, 1993, pp. 236–47).

"Re-inventing History/Imagining the Future," *Black American Literature Forum*, vol. 23, no. 2, 1989, pp. 381–7.

"Proletarian or Revolutionary Literature: C.L.R. James and the Politics of the Trinidadian Renaissance," *South Atlantic Quarterly*, no. 87, Winter 1988, pp. 39–52.

"Ideologies of Black Folk: The Historical Novel of Slavery," in Deborah McDowell and Arnold Rampersad, eds, *Slavery and the Literary Imagination*, Baltimore, MD: Johns Hopkins University Press, 1988, pp. 125–43.

"On Zora Neale Hurston's *Seraph on the Suwanee*," first published as "Foreword" to Zora Neale Hurston, *Seraph on the Suwanee*, New York: Harper-Collins, 1991, pp. vii–xviii.

"The Politics of Fiction, Anthropology and the Folk: Zora Neale Hurston," in Michael Awkward, ed., *New Essays on Their Eyes Were Watching God*, Cambridge: Cambridge University Press, 1991, pp. 71–93. Reprinted with the permission of Cambridge University Press.

"Schooling in Babylon," in Centre for Contemporary Cultural Studies, *The Empire Strikes Back: Race and Racism in Seventies Britain*, London: Hutchinson, 1982, pp. 182–211.

"Multiculture," first published as "Multiculturalism," *Screen Education*, no. 34, Spring 1980, pp. 62–70; reprinted in Manuel Alvarado, Edward Buscombe and Richard Collins, eds, *The Screen Education Reader: Cinema, Television, Culture*, London: Macmillan, 1993, pp. 263–74.

"The Racism behind the Rioting," *In These Times*, vol. 27, (January 1982), p. 18.

"The Blackness of Theory," review of Henry Louis Gates, Jr, *The Signifying Monkey*, *Times Literary Supplement*, December 29, 1989–January 4, 1990, p. 1446.

"The Canon: Civil War and Reconstruction," *Michigan Quarterly Review*, vol. 28, no. 1, Winter 1989, pp. 35–43.

"The Multicultural Wars, Part One," first published as "The Multicultural Wars," *Radical History Review*, vol. 54, no. 7, 1992, p. 18.

"The Multicultural Wars, Part Two," first published as "Can the Tactics of Cultural Integration Counter the Persistence of Political Apartheid? Or, The Multicultural Wars, Part Two," in Austin Sarat, ed., *Race Law and Culture: Reflections on Brown v. Board of Education*, New York: Oxford University Press, 1997, pp. 221–8.

"Imagining Black Men: The Politics of Cultural Identity," *Yale Review*, vol. 80, no. 3, July 1992, pp. 186–97.

Index